MW01125072

Confederate Monuments at Gettysburg

David G. Martin

COMBINED BOOKS
Pennsylvania

Paperback edition published by arrangement with Longstreet House.

Originally published in cloth edition in 1986 by Longstreet House, Hightstown, NJ 08520. This revised paperback edition published in the United States of America in 1995 by Combined Books and distributed in North America by Stackpole Books, Inc., 5067 Ritter Road, Mechanicsburg, PA 17055 and internationally by Greenhill Books, Lionel Leventhal Ltd., 1 Russell Gardens, London NW11 9NN.

For information, address:
COMBINED BOOKS, INC.
151 E. 10th Avenue
Conshohocken, PA 19428

Library of Congress Cataloging-in-Publication Data
Martin, David G.
    Confederate monuments at Gettysburg / David G. Martin.
    p.   cm.
    Includes bibliographical references. (p.)
    ISBN 0-938289-48-9
    1. Gettysburg National Military Park (Pa.) 2. Soldiers'
monuments—Pennsylvania—Gettysburg National Military Park. 3. United
States—History—Civil War, 1861-1865—Monuments.   I. Title
E475.56.M37 1995
973.7'349—dc20   95-22421
                                   CIP

Combined Books Edition   1 2 3 4 5

Printed in the United States of America.

Contents

A fold-out map showing the positions of Confederate monuments at Gettysburg may be found at the back of the book. Monument locations on the map are completely cross-referenced with Texts and Descriptions and all Appendices, including the Organization of the Army of Northern Virginia.

List of Abbreviations

Art.	Artillery
Bat.	Battery
Batn.	Battalion
Brig.	Brigade
c	Captured
Cav.	Cavalry
Inf.	Infantry
k	Killed
mw	Mortally Wounded
OR	United States War Department. *The War of the Rebellion: A Compilation of the Official Records of the Union and Confederate Armies.* Washington: GPO, 1880-1901.
RSLG	Busey, John W. and David G. Martin. *Regimental Strengths and Losses at Gettysburg.* Third Edition. Hightstown, NJ: Longstreet House, 1994.
w	Wounded

Original Preface

Gettysburg battlefield has over 1300 monuments and memorials, more than any other battlefield in the world. The texts and descriptions of the markers erected by several of the Northern states have been published for study, but little attention has been paid individually or collectively to the 203 Confederate markers that have been erected in the past 100 years. This book will attempt to fill this void by giving the texts, locations, and descriptions of the markers that have been set up on Gettysburg battlefield to commemorate the Southern soldiers who fought there for the cause in which they believed.

This work could not have been completed without the assistance of numerous individuals and organizations. I am particularly indebted to Kathleen G. Harrison, Research Historian at the Gettysburg National Military Park, who made available to me the extensive collection of maps and papers in the Gettysburg National Military Park Library. These constitute the single most informative source on the structure and history of the monuments. Kathy was also most helpful by attempting to answer my numerous detailed questions about the monuments and by sharing with me her extensive knowledge of the battle and the battlefield. I am also indebted to Jim Clouse, who helped clear up some last minute details that I could not check myself on the battlefield. During the course of my seven years of research I was aided by the following organizations and individuals, to whom I now publicly express my appreciation: Department of Archives and History, State of Alabama; Arkansas History Commission; State Library of Florida; Georgia Department of Archives and History; Louisiana State Library; Department of Archives and History, State of Mississippi; North Carolina State Archives; South Carolina Confederate Relic Room and Museum; Texas State Library; Virginia State Library; War Library and Museum in Philadelphia; and Donald A. Ramsay Sr. of the Tennessee Monument Commission. Thanks are also owed to Ed Bearss for encouraging me to complete the work, and to Jack Davis for reviewing the introductory section.

Dr. David G. Martin

Preface to the 1995 Edition

This edition includes three new monuments and memorials erected on the battlefield since the first edition of this book was published in 1986 (Nos. 201-203); the entry for the new Maryland Memorial (No. 203) replaces the earlier proposed entry (No. A-20). In addition, the entry for the Lonstreeet Monument (No. A-5) has been updated. Lastly, several additions and corrections to the text have been made where needed. The 1986 edition included a photographic supplement and several technical appendices not included in this edition.

Introduction

Confederate Monuments at Gettysburg

*I*n the years following the Civil War, battle scarred veterans began to commemorate their heroic deeds and their fallen comrades by erecting markers and monuments on the fields on which they had fought. By the 1880s every major battlefield of the war was sprinkled with monuments, but none would have as many as Gettysburg. Eventually over 1300 monuments would be erected near this small Pennsylvania town to show how and where the battle lines seethed back and forth during those bloody first three days of July of 1863. It is no accident that only about fifteen percent of these monuments were erected to honor southern troops. Northern veterans' groups met regularly at Gettysburg in the years following 1878 for two major reasons—it was the closest battlefield to their northern homes, and it was the scene of a significant Union victory. Interest in the battle continued to grow year by year until by 1920 every Yankee regiment and battery had at least one marker erected to show its position on the field. Conversely, southern interest in erecting monuments at Gettysburg grew slowly because the Confederate veterans were reluctant to commemorate a battle they had lost in Pennsylvania. They much preferred to erect memorials at Chickamauga, which they had won, or at Shiloh or Vicksburg, which were much closer to home. The few southerners who did show an interest in erecting monuments at Gettysburg received such cool treatment from the battlefield's administrators that their eagerness died out. Paradoxically, by far the majority of the Confederate markers later erected on the battlefield were set up by the Federal government, not by Confederate veterans or southern states. In later generations all the southern states that fought in the battle did eventually erect their own memorials, but these were in a quite different vein than the monuments erected in the previous century—their purpose was to commemorate the devotion and heroism of the soldiers, not the marking of the movements of individual units. It is for these reasons that the monuments on Seminary Ridge differ so much from those on Cemetery Ridge.

The first markers erected on the battlefield were the temporary wooden headboards set over the hastily dug graves of the fallen during and right after the battle. These headboards helped identify individual Northern soldiers when they were soon afterwards disinterred for reburial at their homes or in the new National Cemetery laid out on Cemetery Hill. Few fallen Southerners had the luxury of individually marked graves. Lee's men were too busy fighting the battle to bury their dead anywhere except along their immediate lines. Since the Confederates were attacking for most of the battle, the majority of their dead lay outside their own lines at or near positions held by the enemy. These casualties were buried by Federal troops in multiple graves several days after the battle. No markers were erected for them except for occasional boards scratched with the number of dead Rebels laid to rest there. Even these rough memorials disappeared within the next few years. By 1872 most of the Confederate dead had been disinterred for reburial in the South, and no Confederate epitaphs remained on the battlefield.

It was not until 1886, twenty three years after the battle, that the first Confederate monument was erected on the battlefield. In the intervening years many northern monuments had been constructed. At first these were erected only in the cemetery. Later, interest developed in commemorating the events of the battle by erecting markers and monuments on lands supervised by the Gettysburg Battlefield Memorial Association, which had been established in 1864 to acquire some of the more noted parts of the battlefield. Under the GBMA, several wooden signs had been set up to mark Union unit positions and locations of interest. The first stone monuments outside the Cemetery were not erected until 1878. In the summer of that year two Pennsylvania chapters of the Grand Army of the Republic (the national organization of Union veterans) erected tablets to mark the spots where Brigadier General Strong Vincent and Colonel Fred Taylor had been killed on July 2nd. The next year the battlefield's first regimental monument was erected by veterans of the 2nd Massachusetts Infantry.

Early Confederate interest in monumentation at Gettysburg had the same goals as the first permanent Union monuments—the marking of regimental unit positions and the commemoration of fallen leaders. The first Confederate monument erected was the regimental monument of the 1st (2nd) Maryland Infantry (CSA), which was put up in 1886 (No. 32). The second Southern monument was erected the next year to show where Brigadier General Lewis Armistead was mortally wounded during Pickett's Charge (No. 124).

The Confederate road to monumentation was not to be a smooth one. The application made by the veterans of the 1st (2nd) Maryland Infantry (CSA) was brought before the GBMA on August 11, 1885. One source[1] claims that the GBMA had to grant special permission for Confederate monuments to be erected. However, no evidence of any such deliberations exists in the surviving minutes of the GBMA. Instead, the application of the 1st (2nd) Maryland appears to have been considered in the same way as any northern unit's application. On May 7, 1886 the GBMA granted the Confederate regiment permission to erect a monument along with an advanced position marker on South Culp's Hill near the monument of the 20th Connecticut. However, the Battlefield Association's Superintendent of Tablets and Legends, Colonel John B. Bachelder, did not approve of the title of the regiment as proposed. The Union army had two 1st Maryland infantry regiments at the battle—the 1st Infantry (Potomac Home Brigade) and the 1st Infantry (Eastern Shore), not to mention another 1st Maryland Infantry that was not present at the battle. For this reason Bachelder thought that it might be confusing to have a monument to a Confederate 1st Maryland Infantry. This situation was even more confused because the Confederates themselves called the regiment by two different names. The 1st Maryland Infantry Battalion that fought at Gettysburg had been formed in September of 1862 as successor to the disbanded 1st Maryland Infantry. In an attempt to avoid confusion with the earlier regiment, the 1st Infantry Battalion was officially redesignated the 2nd Infantry, though its members continued to call it the 1st Battalion.[2] Given this situation, Bachelder thought that it would be best for the monument to be labeled "2nd Maryland." For this reason the inscription on the monument began "1st Md., changed to 2nd. Md. Infantry C.S.A." when it was dedicated on November 19, 1886. Curiously, Bachelder did not require this change to be made on the regiment's advanced position marker or two flank markers. These read "1st Md. Battalion C.S.A." and "1st Md. C.S.A." respectively.

Southerners also experienced some difficulty erecting their second monument on the battlefield. On May 5, 1887, some friends of Confederate Brigadier General Lewis Armistead asked for permission to erect a marker at the spot on Cemetery Ridge where the General had been mortally wounded during Pickett's Charge. The Battlefield Association refused this request at first on the grounds that it violated their rule that all monuments had to be in battle lines; if the monument were erected on Seminary Ridge at Armistead's pre-attack position, it would then be acceptable for a tablet to be placed where Armistead fell on Cemetery Ridge. This response was clearly a case of legal obfuscation. Numerous markers to Union commanders already had been erected without regard to the position of related unit monuments. This double standard was quickly brought to the attention of the Directors of the Gettysburg Battlefield Memorial Association, who reconsidered and approved the Armistead marker on July 12, 1887. It was erected on Cemetery Ridge in the "Angle" early in 1888 (No. 124).

Four years later another quite different marker of Confederate interest was erected on Cemetery Ridge near the "Angle." In 1887 the Directors of the Gettysburg Battlefield Memorial Association asked John B. Bachelder, their Superintendent of Tablets and Legends, to design a monument to mark the "High Water Mark of the Confederacy" at the farthest point reached by Pickett's men during their charge on the afternoon of July 3rd. Bachelder's monument, which was dedicated on June 2, 1892 (No. 197), had as its centerpiece a large open book ("the record of history") that was inscribed with the names of the Confederate commands that had formed or supported Longstreet's assault, and the Union commands that repulsed them. As such, the monument was intended to be a "national memorial," but it was actually more a Union memorial than a Confederate one. This was made clear by the fact that fifteen northern states donated money for its erection, but not one southern state did. The High Water Mark Monument later became somewhat controversial when some Union veterans objected that their regiments were not individually named on the monument, which listed no units below brigade level. These veterans wanted the world to know that they had helped to repulse Pickett's Charge, which then was being viewed as the pivotal point of the war. They finally got their way in 1902, when tablets were added to the monument listing the names of all the regiments and batteries, Union and Confederate, that participated in the assault or its repulse.

Confederate interest in erecting their own monuments continued into the 1890s, though none were actually set up until the end of the decade. With Union monumentation nearing completion, battlefield administrators invited Confederate veterans to visit the battlefield and mark the positions their units held during the battle. For example, members of the old "Stonewall Brigade" came to Gettysburg in 1893 to mark their positions near Culp's Hill. The year 1894 was a very busy one as veterans from Private to General came to the battlefield to mark their positions with wooden stakes. General Harry Heth pointed out the place from which the first Confederate artillery shots were fired on July 1st, and delegations toured the field to show where Barksdale's and Perry's brigades fought. In addition, representatives of the 6th North Carolina, 7th Louisiana and 14th Louisiana regiments marked the points they had reached in their attacks on East Cemetery Hill and Culp's Hill; members of the 43rd North Carolina, 55th North Carolina and 33rd Virginia regiments marked their July 3rd positions. Numerous battery positions were also designated that same year by E.P. Alexander, former commander of a reserve artillery battalion in Longstreet's Corps.[3]

In 1895 the administration of the battlefield was transferred from the GBMA to the United States government, which established the Gettysburg National Military Park under the supervision of the War Department. One of the stated goals of the new park was the "preservation and marking of the lines of battle of the Union and Confederate armies at Gettysburg."[4] The Park Commissioners, John P. Nicholson, William Robbins and C.A. Richardson, took a special interest in marking Confederate positions. They were well aware that the individual southern states were showing little interest in erecting monuments to their units in the way that every northern state involved in the battle had done or planned to do. Consequently, the Commissioners realized that if the Confederate positions were to be marked, this would have to be done by the Federal government.

In order to establish Confederate positions accurately, the Park Commissioners encouraged Confederate veterans to continue visiting the field for this purpose. Their 1895 report to the Secretary of War laid out their intentions in this way: "Surviving Confederate officers and soldiers have been invited to visit the field; also the authorities of the Southern States have been requested to send commissioners representing Confederate commands to point out positions. The responses from the South to these invitations and requests have been very encouraging, and the commission have had the aid of many Confederate soldiers of intelligence, some of high rank, in fixing positions and movements of Confederate troops. Additions to our information on these points are constantly being made. All positions are, of course, carefully noted on our topographical maps, as well as upon the field, so that they can not be lost."[5]

To carry out the marking of the Confederate battle positions, the Commissioners urged the purchase of tracts along Seminary Ridge that were held by Lee's soldiers. Along these lines a new road (the later West Confederate Avenue) would be constructed. Part of Longstreet's lines along Warfield Ridge and southern Seminary Ridge were already owned by the Park. Here the Commissioners marked the positions of Longstreet's batteries by setting two artillery pieces for each battery at locations already marked by E.P. Alexander. The Commissioners then planned to set up "handsome tablets of iron" for each battery outlining its movements during the battle. Such tablets began to be erected in 1898."[6]

Besides erecting battery tablets, the Park Commissioners planned to erect iron tablets for each infantry and cavalry command "along the main lines of battle with brief inscriptions specifying the name of each command, its service in the battle, and referring to auxiliary and subordinate tablets so placed as to indicate successive movements during the conflict."[7] The texts of these tablets were to be carefully written "so as to arrive at the utmost possible historic accuracy with regard to each one as well as perfect consistency and fairness among them as a whole."[8] The first brigade markers planned were for the units of Hood's and McLaws' divisions. These tablets were erected in 1899 at the positions held by these units just before their attack on the afternoon of July 2nd.

Confederate veterans were supportive of the Park's effort to mark their positions, and urged the Commissioners to set up more than the battery and brigade tablets just mentioned. J.F. Means of Macon, Georgia, wrote a *Confederate Veteran* article to suggest that markers be erected to show where Generals and other important officers had been killed or wounded.[9] This had been done at other battlefields, but so far only General Armistead had been so honored at Gettysburg (No. 124). Indeed, Lee's army had many more candidates eligible for such markers at this battlefield—Barksdale, Pettigrew, Trimble, Hood, Semmes, G.T. Anderson, R.B. Garnett, Kemper, Avery, Fry, Heth, Scales and Latimer. Means' suggestion was not to be heeded by the Park Commissioners.

What the Confederate veterans were most interested in marking was their advanced positions. Park policy so far had been to mark only Lee's main battle line along Warfield and Seminary Ridges. To the Confederates, these lines had been only jump-off positions. Their real glory had been in heated conflict with the enemy on Little Round Top, Cemetery Ridge and Culp's Hill. For this reason Lee's veterans argued strongly for advanced position markers to show their forward battle lines and the farthest points reached by their attacks. Minimally, the southerners wanted the erection of iron advance position markers similar to those erected at Chickamauga. Ideally, they wished all their advanced lines marked in the same way that the Union temporary lines in the Wheatfield area had been marked.

The Park Commissioners had originally intended to mark Confederate advanced positions and regimental lines. However, their first efforts to do this met so much northern opposition that they had to give up on the project. By the 1890s almost all the Federal battle lines had been clearly marked down to regimental level. Many northern veterans did not want their lines cluttered or dishonored with Confederate monuments. Feeling was especially strong among the Union regiments that had fought in Sickles' line at Devil's Den, the Wheatfield, the Peach Orchard, and along the Emmitsburg Road. These troops had been swept away by the Confederate attacks on July 2nd, and they did not want this fact emphasized by the erection of Confederate monuments within their lines.

This ill feeling over the placement of Confederate advance position markers came to a head in April of 1902 when William Oates, Colonel of the 15th Alabama Infantry during the battle, proposed to erect at his own expense a small marker at each end of the line held by his regiment at the base of the Round Tops on the evening of July 2nd. His request was denied by the Park Commissioners, ostensibly because, "The Commission should not favor giving any single regiment on either side conspicuous notice over others by special regimental monument apart from other regiments engaged substantially at the, same position."[10]

This response was clearly only a technicality. Since most of the Confederate monuments had been erected on Warfield and Seminary Ridges, any monument erected outside these lines would give conspicuous honor to the unit involved. In addition, two markers—the 1st (2nd) Maryland and Armistead monuments—had already been erected at advance positions at or near Federal lines. What was clearly the issue was that northern interests did not want any more Confederate markers so close to Union lines. This became obvious when Oates gave up his first proposal and offered to erect a different marker: "I acquiesced in the adverse decision not to allow markers where the right and left of my regiment rested, and proposed at my own expense to erect a single inexpensive monument about where the center of my regiment stood at the most advanced spot, and where my brother and other officers were killed, and where I sustained nearly all my losses."[11] This proposal, too, was rejected, chiefly because veterans of the 20th Maine objected to a Confederate monument being erected behind their already monumented line on southern Little Round Top.

The rejection of his second proposal made Oates furious. He threatened to appeal to Congress and take his case to the newspapers. Numerous Union regiments had been permitted to erect markers at secondary or advanced positions—Brooke's brigade of the Second Corps even had monuments at a position near the Rose Farm that had been held for less than half an hour. In addition, the GBMA sixteen years before had approved an advanced position marker for the 1st (2nd) Maryland Infantry on South Culp's Hill (No. 35).

Robbins, the sole Southern representative on the Park Commission, tried to persuade Oates to erect his regimental marker on West Confederate Avenue where his attack had started from rather than at its zenith on Little Round Top.[12] As an example to Oates, Robbins arranged for a tablet to his old regiment, the 4th Alabama Infantry, to be set up on southern Seminary Ridge (No. 13). Robbins' regiment had served in Law's brigade along with Oates' regiment, and Robbins hoped that Oates would consent to setting up a marker to his 15th regiment next to that of Robbins' 4th regiment. Oates, however, refused to take the ploy. Backed now by a committee of veterans from the 15th regiment, he continued to insist on erecting his marker on Little Round Top. On February 2, 1903, the Park Commissioners again refused Oates' request, this time citing the GBMA's directive that monuments had to be "on line of battle held by the brigade unless the regiment was detached.[13] Oates' response to this technicality was to argue that his regiment had fought 200 yards in advance of the rest of his brigade, and therefore qualified to have a marker as a "detached unit." This argument was less strong than his previous claims because the 15th, though on the right of the Confederate line, had still been fighting next to the 4th and 47th Alabama regiments of Law's brigade.

In the end, Oates never did persuade the Park Commissioners to let him erect his monument on Little Round Top. In 1905 he was still arguing with representatives of the 20th Maine over the farthest point reached by his troops on July 2nd. Oates claimed that he personally had reached a large boulder above and behind the 20th Maine's monument, but this was denied by Joshua Chamberlain, the former commander of the Maine regiment.[14] Oates adamantly refused to compromise by erecting his monument as an "ornament to that Avenue" (West Confederate Avenue), and took the quarrel with him to his grave in 1910.

The length and intensity of Oates' vain struggle to erect his 15th Alabama marker discouraged the former Confederates from making any farther similar attempts. The Park Commissioners did give in a little in 1907 when they allowed Confederate brigade tablets to be erected near Devil's Den, the Wheatfield, and the Emmitsburg Road (see page 20). However, these were a far cry from the advanced position and regimental line markers that Oates and his compatriots had been willing to erect. The final result of the Park's policy was that the Confederate battle positions that had been so carefully located in the 1890s were never permanently marked. The wooden stakes set up by Confederate veterans who had fought in the battle disappeared or rotted, and today there is no way for us to trace Lee's advanced battle lines with the preciseness that once had been possible.

Thus the Union regimental positions at Gettysburg are perhaps the best monumented battle lines in the world, while the opposing Confederate lines contain only four widely separated regimental monuments—the 1st (2nd) Maryland on Culp's Hill (No. 32), the 4th Alabama on southern Seminary Ridge (No. 13), the 26th North Carolina at McPherson's Woods (No. 39) and the 43rd North Carolina on Culp's

Hill (No. 201). Southern dissatisfaction at this state of affairs was perhaps most articulately presented in a letter H.R. Hought of Georgia wrote to Daniel E. Sickles on October 17, 1904: "I fought in Benning's Brigade, Hood's Division, at Devil's Den, Gettysburg, and visited the field in September, 1903. I found the Union lines well marked—tablets and monuments showing the position of nearly every Union regiment and battery—but there is nothing on the actual fighting line to show where even one Confederate command fought. True, there are tablets on what is called Confederate Avenue, nearly a mile from the scene of the Infantry fighting, showing where each Brigade formed for the charge, but owing to changes in direction of the march, one can get very little information from there. My brother fought in the 15th Alabama, Law's Brigade, which regiment attacked the east side of Little Round Top, but nothing is there to show what command attacked your left. So with the Texas Brigade, Barksdale, Semmes, Wofford, or Kershaw. The monument to Gen. Armistead is the only one I could find on the field, showing where a Confederate Infantry-man fought. Since in a few years there will be none left to point out these places, it would seem that they ought to be marked for the sake of truth in history."[15]

Though the Park Commissioners had squashed Confederate efforts to mark their regimental lines and advanced positions, they did continue their interest in marking the battery and brigade positions of Lee's troops. This was part of an overall project to erect, at government expense, descriptive tablets marking the general battle lines of the brigades and divisions of both armies. As already discussed on page 11, the Park by 1899 had erected iron brigade and battery tablets along Warfield Ridge and Seminary Ridge south of Millerstown Road. In addition, the positions of McIntosh's batteries on central Seminary Ridge south of Fairfield Road were also marked. The year 1899 also saw tablets erected on East Confederate Avenue in the Culp's Hill area to show the positions of Ewell's brigades on July 3rd.

In 1901-1902 battery and brigade tablets were erected along the central part of West Confederate Avenue from Fairfield Road south to the Millerstown Road. These tablets completed the major portion of Lee's battle lines of July 2nd and 3rd. These lines were made virtually complete about 1905 by the erection of tablets for Latimer's and Nelson's batteries on Benner's Hill. Confederate battery and brigade positions on the East Cavalry Battlefield were marked in 1906.

The last Confederate battle positions marked by the Park were shown by tablets erected in 1907-1908. As has been mentioned on page 12, the Park Commissioners in 1896 had originally planned to erect tablets to show the line of advance of the Confederate attacks. Eleven iron tablets were erected in 1907-1908 on the second day's battlefield to show the advance of Hood's four brigades (Nos. 101, 103, 105 and 107), McLaws' four brigades (Nos. 113, 115, 118 and 120) and Wilcox's, Perry's and Wright's brigades of R.H. Anderson's division (Nos. 166, 163 and 168 respectively). Most of these markers show only the ground over which each brigade advanced during its attack. Only two (J.B. Robertson's and Benning's) show actual battle lines, and none show the farthest point reached by any brigade attack. In most cases, the texts of the advance position markers are simply duplicates of the relevant portions of their respective brigade tablets. It is difficult today to determine why more Confederate advanced position markers were not erected. Surely northern opposition to their construction played a significant factor in the demise of the project. Whatever the reasons, the project of erecting Confederate advanced position markers was left incomplete and has not been resumed since then.

The Park's monumentation interest began to take a different course after 1907. For reasons not fully understood today, the Commissioners decided to replace most of the Confederate iron brigade tablets erected earlier with bronze tablets set on granite pedestals.[16] These tablets, which were set up in 1910-1911, were similar in style to those already being erected for the Union brigades. As far as can be determined, the new tablets were set up on the same sites as their predecessors. In addition, the texts of the new bronze tablets were duplicates of the earlier iron tablets except for one known case.[17]

Another project begun in 1907 was the marking of Confederate division and corps positions. These markers, of course, only show approximate positions since the individual Confederate brigades fought over wide sections of the field. The division and corps tablets were set up primarily for their descriptive texts that outline each unit's general movements in the battle. In addition, these large markers were meant to be compatriots to the similar division and corps tablets being erected at the same time for the units of Meade's army. The Confederate corps tablets (Nos. 95, 129 and 156) were set up in 1907, along with the tablet for McLaws' division (No. 110). The remaining infantry division tablets were set up by 1909 (Nos. 99, 122, 133, 140, 146, 160, 170 and 178). Stuart's cavalry division tablet (No. 185) was set up on the East Cavalry Battlefield in 1913.[18] In addition, a tablet for the Army of Northern Virginia (No. 92) was erected in 1908 on Seminary Ridge near the position from which Lee observed Pickett's Charge. The last Confederate markers that the Park erected on the battlefield were the army and corps headquarters tablets erected in 1920-1921 (Nos. 94, 96, 130 and 157). These consisted of upright cannon barrels set in stone foundations.[19]

Several of the markers erected by the Park Commissioners did not show actual troop positions. One of the most unusual of these was a tablet set up on Warfield Ridge in 1900 (No. 93) to show the right flank of the Army of Northern Virginia. This was placed to match a corresponding marker for the left flank of the Army of the Potomac. The primary purpose of these tablets must have been to show the approximate ends of the battle lines of the two armies to visitors as they traveled the Park's roads. Because of the complex maneuvers that occurred at this end of the battlefield, especially during the cavalry attack on the evening of July 3rd, these two flank markers are actually more misleading than informative by their positions.

In 1901 the Park Commissioners determined to commemorate the movements of the Union army during the campaign by erecting iron narrative tablets in several of the Maryland and Pennsylvania towns through which the Union soldiers had marched. Duplicates of these tablets were erected on East Cemetery Hill. To complete the story of the battle, the Commissioners also decided to erect Confederate "itinerary tablets." These tablets, one for each day of the campaign from June 26th to July 5th, were erected in 1903 on the west side of West Confederate Avenue just south of the Fairfield Road (Nos. X-1 to X-10). These tablets were removed by the Park in 1974 and are presently in storage.

Six tablets were erected to commemorate three Confederate cavalry brigades that participated in the campaign but did not fight in the battle proper. W.E. Jones' brigade was assigned to guard Lee's right and rear, and fought a sharp fight with the 6th U.S. Cavalry between Fairfield and Orrtanna on July 3rd. A tablet commemorating this engagement was erected near Orrtanna about 1905 (No. 190). At the same time a tablet was erected in Orrtanna to commemorate the movement of B.H. Robertson's brigade through that town (No. 193). The same year saw the erection of a small tablet at Cashtown to note the presence of Imboden's cavalry command there on July 3rd (No. 196). Though these three brigades did not reach the battlefield proper, bronze tablets outlining their movements were erected on the battlefield in 1910-1911 west of South Reynolds Avenue near its intersection with Fairfield Road (Nos. 189, 192 and 195).

Three miscellaneous Confederate markers erected by the Park remain to be mentioned. The route taken by McLaws' and Pickett's divisions to the front lines was marked by an iron tablet set up in 1903 on the Fairfield Road west of Gettysburg (No. 111). That same year another iron tablet was erected on northern Seminary Ridge to show where Ewell's divisions formed on July 3rd and 4th after they withdrew from their positions east of Gettysburg (No. 129). A small iron tablet showing the location of Rodes' breastworks on Seminary Ridge (No. 147) may have been erected at about the same time.

The Confederate monuments set up by the Park certainly are informative in their texts and locations. However, in spite of the care taken in composing their inscriptions, a few do contain errors. Most notable among their textual errors are the following:

1) Longstreet was not at his headquarters on southern Seminary Ridge from July 1 to 5 as the marker (No. 96) states, but from the morning of July 2nd to late on July 4th.[20]

2) Ewell was not at his headquarters near Rock Creek from July 1 to 5 as the marker (No. 130) states; he left the area on the evening of July 3 when his Corps withdrew to Seminary Ridge.[21]

3) The descriptions of the activities of several of the batteries on July 3rd appear to be in error, as is discussed in the presentation of these markers.[22]

4) The attack times given by several markers are not now generally accepted. For example, Kershaw is now thought to have attacked at 5:30 P.M. on July 2, not 4:30 as No. 114 states; Semmes is thought to have attacked at 5:40 P.M. on the 2nd, not 5:00 P.M. as No. 117 states.

5) Davis' brigade tablet for July 1 (No. 174) does not mention the fact that the 11th Mississippi regiment was not present on the field during the first day's fight (see No. 175).

6) H. Jones' battalion marker (No. 139) does not mention that Green's battery was detached to serve with Stuart's cavalry on July 2 and 3 (see Nos. 25 and 26).

7) On June 6, 1917, veterans of the Washington (La.) Artillery requested the War Department to change their unit's designation on their marker from "Eshleman's Battalion" to "Battalion of Washington Artillery of New Orleans, Louisiana, commanded by Lieut. Col. B.F. Eshleman." This change was approved by the War Department for No. 98, but was never carried out.

Another major error on the Confederate markers concerns the battle strengths given on each infantry brigade marker. Though some of these figures have been shown to be accurate, most have been demonstrated to be on the low side. This is because the figures given are mostly estimates. In addition, all seem to include only men armed for battle, with officers excluded.[23] This problem has been studied by John Busey and myself in *Regimental Strengths and Losses at Gettysburg*,[24] which is based largely on previously unstudied muster roll returns for June 30, 1863. For example, Hood's Texas Brigade tablet (No. 106) claims a battle strength of 1100, while June 30, 1863 muster rolls show 1839 officers and men present in the brigade, of whom an estimated 1734 were engaged in the battle.[25] Hoke's brigade tablet (No. 137) claims 900 men engaged, but the brigade more probably had approximately 1244 officers and men in the battle.[26] The estimated battle strengths derived for each unit in *Regimental Strengths and Losses at Gettysburg* are given in the commentary to each marker. The casualty figures given on the brigade markers are in most cases derived directly from those given by the army's Medical Director in the *Official Records of the War of the Rebellion*, and as such can only be as accurate as their source.[27] A more exact count of Confederate battle casualties can be made using muster rolls, individual service records, Confederate hospital records, and Union prisoner records. This, however, lies outside the scope of the present study.[28]

Informative as the narrative tablets are, they actually do not tell us significantly more than can be found in unit histories and official battle reports. Their real value is in marking the locations where the events they describe actually occurred. In viewing the monuments, however, we must remember that they show only general positions, and that even these positions were not all held at the same time. The battle lines in neither army were as neat and orderly as the positioning of the monuments would seem to suggest.

This is especially apparent on West Confederate Avenue. Here the positions of the monuments suggest a solid artillery line near the Millerstown Road, when in fact eight of the batteries marked there (Eshleman's and Dearing's battalions) never held positions here, but were three fourths mile to the east near the Emmitsburg Road. In addition, Pickett's three brigades were not formed for their charge at the location of their markers on West Confederate Avenue, but actually formed about three eighths mile southeast of their tablets. Some markers, such as Longstreet's Headquarters (No. 96) and Hill's Headquarters (No. 157) are self admittedly as far as one half mile from the position they describe. Others, such as Semmes' advance position marker (No. 118) do not point out that they are as far as one quarter mile from the position they describe.

It is much to be regretted that all portions of the Confederate line are not marked with equal care. The markers now on the field show mostly the position held on July 2nd along Seminary Ridge, and on July 3rd in the Culp's Hill area and on the East Cavalry Battlefield.

Many of the Confederate battle lines on July 1 are not marked because the Park never purchased the land over which the Confederates advanced here. Today only eight of the sixteen brigades that fought on July 1st have their battle positions marked on this part of the battlefield. These tablets, erected in 1905-1907, are to Archer's brigade at McPherson's Woods (No. 171), to Davis' brigade at the Railroad Cut (No. 174), to Rodes' five brigades at Oak Hill (Nos. 148, 150, 151, 152 and 154), and to Gordon's brigade at Barlow Knoll (No. 134). The only battery positions marked at the same time were T. Carter's four batteries on Oak Hill (Nos. 16, 70, 75 and 77) and H. Jones' four batteries east of the Harrisburg Road (Nos. 25, 57, 58 and 90). It is especially regretful that the Park Commissioners did not make more of an effort to mark the first day's battlefield. Tablets should have been erected to mark the attacks of Pettigrew, Brockenbrough, Hoke and Hays, and especially the fierce assault of Pender's division against the Union First Corps' lines on Seminary Ridge. In addition, the artillery line held by Pegram's, McIntosh's and J. Garnett's batteries on Herr Ridge should have been marked. This position is near where the first Confederate cannon shots were fired on July 1st, and was later one of the most powerful artillery lines of the battle. Yet this historic land has not even been purchased by the Park to make it available for monumentation.[29]

Confederate positions on July 2 are not marked in two principal areas. One is Long Lane (see No. A-17), where parts of Rodes' and Pender's divisions formed prior to their abortive assault on Cemetery Hill. The other is the advanced line reached by Hood's, McLaws' and R.H. Anderson's brigades from Little Round Top to central Cemetery Ridge. As discussed on pages 12-14, the Park's administrators refused to allow Confederate markers at the high points reached by their attacks. In addition, most of the so-called "advance position" markers show only attack routes, not advanced battle lines.

Almost all of Longstreet's troops do not have their July 3rd positions properly marked. Most of the First Corps markers on the field show positions held late on the afternoon of July 2nd, just before the attacks began against Devil's Den and the Peach Orchard. Only a few markers show infantry positions held on July 3 at Devil's Den, the woods west of the Wheatfield, and on the far right facing the Union cavalry lines. Most disappointing is the fact that no markers (and only a handful of cannons) show the line of 75 guns formed by Colonel E.P. Alexander on the morning of July 3 for a distance of 1300 yards north of the Peach Orchard (see No. A-6).

Lastly, it should be mentioned that no markers have been erected to two horse artillery batteries that fought in the battle. Hart's South Carolina battery (see No. A-2) served with Hood's division on the army's right flank, while W. Griffin's Virginia battery (see No A-1) was posted on Oak Hill on July 3. The "A" series of markers is designed to commemorate the deeds of these and other units whose stories are not fully told by the markers now on the battlefield.

The completion of the Confederate headquarters markers in 1921 marked the end of the most prolific phase of Confederate monument building—in the span of twenty-three years the Park Commissioners had erected 175 of the 200 Southern monuments that now grace the battlefield. The Park by then was probably running low on funds, since it also ceased erecting Union monuments at about the same time. The World War I era then saw the beginning of a new phase of Confederate monument building—the erection of state memorials and brigade monuments by non-Federal sponsors.

Only two all granite Confederate brigade markers have been erected on the battlefield. The earlier of the two is the Hood's Texas Brigade Monument (No. 108) which was dedicated on September 27, 1913. This simple granite shaft was erected on Warfield Ridge near the marker of J.B. Robertson's brigade (No. 106) at the location from which the brigade began its attack against Little Round Top and Devil's Den on the late afternoon of July 2nd. The monument was set up by a committee of Texas residents, and as such is one of the few Confederate markers on the field that were erected solely by private citizens. The other all granite brigade marker is the Kershaw's Brigade Marker (No. 116), which was dedicated on July 21, 1970. It was erected by Project Southland in cooperation with the Gettysburg Battlefield Preservation Association, an organization which had been formed as a spiritual descendant of the old GBMA. This monument was set up at the spot where Kershaw's unit crossed the Emmitsburg Road during its attack on the late afternoon of July 2nd. This is the most recent Confederate advanced position marker erected on the battlefield.

The main impetus of twentieth century Confederate monumentation has not been the marking of the movements of individual units or the commemoration of separate brigades, but has been the honoring of the valor of the Confederate soldiers through monuments erected by each Southern state whose sons fought at the battle. The first, and perhaps the noblest, of these state memorials was the Virginia Monument (No. 11). It was sculpted by F. William Sievers and was dedicated on June 8, 1917. This monument had been proposed by the state of Virginia in 1908, but had met difficulties in construction that included opposition by northern veterans' groups.[30] In addition, the Secretary of War used blunt words to refuse the state's application to erect the monument on Cemetery Ridge at the farthest point reached by Pickett's Virginians during their famous charge.[31] The monument was then erected at an alternate site on central Seminary Ridge, at the approximate point from which Lee observed Pickett's Charge. Virginia's soldiers are commemorated by seven figures on a pedestal at the monument's base; on top of the monument stands an impressive statue of General Robert E. Lee astride his war-horse Traveler. Quite appropriately, Lee's statue faces across the battlefield towards a similar equestrian statue of his opposing army commander, George G. Meade.

The battlefield's second Confederate state memorial is that of North Carolina, the Southern state that furnished the most troops to the battle after Virginia. This monument (No. 7) was sculpted by noted artist Gutzon Borglum, who is also famous for his gigantic sculpture at Mount Rushmore. The North Carolina Monument was dedicated on July 3, 1929. It consists of a group sculpture of five soldiers advancing towards the Union lines. It is located on the exact ground over which men of Pettigrew's and Scales' North Carolina brigades advanced from McMillan Woods to join up with the Virginians of Pickett's division during the famous assault of July 3rd.

The Alabama Monument (No. l), which was dedicated on November 12, 1933, continued the tradition of commemorating the valor and patriotism of the Confederate soldier. This monument, erected by the Alabama Division of the United Daughters of the Confederacy, features a group sculpture containing three figures—a female "Spirit of the Confederacy" urges forward an older soldier while she comforts a wounded young soldier. The monument was erected near the position from which Law's Alabama brigade began its attack on the afternoon of July 2nd.

Five years later one of the battlefield's largest monuments, the Eternal Light Peace Memorial (No. 199), was dedicated as part of the celebrations marking the battle's 75th anniversary. It was erected to commemorate the country's unity after the divisive civil war. Quite appropriately, the Peace Memorial is the only monument on the battlefield erected jointly by both northern and southern states. In 1935 Virginia was the first state to respond to Pennsylvania's request for contributions to the project; Tennessee also sent funds later. Altogether five northern states (Pennsylvania, New York, Wisconsin, Indiana and Illinois) also appropriated money for the Peace Memorial. The memorial is conspicuously located on Oak Hill on land occupied by part of Rodes' division on July 1st. It consists of a large base supporting a forty foot tower adorned with a symbolic bas relief sculpted by Lee Lawrie. The relief depicts two figures holding a wreath of peace; in front of them stands an eagle, symbolizing the reunified Federal government. The memorial was dedicated on July 3, 1938, at ceremonies attended by well over 100,000 people. President Franklin D. Roosevelt was the featured speaker. At the moment of dedication a huge garrison flag that draped the memorial was lowered by two aged veterans, one from the North and one from the South. At the same time the monument's "eternal flame" was lighted. This gas flame burned continuously until 1973, when it was extinguished because of an energy crisis. It was rekindled in 1978 as a sodium vapor light.

World War II almost brought an end to all the metal monuments at

Gettysburg. On September 11, 1942, eighteen tons of "miscellaneous metal, obsolete signs, iron fence, and worn out equipment" were donated to a government scrap metal drive. Another 38 tons of post Civil War cannon balls were also sent to the scrap heap. The Park's director was then instructed to draw up priorities for scrapping the remaining metal in the Park. First on his list, which was submitted on January 19, 1943, were the Union and Confederate itinerary markers. The remaining items, listed on the next page, are given in priority with their weights. The Virginia, North Carolina and Alabama monuments are listed last because they were paid for by state or private funds, not by Federal moneys. Fortunately the war began going better in 1943, and no markers, Union or Confederate, had to be sacrificed to it.[32]

Priority List of Metals for the Scrap Heap (1943)
1. Itinerary markers; 231 pounds each.
2. 197 cannons; 229,300 pounds.
3. 256 position markers: 59,163 pounds.
4. Bronze on monuments; 20,950 pounds.
5. Statues; 57,800 pounds.
6. Inscriptions on monuments; 53,344 pounds.
7. Artistic reliefs on monuments; 4254 pounds.
8. Portraits on monuments: 141,674 pounds.
9. Virginia, North Carolina & Alabama memorials, 48, 500 pounds.

After World War II, interest in Confederate monumentation lay dormant for a generation until it was revived by the spirit of the war's centennial. Four major state memorials were dedicated during the years of the centennial, with four more set up soon afterwards. The first of the centennial era memorials was dedicated by Georgia on September 21, 1961. This monument (No. 4) stands on Warfield Ridge at the position from which Semmes' Georgia brigade began its attack on July 2nd. In addition, the Georgia brigades of G.T. Anderson, Benning, Wofford and Wright all held positions only a short distance from this monument. These troops altogether constituted over half of Georgia's 11,000 man contingent at the battle.

Two memorials were dedicated precisely at the battle's centennial. July 2, 1963 saw the dedication of the South Carolina Monument (No. 8). It was erected on southern Seminary Ridge at the point from which Kershaw's South Carolina brigade began its attack on July 2nd. The monument features no sculpture, but has an outline of the state and the state seal. Its inscription speaks of the "sacredness of states rights," a phrase appropriate to the first southern state to leave the Union. This is in fact the only inflammatory phrase on any of the southern monuments on the battlefield. The other Confederate monument dedicated at the battle's centennial was Florida's, whose ceremonies took place on July 3, 1963 (No. 3). This simple granite memorial to Florida's three battle regiments has the Florida state seal as its focus. It was erected on the ground from which Perry's Florida brigade advanced to the support of Pickett's division on July 3, 1863.

The Texas Monument (No. 10) was dedicated in September 1964. It is a granite shaft with a long inscription, and was one of seven similar monuments erected by the state of Texas at prominent Civil War battlefields. It is located at the position from which J.B. Robertson's Texas and Arkansas brigade advanced to the attack on the afternoon of July 2nd.

The Memorial to the Soldiers and Sailors of the Confederacy (No. 12), which was dedicated on August 25, 1965, is unique in several ways. Firstly, it is the only memorial on the battlefield dedicated specifically to the southern soldiers and the cause for which they fought. Secondly, the memorial was paid for not only by the eleven states of the old Confederacy, but also by donations from the border states of Missouri, Kentucky, and Maryland. The sculpture on the memorial was executed by Donald DeLue and is quite symbolic. It consists of a larger than life size soldier who has dropped his weapons to carry a Confederate flag; while he advances toward the enemy he looks back to urge on his followers with his right hand. The memorial's text honors the last surviving Confederate veteran, Walter Washington Williams, who died in 1959 at the age of 117.

The next Confederate memorial erected on the battlefield was the Arkansas Memorial (No. 2), which was dedicated on June 18, 1966. This large stone monument marks the position from which the 3rd Arkansas Infantry advanced to attack the Union lines on July 2nd. It features a carved outline of the state and a low relief etching of charging troops.

Two Confederate state monuments were erected in the 1970s. The Louisiana Monument (No. 5) was dedicated on June 11, 1971. It is perhaps the most abstract of the Confederate memorials on the field. It features a statue of a larger than life size female who is blowing a trumpet above a fallen soldier; the soldier holds a Confederate flag to his heart. The female figure represents the "spiritual ideal of peace and memory who is flying over the embodiment of the fallen Confederacy. The fallen soldier is an artilleryman, since the monument is located near the position held by Moody's Louisiana battery. The monument was sculpted by Donald DeLue, who also did the Memorial to the Soldiers and Sailors of the Confederacy (No. 12). DeLue was also the sculptor of the nearby Mississippi Monument (No. 6). This monument features statues of two infantrymen—one is fallen and the other is swinging his musket as a club. The soldiers represent the men of

Barksdale's Mississippi brigade, which advanced from this position to attack the Sherfy and Trostle farms on July 2nd. The Mississippi Monument was dedicated on June 11, 1971.

With the erection of the Mississippi Monument, all of the old Confederate states except Tennessee had monuments on the battlefield. It was not long thereafter that a movement began to erect a Tennessee Monument. This was originally planned for construction on ground held by Archer's brigade on July 1st, but no suitable location could be found. The monument was then erected on Seminary Ridge between the North Carolina and Virginia monuments, on ground held by the three Tennessee regiments of Archer's brigade before they advanced to join Pickett's Charge. The monument, which was dedicated on July 3, 1982 (No. 9), features a large polished monolith with a lightly etched relief of three Tennessee soldiers. The monolith is set on a base cut in the shape of the state of Tennessee.

Two Confederate monuments honoring individual regiments were erected in the late 1980s, so giving a new thrust to Confederate monumentation on the battlefield. On October 5, 1985, a granite marker was dedicated to the memory of the men of the 26th North Carolina Infantry (No. 39) on McPherson's Ridge at the location where the regiment lost most of its 588 battle casualties, the greatest loss of any individual regiment on either side in the battle. It was erected by the North Carolinian Society, the North Carolina Historical Commission, and the North Carolina Department of Cultural Resources. On October 22, 1988, a similar granite marker was dedicated near Culp's Hill to honor the men of the 43rd North Carolina (No. 401). It was erected by the State of North Carolina largely from funds donated by the descendants of Colonel Thomas S. Kenan of the 43rd, who was wounded on July 3 during the fighting on Culp's HIll.

The theme of brotherhood between the soldiers of the North and the South is the message of the Masonic Memorial (No. 202), which was dedicated on August 21, 1993, to honor the 18,000 Freemasons who fought in the battle on both sides. Sculpted by Ron Tunison, the memorial features two larger than life size figures that depict Union Captain Henry Bingham giving aid to a fellow Freemason, Confederate Brigadier General Lewis A. Armistead, immediately after the latter was mortally wounded on nearby Cemetery Ridge at the height of Pickett's Charge on July 3. The two bronze figures are the Park's first polychromed statues—Bingham's uniform is chemically treated to have a bluish tint and Armistead's is similarly treated to appear grayish.

The last Southern state to commemorate its troops that fought in the battle was Maryland, whose memorial was dedicated near the Park's Visitor Center on Taneytown Road on November 13, 1994 (No. 203).

Sculpted by Lawrence M. Ludkte, the memorial features two larger than life size figures that honor all the state's units. both Southern and Northern, that fought in the battle. This is only the second monument on the battlefield to specifically honor both Northern and Southern units, the other being the High Water Mark Monument (No. 197).

The recent erection of these monuments shows that Confederate monumentation at Gettysburg has not ended. Under present Park policy, more monuments can be erected, though the application process is lengthy and requires a great deal of supporting historical documentation. The next Confederate monument to be erected might well be to Lee's "Old War Horse," Lieutenant General James Longstreet. Recently a movement has begun to erect a Longstreet monument, reviving plans that had been made but dropped several decades ago (see No. A-5).

What is most clear, unfortunately, is that the part at present has no plans to erect any more Confederate markers at Federal expense. What moneys the Park does have to spend on monuments are quite understandably being spent to clean and restore existing monuments. However, it seems a shame that every Southern battery except for Hart's and W. Griffin's should have a tablet—and some even have two markers.[33] In addition, it would be only fair that all the Confederate brigade positions on the first day's battlefield should be marked, since all the Federal positions there are fully documented. Since monumentation began at Gettysburg, the marking of Confederate positions has played second fiddle to the marking of Meade's lines, even in the eyes of the Federal government. It is not too late even now to make some effort to atone for this discrimination.

Confederate Monuments at Gettysburg

Texts and Descriptions of Monuments

The monuments that follow are divided into seven groups:

1) State monuments and memorials (Nos. 1-12), arranged alphabetically, with the exception of Maryland's which is No. 403.

2) Regimental and battery monuments and tablets (Nos. 13-91), arranged alphabetically by state and then by number, with the exception of the 43rd North Carolina's monument, which is No. 401.

3) Brigade and higher organization tablets (Nos. 92-196), listed by Corps.

4) Miscellaneous markers (Nos. 197-200)

5) Monuments erected from 1988 to 1994 (Nos. 201-203).

6) Tablets no longer on the battlefield (Nos. X-1 to X-10).

7) Proposed new markers and monuments (Nos. A-1 to A-19).

The beginning of each monument entry gives the following summary information: its number (keyed to the accompanying map), and title; its location and dedication or construction date; and its designer or sculptor if there is sculpture on it. After the text is given any relelvant notes or comments concerning the monument's structure and the accuracy of its text and position.

1.   ALABAMA MONUMENT

Granite monument supporting group of three bronze figures. Located west of South Confederate Avenue, .25 mile south of intersection of South Confederate Avenue and Emmitsburg Road.
Sculpted by Joseph W. Urner.
Dedicated November 12, 1933.

TEXT

Alabamians! Your names are inscribed on fame's immortal scroll. By the Alabama Division, United Daughters of the Confederacy. Unveiled November 12, 1933.

COMMENTARY

This monument was erected in 1933 by the Alabama Division of the

United Daughters of the Confederacy to commemorate the valor of the state's 16 infantry regiments, one infantry battalion, and two batteries that participated in the battle. It is located on ground occupied by Law's Alabama brigade of Hood's division about 4:00 P.M. on July 2nd, immediately prior to its attack on the Union left flank at Little Round Top.

The monument weighs 28.5 tons and is 12 feet high. It consists of a base of Vermont granite 19 feet long and 8 feet 3 inches wide that supports a plinth, a die, and a bronze sculptural group. The sculpture consists of three figures, each slightly smaller than life size. Its central figure is a standing female figure who personifies the State of Alabama. She gives comfort to a wounded young soldier who kneels at her right, and urges into battle an older soldier who kneels at her left. All three figures appear to be filled with determination and a sense of duty. The monument's sculptor was Joseph Walker Urner, a native of Frederick, Maryland, who was born in 1898. His other works include the Taney monument in Frederick. The Alabama Monument was designed by the firm of Hammaker Brothers of Thurmont and Hagerstown, Maryland, and was cast by the Roman Bronze Works of New York City.

Most of the $12,000 cost of the monument was paid for by the State of Alabama, which made its first appropriation for that purpose on September 9, 1927.[1] It was dedicated before a crowd of 1500 in ceremonies held from 2:00 to 5:00 P.M. on November 12, 1933. The monument was unveiled by Mrs. Lewis Sewall of Mobile, and was accepted on behalf of the government by Arno B. Cammerer of the National Park Service. Among the speakers at the dedication was Alabama's Senator Black, who in his address made a plea for all sections of the nation to unite and insure social justice throughout the country.

2. ARKANSAS MEMORIAL
Granite memorial with light bas relief. Located west of West Confederate Avenue, .06 mile north of intersection of West Confederate Avenue and Emmitsburg Road. Dedicated June 18, 1966.

TEXT
Arkansas. The grateful people of the State of Arkansas erect this memorial as an expression of their pride in the officers and men of the Third Arkansas Infantry, Confederate States Army, who by their valor and their blood, have made this ground forever hallowed. Third Arkansas Infantry, Confederate States Army.

COMMENTARY
The Arkansas Memorial was erected to honor the state's only unit present on the battlefield, the 3rd Arkansas Infantry of J.B. Robertson's "Texas" Brigade. It was erected on June 3-9, 1966 on the approximate

line held by the regiment before it began its attack against Devil's Den about 4:30 P.M. on July 2nd. For the regiment's movements, see Numbers 106 and 107. The 3rd Arkansas was commanded by Col. Van H. Manning and lost at least 142 casualties of its 479 officers and men engaged.

Erection of the memorial was authorized by the Arkansas State Legislature on March 19, 1965.[1] A ten man Arkansas Gettysburg Memorial Commission was set up at the same time to supervise the project. The actual construction of the monument was contracted to Cobb Memorials of Marietta, Georgia, at a cost of $50,000. The memorial, which was dedicated on June 18, 1966, consists of a 20 foot long monolith set on a three step platform. The stone is Mt. Airy granite. Overall, the memorial is 8 feet 6 inches high, 28 feet long, and 8 feet wide. At the center of the monolith is a carved outline of the state; the remainder of the monolith is adorned with a low bas relief carving of charging Alabama troops. At each of the four corners of the memorial are placed aluminum cubes that measure two feet on each side. They are engraved with a Confederate battle flag design, and symbolize Arkansas as a great aluminum producing state.

3. FLORIDA MEMORIAL
Polished granite monument.
Located west of West Confederate Avenue, .3 mile southwest of Virginia Monument; it is opposite Spangler's Woods.
Dedicated July 3, 1963.

TEXT
Florida. Floridians of Perry's Brigade, comprised of the 2nd, 5th and 8th Florida Infantry, fought here with great honor as members of Anderson's Division of Hill's Corps, and participated in the heaviest fighting of July 2 and 3, 1863. The Brigade suffered 445 casualties of the 700 men present for duty. Like all Floridians who participated in the Civil War, they fought with courage and devotion for the ideals in which they believed. By their noble example of bravery and endurance, they enable us to meet with confidence any sacrifice which confronts us as Americans. Gettysburg Memorial Commission. Adam G. Adams, Chairman. Mrs. Wilson L. Baker. Paul W. Danahy, Jr. Farris Bryant, Governor.

COMMENTARY
The Florida Memorial is one of two Confederate monuments that were dedicated on the exact centennial of the battle. It was erected on ground held by the Florida Brigade on July 2nd and 3rd. From this position the Floridians advanced to attack Cemetery Ridge about 7:15 P.M. on July 2nd, and then advanced to the support of Pickett's Charge about 3:30 P.M. on July 3rd. The memorial was dedicated at 4:30 P.M.

on July 3, 1963, exactly one hundred years after the Florida Brigade was repulsed from Cemetery Ridge. The dedication address was given by Florida Congressman Sam Gibbons of Tampa.

Construction of this memorial was authorized by the State of Florida in a bill approved by the Governor on May 30, 1963.[1] In accordance with the terms of this bill, the Governor created a Gettysburg Memorial Commission chaired by Adam G. Adams; other members of the Commission included Paul W. Danahy of Tampa, and Mrs. Wilson L. Baker, President of the Florida Chapter of the United Daughters of the Confederacy. On June 6, 1963 the committee approved a design submitted by architect J.B. Hill of Tate, Georgia. Construction of the memorial was contracted to the Bruns Monument Company of Columbia, South Carolina, at a cost of $20,000. These were the same architect and contractor who worked on the South Carolina Monument.

The completed memorial consists of two plinths on a granite base that measures 11 feet 8 inches long by 4 feet 6 inches wide. The total height of the memorial is 14 feet 3 inches; the two plinths measure 4 feet 8 inches by 1 foot 6 inches, and 4 feet 6 inches by 1 foot 2½ inches. The stone used is Select Southern Granite. The only decoration on the memorial is the Florida state seal on the taller plinth. The shorter plinth contains the historical inscription engraved below three stars, one for each of the state's regiments that fought in the battle. The text of the inscription claims that the brigade suffered over 60% casualties in the battle, but more exact sources show 250 casualties[2] out of an engaged battle strength of about 742.[3]

4. GEORGIA MONUMENT

Granite monolith.
Located west of West Confederate Avenue, .2 mile south of intersection of West Confederate Avenue and Millerstown Road.
Dedicated September 21, 1961.

TEXT

Georgia Confederate Soldiers. We sleep here in obedience to law. When duty called, we came. When country called, we died.
Georgia Confederate Soldiers. We sleep here in obedience to law. When duty called, we came. When country called, we died.

COMMENTARY

The advent of the Civil War Centennial brought increased interest in the study and commemoration of the war, especially in the South. In 1961 the Georgia Centennial Hall of Fame Committee brought it to the attention of the state legislature that no monument had been erected to honor the Georgians who had been killed at the great battles of Antietam and Gettysburg. Pursuant to their request, the Georgia General Assembly on March 1, 1961 passed a resolution to erect a monument at Antietam and one at Gettysburg.[1] The law was signed by Governor S. Ernest Vandiver on March 28, 1961.

Arrangements for the construction and dedication of the two monuments were handled by the "Centennial Hall of Fame Committee for Placing Monuments at Gettysburg and Antietam." This committee was chaired by Mrs. Forrest E. Kibler of Atlanta, who was the Honorary President of the Georgia Division of the United Daughters of the Confederacy; Mrs. Max S. Flynt of Decatur served as co-chairman. The Gettysburg monument was designed by Harry Sellers and was constructed by Marietta Memorials of Atlanta. It consists of a granite shaft set on a two step plinth. The base of the monument is 7 feet 7 inches square, the shaft is 3 feet square, and the total height of the monument is 15 feet 6 inches. All the stone is Georgia blue granite, quarried in Elberton, Georgia. The only adornment of the monument is the Georgia state seal, which appears on the upper portion of the east and the west faces of the shaft. These two faces are inscribed with identical texts as given above.

The monument specifically honors the 3000 Georgia troops who fell casualty at the battle. It is located near the position from which Brigadier General Paul Semmes led his Georgia brigade into action about 5:45 P.M. on July 2nd. Semmes was mortally wounded during this attack, the highest ranking Georgian to fall during the battle. Altogether, 7500 of Georia's 13,000 troops at Gettysburg fought within a mile of this monument. G.T. Anderson's and Benning's Georgia brigades of Hood's division began their July 2nd attacks one half mile south of the monument, while Wofford's brigade of McLaws' division was posted one half mile to the north; Wright's brigade of R.H. Anderson's division was in line one mile to the north. These brigades included 18 of the 36 infantry regiments Georgia had in the battle. The state also contributed two cavalry regiments and six batteries.

The Georgia monument at Gettysburg was dedicated in ceremonies held at 11:00 A.M. on Thursday, September 21, 1961. Its sister monument at Antietam was dedicated with a similar ceremony on the previous day. Ben W. Fortson, Jr., Secretary of State of Georgia, presided over the ceremonies. Among those giving remarks were U.S. Senator Richard B. Russell of Georgia, and Georgia Congressman Robert G. Stephens, Jr. The monument was presented to the National Park by Governor Vandiver, and was unveiled by Mrs. C. Robert Walker and Mrs. Max S. Flynt of the Hall of Fame Committee.[2]

5. LOUISIANA MEMORIAL

Two large bronze figures on granite base.
Located east of West Confederate Avenue, .1 mile north of intersection of West Confederate Avenue and Millerstown Road.

Sculpted by Donald DeLue.
Dedicated June 11, 1971.

TEXT

Louisiana. July 1, 2, 3, 1863.

Louisiana State Memorial. This Memorial was erected by the State of Louisiana to honor her sons who fought and died at Gettysburg July 1-2-3, 1863. In particular it memorializes the 2300 infantrymen of Hays' and Nicholls' Brigades, the cannoneers in the Washington Artillery of New Orleans, and those in the Louisiana Guard, Madison, and Donaldsonville Artillery Batteries.

This Memorial is presented to the Gettysburg National Military Park by the State of Louisiana under the administration of the Honorable John J. McKeithen, Governor State of Louisiana, Honorable Lamar Gibson, Director Louisiana State Parks and Recreation Commission, and the Gettysburg Memorial Commission, Mrs. Clarence R. Letteer, Chairman, Joseph A. Winkler, Vice Chairman, Mrs. Robert Jones, Secretary, Representative Nicholas Cefalu, Mrs. Felix D. Catha, Conner Sanders Davis, Senator W.D. Folkes, Mrs. J. Wallace Kingsbury, Senator Feldon H. Mitchell, Representative Harold Montgomery, Representative Ernest Singleton, Angela Gregory, Consultant.

COMMENTARY

This monument is the second, and most abstract, of the three monuments on the battlefield sculpted by Donald DeLue. The others are the Memorial to the Soldiers and Sailors of the Confederacy (No. 12) and the nearby Mississippi Monument (No. 6). For a description of DeLue's life and career, see page 47.

The memorial is 22 feet tall and consists of a bronze sculptural group on a granite pedestal. The pedestal, which is made of polished green granite, stands 3 feet high and is 9 feet 10 inches square. The sculpture consists of two figures, a reclining male figure 9 feet long, and a female figure 10 feet 6 inches high that appears to float over him as she blows a trumpet. The symbolism of the figure is perhaps best explained by the artist himself: "A great symbolic figure representing the spiritual idea of peace and memory, also a resurgent Confederacy, strong, confident and prosperous flies over the battlefield at Gettysburg, blowing the long shrill clarion call on the trumpet over the long forgotten shallow graves of the Confederate dead. It is taps for the heroic dead at Gettysburg. Beneath this figure lies a recumbent figure of a young Confederate soldier from the Washington Artillery who has paid the full price of his devotion to the cause. A comrade has laid the Confederate battle flag lovingly over the prostrate form who has clutched the flag to his heart. This is a tribute to all men who fought and died on the field of battle. In a way, it recalls to mind the tombs of the Knight Crusaders. This memorial proclaims that generations unborn at the time of Gettysburg, over one hundred seven years ago have seen fit not to forget their gallant men and that their memory shall endure for thousands of years."[1]

The movement to erect this memorial was begun by the Louisiana State United Daughters of the Confederacy on May 12, 1966, when Mrs. Clarence R. Letteer of Kentwood, Louisiana, was elected chairman of The Committee for the Louisiana Confederate Monument. This committee's proposal to the state legislature soon met a favorable response, and on September 20, 1966 the project was approved by the state. Altogether the state legislature appropriated $100,000 for the construction of the memorial. The sum of $85,000 was paid to DeLue, who won the design contest in 1968 over entries by James Rice of Hammond, Mississippi, and Jean Seidenburg of New Orleans.

In March 1969 a site for the memorial was chosen near the markers of the Washington Artillery. Quite appropriately, the fallen figure on the monument is represented as an artilleryman. However, no Louisiana troops fought at the position of the memorial. The four batteries of the Washington Artillery were actually posted five eighths mile northeast of their markers at a position near the Emmitsburg Road. This Emmitsburg Road location for the Memorial was probably not deemed suitable because there are no other markers there, and because it is not on the principal line of Confederate monuments located on West Confederate Avenue. The Louisiana unit that actually fought the closest to the site of this memorial was Moody's battery of the Madison Light Artillery, which was posted about .1 mile to the south, just north of the junction of West Confederate Avenue and Millerstown Road.

After the site was picked, the memorial's sculpture was cast in Italy. The memorial was then erected in June 1971, shortly before the dedication ceremonies that were held on Friday, June 11, 1971. At that time it was presented to the National Park Service by John J. McKeithen, the Governor of Louisiana.

6. MISSISSIPPI MONUMENT
Two large bronze soldiers on granite base.
Located east of West Confederate Avenue, .08 mile north of intersection of West Confederate Avenue and Millerstown Road.
Sculpted by Donald DeLue.
Dedicated October 19, 1973.

TEXT
Mississippi. July 1st, 2nd, 3rd, 1863. On this ground our brave sires fought for their righteous cause. In glory they sleep who gave to it their lives: to valor they gave new dimensions of courage, to duty its noblest

fulfillment, to posterity the sacred heritage of honor. Mississippi. Donald DeLue Sc. 1973.

Presented by the State of Mississippi to the National Gettysburg Military Park. Administration of Governors John Bell Williams and William L. Waller. Mississippi Gettysburg Memorial Commission. Dr. M. Ney Williams, Jr.—Chairman, Tom White Crigler, Jr.—Vice Chairman, Gray Evans—Secretary, Justice Tom P. Brady, Ed. C. Sturdevant, Clarence Pierce, Dr. Byrle A. Kynerd, Donald F. Garrett, Alfred P. Andres, Stone Barefield.

COMMENTARY

This monument, which was erected in 1973, is the third of the three Gettysburg monuments sculpted by Donald DeLue. DeLue's previous works on the battlefield were the Memorial to the Soldiers and Sailors of the Confederacy (No. 12) and the Louisiana Memorial (No. 5). His career and style are discussed on page 47.

The monument is 16 feet 2 inches tall and consists of a bronze statuary group on a granite pedestal. The pedestal is made of Lac Dubonnet granite and measures 7 feet 11 inches by 3 feet 11 inches at the base. The sculpture, which was cast in Italy, consists of two larger than life size soldiers. One lies fallen on the left, while on the right the other strains to wield his gun as a club. The work is a masterpiece in design as the tension of the fighting figure contrasts with the limpness of the fallen figure. This tension is increased by the angle at which the lines of the two figures meet. Nevertheless unity is achieved by the way that the gun of the standing figure is roughly parallel to the fallen figure. Art historian Wayne Craven points out the unity of motif gained by the fact that the standing figure on this monument has a pose very similar to the third figure from the right on the base of the Virginia Monument.[1]

Construction of the monument was authorized by the Mississippi State Legislature on May 22, 1968.[2] This same bill set up a Mississippi Gettysburg Memorial Commission of nine members to oversee the erection of the monument; the Commission was chaired by Dr. M. Ney Williams of Jackson. In 1970 the legislature appropriated the sum of $100,000 for the construction of the monument.[3]

Altogether fourteen units from Mississippi fought in the battle—eleven infantry regiments, one infantry battalion, one cavalry legion and one artillery battery. The monument is located at the position held by Barksdale's brigade of Mississippi infantry from 3:00 to 6:00 P.M. on July 2nd before its attack on the Union line at the Peach Orchard one half mile to the east (see Nos. 112 and 113). Mississippi Senator James O. Eastland was the principal speaker at the monument's dedication ceremonies, which were held at 10:00 A.M. on October 19, 1971.

7. NORTH CAROLINA MONUMENT
Five large bronze figures on a bronze base.
Located east of West Confederate Avenue, .83 mile south of Fairfield Road.
Sculpted by Gutzon Borglum.
Dedicated July 3, 1929.

TEXT
North Carolina 1863. To the eternal glory of the North Carolina soldiers, who on this battlefield displayed heroism unsurpassed, sacrificing all in support of their cause. Their valorous deeds will be enshrined in the hearts of men long after these transient memorials have crumbled into dust.

Thirty-two North Carolina regiments were in action at Gettysburg July 1, 2, 3, 1863. One Confederate soldier in every four who fell here was a North Carolinian. This tablet erected by the North Carolina Division, United Daughters of the Confederacy.

North Carolina Organizations in the Army of Northern Virginia at the Battle of Gettysburg July 1-3, 1863. 6th, 21st, 57th Infantry, Hoke's Brigade of Early's Division. 1st, 3rd Infantry, Steuart's Brigade of Johnson's Division. 32nd, 43rd, 45th, 53rd Infantry and 2nd Battalion, Daniel's Brigade of Rodes' Division. 5th, 12th, 20th, 23rd Infantry, Iverson's Brigade of Rodes' Division. 2nd, 4th, 14th, 30th Infantry, Ramseur's Brigade of Rodes' Division. 11th, 26th, 47th, 52nd Infantry, Pettigrew's Brigade of Heth's Division. 55th Infantry, Davis' Brigade of Heth's Division. 7th, 18th, 28th, 33rd, 37th Infantry, Lane's Brigade of Pender's Division. 13th, 16th, 22nd, 34th, 38th Infantry, Scales' Brigade of Pender's Division. 1st North Carolina Artillery Battery A, McLaws' Division. Branch (North Carolina) Artillery, Rowan (North Carolina) Artillery, Hood's Division. Charlotte (North Carolina) Artillery, Pender's Division. 1st Cavalry, Hampton's Brigade. 2nd, 4th Cavalry, Robertson's Brigade. 5th Cavalry, W.H.F. Lee's Brigade, Stuart's Division of Cavalry.

N.C. 1863.

COMMENTARY
The North Carolina Monument is considered by some art historians to be the most "sculptural" of all the monuments on the battlefield.[1] Its main feature is a group of five larger than life size figures who are huddled together as they strive forward to attack the Union lines. The pose is ideally suited to the monument's location, which is at the point where part of Pettigrew's North Carolina brigade of Heth's division emerged from the nearby woods at about 3:00 P.M. on July 3rd as part of the left wing of Longstreet's Assault (also known as "Pickett's

Charge") against the Union center. The scene is one filled with tension as the men lean forward in anticipation against a veritable storm of shot and shell. They are all aware that their charge will be a desperate one—and in fact over 60% of its participants did not return to their lines.[2] The poses of the figures have been perhaps described best in the following words from a speech given by former North Carolina Governor Angus McClean at the monument's dedication ceremonies: "The heroic group represents five typical North Carolina soldiers. Four of the group have just emerged from a small wooded area. As they come out of it into the open, they suddenly see the awful struggle in front of them—the Federals are just across a small ravine, both sides of which are covered with fighting men, many of whom have been wounded. The field has been torn with shot and shell. The leader of the group pushes forward determined on his grim task; the younger man just behind him is stunned momentarily at the awful sight; the bearded soldier to his left, realizing what is taking place in the youth's mind, draws close to him and whispers confidence. The color bearer in the rear presses forward, holding the flag aloft and well to the front of the group. At their right, one knee on the ground, is an officer encouraging his men, his presence and wounds indicating that the struggle has been in progress some time. The whole group discloses spirited action and typifies North Carolina troops as they charge up the heights of Cemetery Ridge."[3]

The artistry of the monument is due totally to the skill of its sculptor, Gutzon Borglum. Borglum (1867-1941) is most noted for his colossal work on Mt. Rushmore, but he is also noted for his marble bust of President Lincoln in the United States' Capitol and for equestrian statues of General Philip Sheridan in Chicago and Washington D.C. He was born in Chicago and received his training in Paris. There he came to appreciate the realistic modeling that could be achieved on bronze surfaces. This careful modeling appears on this monument not just on the faces and skin of the figures, but even on their clothing. The tension of the moment is emphasized by the motion of the figures and the unity of the group, which contrasts noticeably with the individual poses of the figures at the base of the Virginia Monument. The figures here also differ from those on the Virginia Monument in the way that Borglum does not concentrate on details of equipment the way Sievers does. Borglum depicts just enough weaponry to establish the scene, and so does not draw the viewer's attention away from the faces of the figures, which form the focus of the sculpture. Borglum added extra realism to the faces of the figures by modeling them after photographs of actual Confederate veterans. The face of the color bearer is based on a photograph of Randolph Smith of Henderson, North Carolina, who was the designer of the "Stars and Bars."

The movement to construct the monument was begun by the North Carolina Division of the United Daughters of the Confederacy in 1927. Soon the state legislature was persuaded to take up the project—one that had been delayed, in the words of Governor Gardner, "Due to a proud poverty now proudly overcome." Soon the sum of $50,000 was appropriated to pay for Borglum's design. The sculpture was cast by the A. Kunst foundry of New York and was set up in the spring of 1929. Its dedication ceremonies were held on July 3, 1929. They were presided over by North Carolina's Governor 0. Max Gardner. Former Governor Angus McClean gave the dedication speech, and the monument's sculptor, Gutzon Borglum, also spoke a few words. The monument was shrouded by three flags—the "Stars and Stripes" the "Stars and Bars," and the North Carolina state flag—and was unveiled by four children who were descendants of Confederate soldiers. It was then accepted on behalf of the government by General B.F. Cheatham (U.S.A.), the son of the former Confederate General of the same name.

The monument actually consists of a complex of markers. At each corner of the plot on which it stands is a marker that is 2 feet square and 5 feet 6 inches high; each is inscribed "N.C. 1863." The sculpture is 15 feet 9 inches high and stands on a base that measures 9 feet 9 inches by 6 feet 6 inches. At the head of a flagstone ledge is a granite slab inscribed with a list of the state's units that fought in the battle—twenty-three infantry regiments, one infantry battalion, three cavalry regiments and three batteries; the state was second only to Virginia in the number of Confederate troops furnished to the battle. This slab measures 6 feet high, 10 feet long and 6 feet deep. Nearby is a granite monolith of the same pink stone that was donated by the United Daughters of the Confederacy. It was erected by the Johnson Memorial Company at a cost of $15,000 and measures 6 feet 3 inches in height, 9 feet 7 inches in length and 1 foot 5 inches in width. This monolith was dedicated in separate ceremonies following the monument's dedication on July 3, 1929. Its dedicatory address was given by Mrs. Marshall Williams, Chairman of the marker committee of the North Carolina Gettysburg Memorial Commission.

8.   SOUTH CAROLINA MONUMENT
Granite monument.
Located west of West Confederate Avenue, .33 mile north of intersection of West Confederate Avenue and Emmitsburg Road.
Dedicated July 2, 1963.

TEXT
South Carolina. That men of honor might forever know the

responsibilities of freedom. Dedicated South Carolinians stood and were counted for their heritage and convictions. Abiding faith in the sacredness of states rights provided their creed here. Many earned eternal glory. South Carolina. South Carolina Confederate War Centennial 1861-1961. Commission. Rep. John A. May, Chairman, Sen. Wilbur R. Grant, Vice-Chairman, Hon. Roddey L. Bell, Sen. John D. Long, Sen. Walter J. Bristow, Jr., Gov. Ernest F. Hollings, Ex-Officio, Dr. Daniel W. Hollis, Mrs. W.A. King, Hon. Julian Metz, Mrs. Archie C. Watson, Dr. J.H. Eastersby, Gov. Donald S. Russell, Ex-Officio. South Carolina Gettysburg Memorial Committee. Payne Williams, Chairman, Miss Louise de Saussere Lang, Mrs. J.C. Long, Rep. John A. May, S.C.V., Mrs. W. Bedford Moore, Jr., Donald S. Russell, Jr., Mrs. Robert D. Wright, Mrs. Archie C. Watson, U.D.C. "The material in this memorial is native to the State it represents."

First Army Corps. Lieut. Gen. James Longstreet. McLaws' Division, Kershaw's Brigade, Brig. Gen. J.B. Kershaw. 2nd South Carolina Infantry. 3rd South Carolina Infantry. 7th South Carolina Infantry. 8th South Carolina Infantry. 15th South Carolina Infantry. 3rd South Carolina Infantry Battalion. Hood's Division Artillery. German Artillery. Palmetto Light Artillery. Artillery Reserve, Alexander's Battalion. Brooks Artillery. Third Army Corps. Lieut. Gen. A.P. Hill. Pender's Division, First Brigade. 1st (Gregg's) South Carolina Infantry. 1st South Carolina Rifles. 12th South Carolina Infantry. 13th South Carolina Infantry. 14th South Carolina Infantry. Artillery Reserve, Pegram's Battalion. Pee Dee Artillery. Cavalry. Stuart's Division. Maj. Gen. J.E.B. Stuart. Hampton's Brigade. Brig. Gen. Wade Hampton. 1st South Carolina Cavalry. 2nd South Carolina Cavalry. Stuart Horse Artillery. Hart's Battery.

There is no holier spot of ground Than where defeated virtue lies. Timrod.

COMMENTARY

The South Carolina Monument is one of two Confederate monuments that were dedicated on the exact centennial of the battle. It is located on ground on which Kershaw's South Carolina brigade camped on the night of July 2nd, and is near the position from which Kershaw advanced to attack the Union lines at about 5:30 P.M. on July 2nd (see No. 114). The monument's dedication ceremonies were held at 4:30 P.M. on July 2, 1963.

The monument was erected by the South Carolina Confederate War Centennial Commission at a cost of $15,000. It was designed by J.B. Hill of Tate, Georgia, and was constructed by the Bruns Monument Company of Columbia, South Carolina. These were the same architect and contractor who worked on the Florida Memorial. The monument, which is surrounded by a patio and is flanked by two marble benches, is made of Winsboro Blue Granite. It consists of several monoliths set on a base 23 feet long and 3 feet 9 inches wide. The central monolith is 14 feet 2 inches high, and measures 5 feet 5 inches by 2 feet 6 inches. On it is carved the South Carolina state seal superimposed on an outline of the state. On each side of the tall shaft are tablets listing South Carolina's eleven infantry regiments, two cavalry regiments and five batteries that fought in the battle. At the left and right ends of the monument are blocks carved with a Palmetto tree, symbolizing South Carolina as the "Palmetto State."

The text of the monument speaks of the "abiding faith in the sacredness of states' rights" held by the South Carolinians who fought here. This phrase is totally appropriate to the first state to leave the Union at the start of the war. There is no question that this was the feeling of South Carolinians 125 years ago, but its phrasing might seem anachronistic today. The two lines of poetry at the base of the central shaft are by Henry Timrod, the "Poet Laureate" of the Confederacy. He was a native of Charleston, S.C., and lived from 1829 to 1867.

9.   TENNESSEE MONUMENT
Granite monument.
Located east of West Confederate Avenue, .9 mile south of Fairfield Road.
Dedicated July 3, 1982

TEXT
Tennessee. Valor and Courage were virtues of the three Tennessee Regiments.
The Volunteer State. This Memorial is dedicated to the memory of the men of the 1st (PACS), 7th and 14th Tennessee Infantry Regiments, Archer's Brigade, Heth's Division, Third Army Corps, Army of Northern Virginia. They fought and died for their convictions performing their duty as they understood it.

	Killed	Wounded	Wounded & Missing	Missing
1st Tennessee	6	67	1	104
7th Tennessee	5	26	20	60
14th Tennessee	5	25	16	81
	16	118	37	245

Present June 30, 1863.

1st Tennessee Prov.	29 officers, 238 men	= 267
7th Tennessee	33 officers, 243 men	= 276
14th Tennessee	25 officers, 207 men	= 232
		775

COMMENTARY

After the erection of the Mississippi Monument (No. 6) in 1973, Tennessee was the only state of the old Confederacy which did not have a monument on the battlefield to her troops that fought in the battle. The cause of building the state monument to "complete the circle of stars" was taken up by Donald A. Ramsay Sr. of the Confederate High Command. He organized the Tennessee Monument Commission to oversee the project, which took nine years to reach fruition.

The original design for the monument was made by noted sculptor Felix de Weldon, the sculptor of the "Iwo Jima" memorial in Arlington, Virginia. The monument was to feature a group of three Confederate soldiers each 12 feet in height, and was to cost some $175,000. A bill to support this monument was passed by the Tennessee legislature in 1974, but it was vetoed by the governor. When the state continued to refuse to contribute to the project, plans for the monument had to be scaled down considerably. As constructed in 1982 the monument consisted of a granite slab 6 feet high, 8 feet 10 inches wide and 10 inches thick. The slab is adorned with a light relief of three charging soldiers, and supports three ten inch stars, one for each of the Grand Divisions of Tennessee. The stars are made of Elbertson gray marble and the rest of the monument is made of Carnelian select granite from the Royal Melrose Quarry in St. Cloud, Minnesota. The whole monument rests on a base shaped like the state of Tennessee. The base is 16 feet long (signifying the fact that Tennessee was the sixteenth state to join the Union) and 6 feet wide. The final cost of the monument was about $25,000, all of which was raised through private contributions.

At one point there were plans to set up a series of stepping stones to the monument. Each state whose residents contributed $500 to the monument was to be entitled to erect a stepping stone. Indiana did so in 1979, followed by the Confederate Historical Association of Belgium. When no other states followed suit, this part of the project was dropped.

The monument commemorates the role of the state's three infantry regiments (1st P.A.C.S., 7th and 14th) that served in Archer's brigade during the battle. It is located slightly to the south of where the regiments formed about 1:00 P.M. on July 3rd before advancing as part of the left wing of Longstreet's assault against the Union center. Earlier plans for the monument had been to erect it on McPherson's Ridge, where the brigade fought on July 1st (see No. 171); another proposed site was west of West Confederate Avenue just across the road from its present location.

The June 30, 1863 strength given by the monument does not include Company D or the regiment's field and staff contingent; the total strength of the regiment on June 30 was 310 (39 officers and 271 men). The June 30 strength given by the monument for the 14th regiment does not include the regiment's field and staff contingent, which is estimated to have been 5 officers and 6 men; this gives the regiment a June 30 estimated strength of 30 officers and 213 men. The total June 30 strength of Archer's three Tennessee regiments was about 829, not 775 as stated on the monument.[1]

The monument was dedicated amidst elaborate ceremonies during a steady rain on Saturday, July 3, 1982. The dedication speech was given by Donald Ramsay, Sr., and the monument was received by James W. Coleman on behalf of the United States Park Service.

10. TEXAS MONUMENT
Granite monument.
Located west of South Confederate Avenue, 450 feet south of intersection of South Confederate Avenue and Emmitsburg Road.
Dedicated September 1964.

TEXT
Texas remembers the valor and devotion of her sons who served at Gettysburg July 2-3, 1863. From near this spot the Texas Brigade at about 4:30 P.M. on July 2 crossed Emmitsburg Road and advanced with Hood's Division across Plum Run toward Little Round Top. The Texas Brigade after severe fighting on the slopes of Little Round Top retired to a position on the south side of Devil's Den. The Brigade held this position the night of July 2 and during the day of July 3. The Brigade then fell back to a position near this memorial on the evening of July 3. On the field at Gettysburg the Texas Brigade suffered 597 casualties. Texas troops at Gettysburg were: 1st Texas Inf., Lt. Col. P.A. Work; 4th Texas Inf., Lt. Col. J.C.G. Key, Lt. Col. B.F. Carter, Major J.P. Bane; 5th Texas Inf., Col. R.M. Powell, Lt. Col. K. Bryan, Maj. J.C. Rogers. The Texas Brigade included the 3rd Arkansas Inf., Col. Van H. Manning (Brig. Gen. J.B. Robertson's Texas Brigade, Hood's Division, Longstreet's Corps). Of all the gallant fights they made, none was grander than Gettysburg. A memorial to Texans who served the Confederacy. Erected by the State of Texas, 1964.

COMMENTARY
This monument was erected by the Texas State Civil War Centennial Commission to honor the role played in the battle by the 1st, 4th and 5th Texas Infantry regiments of Hood's old brigade, then led by J.B. Robertson. Its construction was due largely to the efforts of noted Texas

Brigade historian Harold B. Simpson. Simpson was a member of the Marker Committee of the Centennial Commission. This committee was chaired by Dr. Rupert N. Richardson and also had as members Professor John T. Dimean of Texas A&M University, attorney Cooper Regan of Houston, and Frank LaRue Jr. of Athens. Simpson had observed that Hood's Texas Brigade had only two small monuments (No. 108 here at Gettysburg and one at the Wilderness battlefield in Virginia), even though it had been one of the most famous units in Lee's Army of Northern Virginia. Simpson proposed that appropriate monuments to the brigade be erected at Gaines' Mill, Second Manassas, Antietam, Chickamauga, and the Wilderness, with a more elaborate memorial at Gettysburg. At one point the Texas Legislative Budget Board recommended $60,000 for the Gettysburg monument, but this amount was not appropriated by the state legislature. Instead, the Gettysburg monument finally approved was to be the same size and shape as ten other Texas monuments to be set up at the following other Civil War battle sites—Antietam, the Wilderness, Bentonville, Chickamauga, Fort Donelson, Kenesaw Mountain, Mansfield, Pea Ridge, Shiloh, and at Anthony, Texas. Those at Antietam, Gettysburg, and the Wilderness specifically honored Hood's old Texas Brigade; another monument to the brigade was planned for Second Bull Run battlefield but was never erected. The only large scale Civil War memorial Texas was to erect was to be at Vicksburg, not at Gettysburg as Simpson hoped.

The monument is 7 feet 8 inches high and consists of a red granite shaft on a marble base. The shaft measures 2 feet 7 inches by 1 foot and the base is 3 feet 6 inches by 2 feet 6 inches. It was made by the Stasswender Marble and Granite Works of Austin, Texas at a cost of approximately $1000. The monument's only adornment is the "Star of Texas" encircled by a wreath. It was dedicated in September 1964 and stands near the position from which the brigade began its attack against Devil's Den and Little Round Top at about 4:30 P.M. on July 2nd. The brigade's movements on the battlefield are outlined on No. 106 and its combat at Devil's Den is noted by No. 107.[1]

11. VIRGINIA MONUMENT

Granite monument with seven bronze figures at its base and surmounted by a bronze equestrian statue of Robert E. Lee.
Located east of West Confederate Avenue, 1.2 mile south of Fairfield Road.
Sculpted by F. William Sievers.
Dedicated June 8, 1917.

TEXT
Virginia to her Sons at Gettysburg. Memorial of the State of Virginia to the Virginia Troops at Gettysburg.
Virginia Memorial. General Robert E. Lee, Mounted on "Traveler." The

group represents various types who left civil occupations to join the Confederate Army. Left to right: a professional man, a mechanic, an artist, a boy, a businessman, a farmer, a youth. Dedicated June 6, 1917. Sculptor, F.W. Sievers.

COMMENTARY

The Virginia Monument is perhaps the noblest of the Confederate monuments on the Gettysburg battlefield. By its inspired design and location the monument commemorates all of Virginia's sons who fought in the battle—from the common Privates in each branch of the service to the commander of the Army of Northern Virginia, General Robert E. Lee. At the base of the monument seven soldiers show the tension of battle while above them General Lee, calmly astride his war horse Traveller, surveys the battlefield. These poses are especially appropriate since it was from the approximate location of this monument that Lee watched 6000 Virginians advance against Cemetery Ridge in what is commonly called "Pickett's Charge". It is also significant that Lee's statue faces directly across the once blood soaked fields to an equestrian statue of General George G. Meade, Lee's opposing commander at the battle.

The movement to erect a Virginia Monument at Gettysburg began in earnest on October 23, 1907, when the Grand Camp of the Confederate Veterans of Virginia then meeting at Norfolk passed a resolution proposed by General Lindsay L. Lomax to erect a Gettysburg Memorial "not to leaders only, but to Confederate followers worthy of great leaders."[1] This proposal soon received the favorable support of Governor Claude A. Swanson and the state's General Assembly, which on March 9, 1908 unanimously passed a bill for "the erection of a suitable monument in the National Military Park at Gettysburg, Pennsylvania, to commemorate the deeds of Virginia soldiers on that field." The bill also created a five man committee chaired by the Governor to supervise the project, and appropriated $10,000 for its construction. This amount was later increased to $50,000, with an additional $8000 for dedication expenses.

The Commission's first action was to determine a suitable location for the monument. After much consideration, the Commissioners decided that either of two sites would be acceptable. One was near Spangler Woods on West Confederate Avenue at the location from which Lee watched the charge of Pickett's Virginians on July 3rd; the other was on Cemetery Ridge inside the "Angle" at the farthest point reached by Pickett's men at the height of their charge. When these sites were discussed with the Park Commissioners and the Secretary of War, the Virginia Commissioners were told bluntly that the Cemetery Ridge site was out of the question. The Spangler Woods site, however, was acceptable to the government, and this location was accepted by the Virginia Commission.

The Commission's next step was to solicit designs for the monument. Requirements were advertised in the newspapers, and artists were invited to submit their plans. One unusual stipulation was that submitted plans had to include two alternate forms—one with an equestrian statue of General Lee and one without. Some Confederate veterans had been lobbying for a memorial to General Lee for several years, but the Virginia Commission was not totally convinced that the Lee memorial should be included as part of the Virginia Monument.

Some forty artists from all over the country submitted designs for the monument. The best plan was judged to be that of F. William Sievers. Sievers was a Northerner who had been born in Fort Wayne, Indiana in 1872 and had his studios in New York; however, he had grown up in Atlanta and Richmond, a fact that pleased the Commissioners. He had studied sculpture in Rome and in Paris, and was still in the beginning stages of his career when he received the commission for the Virginia Monument. His first public commission had been for the Confederate monument in Abington, Virginia.

Sievers' original plan had been for a monument surmounted by an equestrian statue of General Lee and having three sculptural groups at its base. Two, one on each flank of the monument, would be of Virginia soldiers, while the central group would show a Minerva-like personification of Virginia standing with a young soldier. The lower section of the monument was to undergo extensive revision before it reached its final form. Sievers' final design abandoned the side groups and Minerva figure in favor of one large group at the front of the monument's base. The central figure here was to be a mounted cavalryman; on each side of him are three figures, one artilleryman and two infantrymen. Each figure has a different pose characteristic of battle, and each shows character and emotion. The artist himself describes the figures as follows: "The group is intended to represent the three branches of military service that took part in the Battle,—infantry, artillery and cavalry. The several characters are drawn from various walks of life. The figure to the extreme left, biting off the end of a paper cartridge might well be the average man about town; the next, a mechanic. The bearded figure is of the professional type; and the gawky figure with charging bayonet, a farmer. These four characters are infantrymen. The figures with the pistol and the bugler are artillerymen. The mounted youth, a cavalry standard bearer, shows refinement, supposedly from the well-to-do class, and being possessor of a saddle horse landed him in the cavalry. The figures, in general, are intentionally robust, to symbolize the vigor of the Confederate Army.

The battered and scattered military equipment merely records incidents of the battle—symbolic of the struggle.[2]

Only two major alterations were made in this design before this section of the monument was cast in 1916. The pose of one infantryman was changed slightly, and the flag carried by the mounted cavalryman was changed from the "Stars and Bars" to the Virginia state flag. As finally sculpted, the figures are larger than life size, and each is realistic in its pose and details of equipment. Indeed, Sievers modeled the arms and accoutrements after original items used in the war. The figures appear to be grouped for combat, but the combined effect of their poses is unnatural, almost baroque—quite a contrast to the natural unity of the figures in the nearby North Carolina Monument. The mounted cavalryman's horse appears to be about to step on the artilleryman standing to his right, and seems to be slipping on all the war debris shown under his feet—a shattered cannon, broken wheel, knapsack, exploded shell, and cannon sponge. Another figure seems to be about to club one of his own fellows with his upraised musket. Thus this part of Sievers' work succeeds in its symbolism and detail, but is not totally satisfying in its overall conception.

The Lee statue is much more successful in its effect. The General is shown calmly surveying the field, a pose that is in marked contrast to the mayhem of poses in the soldiers below. Yet Lee is tense about the outcome of the conflict, a mood reinforced by the alertness of Traveler's ears. Sievers took great pains to give a realistic image of Lee and his war horse. He studied photographs of both, and paid special attention to a life mask of Lee's face that was made in 1869. Details of Lee's coat were modeled after one in the collection of the Confederate Museum in Richmond. To aid in the sculpting of Traveler, Sievers studied the horse's skeleton, which had been preserved at Washington and Lee University. He also took a great deal of time to locate a live horse of Traveller's size and characteristics to use as a model. The artist's efforts to depict both General Lee and his horse were so successful that they have been praised to this day for their expression and realism.

The ground breaking ceremonies for the monument were held on May 6, 1912. The pedestal, which is made of Mt. Airy granite, was made by the Van Amringe Granite Company and was set up in 1913 by Charles Kappes of Gettysburg. The pedestal is 24 feet high, 10 feet wide and 13 feet 7 inches long. The monument's base is 28 feet 2½ inch wide and 32 feet 62½ inches long. Completion of the monument was held up by delays in the finishing of the bronzework, which was being cast by Tiffany Studios of Long Island. When completed in 1917, the monument stood 41 feet tall. The group of soldiers at the monument's base is 18 feet long and 5 feet wide, with an overall height of 16 feet;

each soldier has a height of 8 feet. The Lee and Traveler groups stands 14 feet high. Some of the bronze accoutrements originally attached to the statue are now missing. Originally there had been a plan to inscribe on the sides of the monument the names of all Virginia's organizations and soldiers who fought in the battle, but this had to be dropped as unrealistic. The monument itself now has only a short inscription. A brief description of it is inscribed on a small tablet erected to the ease of the monument.

The Virginia Monument was dedicated on June 8, 1917, a date that was picked to coincide with a large Confederate reunion being held in Washington D.C. The principal address of the day was given by Leigh Robinson. After this the monument was unveiled by Anne Carter Lee, a granddaughter of General Lee. It was then presented to Secretary of War William M. Ingraham by Virginia's Governor, Henry Carter Stuart.[3]

12. MEMORIAL TO THE SOLDIERS AND SAILORS OF THE CONFEDERACY

Bronze statue of soldier with flag on granite pedestal.
Located west of South Confederate Avenue, .35 mile south of intersection of South Confederate Avenue and Emmitsburg Road.
Sculpted by Donald DeLue.
Dedicated August 25, 1965.

TEXT

A Memorial to the Soldiers and Sailors of the Confederacy. Heroic defenders of their country, their fame shall be an echo and a light into Eternity.

Walter Washington Williams, who was recognized by the Government of the United States as the last surviving Confederate Veteran, died 1959, at the age of 117 years. South Carolina, Florida, Georgia, Texas, Arkansas, North Carolina, Kentucky, Mississippi, Alabama, Louisiana, Virginia, Tennessee, Missouri, Maryland.

COMMENTARY

This memorial is the only one on the battlefield that specifically honors the valor of all the Confederate soldiers and sailors who served in the war. It was constructed in the summer of 1965 with funds contributed by all eleven states of the old Confederacy and the border states of Missouri, Kentucky and Maryland. The memorial was dedicated on August 25, 1965, and stands on ground occupied on July 2 and 3 by Hood's division on the extreme right flank of Lee's army.

The memorial is 19 feet 3 inches high and consists of a pedestal supporting a larger than life size figure of a charging Confederate soldier. The pedestal is made of fleshed toned granite and stands 6 feet 1 inch high with a circumference of about 12 feet. The figure has dropped his weapons and holds aloft a battle flag in his left hand; with his right hand he turns back to beckon on his followers. The figure's scale and heroic pose remind at least one critic of the powerful work of Michelangelo.[1]

The memorial's architect was William Henry Dacy, and its sculptor was Donald DeLue. DeLue was born in Boston in 1897 and has had a distinguished career that included election to the presidency of the National Sculptural Society. Two of his most famous works are Valley Forge's "Washington at Prayer," and the "Spirit of American Youth" at Omaha Beach in Normandy, France. His training included study at the school of the Museum of Fine Arts in Boston and five years' study in Paris. This combination of American and European influence produced a style that was a melding of abstraction and naturalism—a moderate voice in the turmoil of twentieth century art.

The scale and passion of this memorial and of his other two works here at Gettysburg the Louisiana and Mississippi Monuments (Nos. 5 and 6) are totally appropriate to their setting and purpose. These monuments do not memorialize specific generals or units, but instead commemorate the courage and valor of each and every soldier. Representative of these soldiers was Walter Washington Williams, who is cited on the base of this monument as the last surviving Confederate veteran. In the war Williams served as a forage master in a Texas outfit. He died on December 19, 1959, at the age of 117 years, 1 month and 5 days.

13. 4th ALABAMA INFANTRY
Bronze tablet.
Located west of South Confederate Avenue, .17 mile south of intersection of South Confederate Avenue and Emmitsburg Road.
Erected March 4, 1904.

TEXT
Army of Northern Virginia. Longstreet's Corps, Hood's Division, Law's Brigade. Fourth Alabama Infantry. July 2. Left New Guilford 25 miles distant at 3 A.M. Arrived here and formed line about 4 P.M. and under fire from Smith's Union Battery on Rocky Ridge and the sharpshooters in Plum Run Valley advanced at once against the Union position on Little Round Top. The Regiment encountered the 83d Penna. and right wing of the 20th Maine. The conflict lasted until nightfall.
July 3. Occupied breastwork on western slope of Round Top with firing on skirmish lines. At 5 P.M. intercepted near the Slyder House and aided in repulsing the Union Cavalry under Brig. Gen. Farnsworth and pursued it into the forest south of the valley. About 11 P.M. the regiment under orders resumed position near here and lay inactive the next day and night.

July 5. About 5 A.M. began the march to Hagerstown. Present Officers and Men about 275. Killed and wounded 87.

COMMENTARY

This marker shows the position taken by the regiment at 4 P.M. on July 2 immediately prior to its attack against Little Round Top; the regiment also occupied this position from 11 P.M. on July 3 to 5 A.M. on July 5. For the course of the regiment's advance against Little Round Top, see No. 105. In the text of this marker, Smith's Union battery is the 4th New York Battery, and "Rocky Ridge" is Devil's Den/ Houck's Ridge. The regiment was commanded by Lieutenant Col. L.H. Scruggs and had 367 officers and 62 men at its June 30 muster; its battle strength is estimated to have been 346.[1] Its casualties were reported by the army's Medical Director to be 66—17 killed and 49 wounded.[2]

This marker consists of a bronze tablet measuring 3 feet by 2 feet 6 inches that rests on a polished cylindrical granite pedestal 3 feet 6 inches high. It was set up by the Van Amringe Granite Company on March 4, 1904. It was apparently ordered by Major William Robbins of the Gettysburg National Military Park Commission, who had formerly served in the regiment. Robbins erected the marker as an example of the type of Confederate regimental marker he hoped would be set up for each unit. However, no one followed this example—not even his friend Colonel William Oates, who was attempting at that time to set up a marker to the 15th Alabama on Little Round Top (see pages 13-14).

14. HARDAWAY (ALA.) ARTILLERY (HURT'S BATTERY)

Cast iron tablet.
Located 60 feet west of West Confederate Avenue, .11 mile south of Fairfield Road (in Schultz Grove).
Erected 1898-1899.

TEXT

Army of Northern Virginia. Hill's Corps, Artillery Reserve. McIntosh's Battalion, Hurt's Battery. Hardaway Alabama Artillery. Two whitworths and two 3 inch rifles. July 1. The Whitworths were in position near Chambersburg Pike west of Herr's Tavern and actively engaged. The 3 inch rifles occupied the hill near Fairfield Road west of Willoughby Run but did no firing though sometimes under fire.
July 2. All the guns were in position here and actively engaged under heavy fire of sharpshooters and artillery. July 3. The 3 inch rifles remained here. The Whitworths were moved to position on Oak Hill. All were actively engaged. The Whitworths were beyond the range of Union guns whilst their own fire reached all parts of the field. July 4. Withdrew at evening to Marsh Creek on Fairfield Road. Losses not reported in detail.

COMMENTARY

This marker shows the position held by the entire battery on July 2, and by the 3 inch rifles on July 3 and 4. The battery's two whitworth guns were located at the position marked by No. 15 on July 3 and 4. The battery had an estimated battle strength of 71.[1]

15.   HARDAWAY (ALA.) ARTILLERY (WHITWORTH SECTION) (HURT'S BATTERY)

Cast iron tablet.
Located on Oak Hill, 110 feet northwest of Peace Memorial. Erected ca. 1906.

TEXT

Army of Northern Virginia. Hill's Corps, Artillery Reserve. McIntosh's Battalion, Hurt's Battery. Hardaway's Alabama Artillery. Two whitworths, two 3 inch rifles. July 1. The Whitworths were in position to the right of the Chambersburg Pike near the position of Pegram's Battalion. Opened fire slowly and effectively shelling the woods occupied by the Union troops to the right of the Town.
July 2. The Battery in position on Seminary Ridge south of the Hagerstown Road, exposed to a heavy fire from the Union Sharpshooters and Artillery.
July 3. The Whitworth guns were moved to this position and fired with great effect. The 3 inch rifles remaining on Seminary Ridge south of the Hagerstown Road.
July 4. Withdrew at evening to Marsh Creek on the Fairfield Road.
Losses not reported in detail.

COMMENTARY

This marker shows the position held by the battery's two whitworth guns on July 3 and 4. On July 1, the battery fought against the line of the Union First Corps from a position on Herr Ridge 1 1/4 mile southwest of this marker (see No. A-9). On July 2 the whitworths were posted with the rest of the battery at the position marked by No. 14. The battery had an estimated battle strength of 71.[1]

16.   JEFF DAVIS (ALA.) ARTILLERY (REESE'S BATTERY)

Cast iron tablet.
Located on Oak Hill, 190 feet north of North Confederate Avenue and .1 mile east of Peace Memorial.
Erected 1906.

TEXT

Army of Northern Virginia. Ewell's Corps, Rodes's Division. Carter's Battalion, Reese's Battery. The Jeff Davis Artillery. Four 3 inch rifles.
July 1. Was placed in position near here in support 'of Doles's Brigade against two Divisions of the Eleventh Corps which were massing on his front and left flank. It rendered effective service not only in

protecting Doles's flank but also aided in dislodging the Union Infantry and Artillery from their position in the fields north of the town.
July 2. Remained in reserve.
July 3. In position on Seminary Ridge near the railroad cut and took part in the cannonade preceding Longstreet's assault.
July 4. After nightfall began the march to Hagerstown. Losses not reported. Ammunition expended 229 rounds.

COMMENTARY

This marker shows the position held by the battery from noon July 1 until the end of the day. For its positions on July 2 and 3, see No. 155. The battery had an estimated battle strength of 79.[1]

17. MILLEDGE'S (GA.) BATTERY
Cast iron tablet.
Located on Benner's Hill, 80 feet north of Hanover Road.
Erected 1905.

TEXT

Army of Northern Virginia. Ewell's Corps, Artillery Reserve. Nelson's Battalion, Milledge's Battery. Georgia Artillery. One 10 pounder Parrott, two 3 inch rifles. July 1. The Battery arrived on the field too late to participate in the engagement of the day.
July 2. Took position on the Seminary Ridge 1/4 mile north of Chambersburg Pike. About 11 A.M. moved to the rear of Pennsylvania College and remained until night when the Battery returned to the position of the morning. July 3. Ordered to the extreme left of Confederate line to find a position to withdraw the fire from the Confederate Infantry. Opened about 12 M. firing from 20 to 25 rounds.
July 4. Took position west of town and at midnight moved on the march to Hagerstown.
Ammunition expended 48 rounds.

COMMENTARY

On July 3 this battery held a position ¼ mile north of this marker. The battery had a battle strength of about 73.[1]

18. PULASKI (GA.) ARTILLERY (FRASER'S BATTERY)
Cast iron tablet.
Located east of West Confederate Avenue, .2 mile north of intersection of West Confederate Avenue and Emmitsburg Road.
Erected 1898-1899.

TEXT

Army of Northern Virginia. Longstreet's Corps, McLaws's Division, Cabell's Battalion. Fraser's Battery. The Pulaski Artillery. Two 10 pounder Parrotts, two 3 inch rifles.

July 2. Took position here 3:30 P.M. and opened fire on Peach Orchard and the Union batteries east of it. At 4 P.M. the Rifles were silenced by loss of men. The fire of the Parrotts continued until Peach Orchard was taken.

July 3. The Parrotts were moved to crest north of Peach Orchard in main artillery line; took part in the great cannonade; aided in checking pursuit after Longstreet's assault and retired from front after dark. The Rifles were placed under command of Capt. Manly of the N.C. Artillery and served by his men in position with his own Rifles.

July 4. In position near here. After night withdrew from the field. Their ammunition was nearly exhausted. Losses. Killed 6, wounded 13. Horses killed or disabled 18.

COMMENTARY

This marker shows the position held by the battery from 3:30 P.M. on July 2 until the morning of July 3. The battery then moved ¾ mile to the northeast to the long artillery line then being formed along the Emmitsburg Road. The battery was near the right end of this line, 1/8 mile north of the Peach Orchard. The battery had a battle strength of about 63.[1] According to the report of the army's Medical Director, it had 18 casualties 4 killed and 14 wounded.[2]

19. Company "A" Sumter (Ga.) Artillery (Ross' Battery)

Cast iron tablet.
Located east of West Confederate Avenue, .42 mile northeast of Virginia Monument.
Erected 1901-1902.

TEXT

Army of Northern Virginia. Hill's Corps, Anderson's Division. Lane's Battalion, Ross's Battery. One Napoleon, three 10 pounder Parrotts, one 3 inch Navy Parrott, one 12 pounder howitzer.

July 2. Five of the guns were in position here and actively engaged under a heavy fire of artillery. The Howitzer was detached and served with Patterson's Battery south of Spangler's Woods.

July 3. Remained here and participated in all the operations of the artillery including the cannonade preceding Longstreet's assault.

July 4. Withdrew about sunset and began the march to Hagerstown. Losses. Killed 1, wounded 7, missing 2. Ammunition expended 506 rounds. Horses killed or disabled 9.

COMMENTARY

This marker shows the position occupied by most of the battery on July 2, 3 and 4; during this period the battery's howitzer was detached and served with Patterson's battery at the position marked by No. 20. The battery's battle strength was about 130.[1]

20. COMPANY "B" SUMTER (GA.) ARTILLERY (PATTERSON'S BATTERY)

Cast iron tablet.
Located east of West Confederate Avenue, .36 mile north of intersection of West
Confederate Avenue and Millerstown Road.
Erected 1901-1902.

TEXT

Army of Northern Virginia. Hill's Corps, Anderson's Division. Lane's Battalion, Patterson's Battery. Two Napoleons, four 12 pounder howitzers.

July 2. Was detached from the Battalion in the morning together with the Howitzer of Ross's Battery and ordered into position here. In the afternoon opened fire upon the Union positions north of Peach Orchard and when the infantry advanced at 6 P.M. moved forward with it beyond the Emmitsburg Road and was engaged there until dark.

July 3. Occupied a position near here in reserve and did not take part in the active operations of the day.

July 4. Withdrew about sunset and began the march to Hagerstown.

Losses. Killed 2, wounded 5, missing 2. Ammuniton expended 170 rounds. Horses killed or disabled 7.

COMMENTARY

This marker shows the position held by the battery on July 2 from the morning until 7 P.M. The battery had an estimated battle strength of 124.[1]

21. COMPANY "C" SUMTER (GA.) ARTILLERY (WINGFIELD'S BATTERY)

Cast iron tablet.
Located east of West Confederate Avenue, .35 mile northeast of Virginia Monument,
just south of North Carolina Monument. Erected 1901-1902.

TEXT

Army of Northern Virginia. Hill's Corps, Anderson's Division. Lane's Battalion, Wingfield's Battery. Two 20 pounder Parrotts, three 3 inch Navy Parrotts.

July 2. In position here actively engaged and exposed all the while to a heavy fire from the Union Artillery.

July 3. Remained here and took part in all the artillery conflicts of the day including that which preceded Longstreet's assault.

July 4. Withdrew about sunset and began the march to Hagerstown.

Losses. Wounded 9, missing 2. Ammunition expended 406 rounds. Horses killed or disabled 20.

COMMENTARY

This marker shows the position held by the battery on July 2, 3 and 4. It had an estimated battle strength of 121.[1]

22.   TROUP (GA.) ARTILLERY (FIRST SECTION) (CARLTON'S BATTERY)

Cast iron tablet.
Located west of West Confederate Avenue, .3 mile south of intersection of West Confederate Avenue and Millerstown Road.
Erected 1898-1899.

TEXT

Army of Northern Virginia. Longstreet's Corps, McLaws's Division, Cabell's Battalion. Carlton's Battery. The Troup Artillery. First Section. Two 10 pounder Parrotts.

July 2. This section took position here 3:30 P.M. and was actively engaged until near dark.

July 3. In position on the main artillery line on ridge in front of Spangler's Woods. Took part in the great cannonade and after repulse of Longstreet's assault advanced 300 yards and aided in checking pursuit. Retired from the front after dark.

July 4. Remained near here all day inactive, short of ammunition. After night withdrew from the field.

Losses of both sections. Killed 1, wounded 6. Horses of both sections killed or disabled 17.

COMMENTARY

This marker shows the general position held by the Parrott section of this battery from 3:30 P.M. on July 2 to the morning of July 3. On the 3rd it moved east to the Corps artillery line then being formed along the Emmitsburg Road (called "the ridge in front of Spangler's Woods" on the marker). There it was on the left of the line, one mile north-northeast of the Peach Orchard. The battery had a battle strength of about 90.[1]

23.   TROUP (GA.) ARTILLERY (SECOND SECTION) (CARLTON'S BATTERY)

Cast iron tablet.
Located west of West Confederate Avenue, .18 mile south of intersection of West Confederate Avenue and Millerstown Road.
Erected 1898-1899.

TEXT

Army of Northern Virginia. Longstreet's Corps, McLaws's Division, Cabell's Battalion. Carlton's Battery. The Troup Artillery. Second Section. Two 12 pounder howitzers.

July 2. This section took position here at 4 P.M. and was actively engaged until near dark.

July 3. In position near main artillery line but under cover of hill in front of Spangler's Woods. After repulse of Longstreet's assault advanced 300 yards and aided in checking pursuit. Retired from the front after dark.

July 4. In position here all day and withdrew from the field after night. Their ammunition was nearly exhausted.

Losses of both sections. Killed 1, wounded 6. Horses of both sections killed or disabled 17.

COMMENTARY

This marker shows the general position held by the howitzer section of this battery from 3:30 P.M. on July 2 to the morning of July 3. On the 3rd it moved one mile northeast to the Corps artillery line then being formed near the Emmitsburg Road, where it was posted near the left end of the position 3/8 mile east of Spangler's Woods. The battery had a battle strength of about 90.[1]

24. DONALDSONVILLE (LA.) ARTILLERY (MAURIN'S BATTERY)

Cast iron tablet.
Located east of West Confederate Avenue, .25 mile south of Fairfield Road.
Erected 1901-1902.

TEXT

Army of Northern Virginia. Hill's Corps, Heth's Division. Garnett's Battalion, Maurin's Battery. The Donaldsonville Artillery. One 10 pounder Parrott, two 3 inch rifles.

July 1. About 3:30 P.M. relieved some of Pegram's guns whose ammunition was exhausted on the ridge west of Herr's Tavern and from that time took an active part in the conflict.

July 2. In position here all day but not actively engaged until 3 P.M. when it opened and maintained a steady fire on Cemetery Hill until near sunset and vigorously renewed it at dusk for the purpose of diverting the fire of the Union Artillery from the Confederate infantry then assaulting East Cemetery Hill.

July 3. Ordered to a position south of McMillan's Woods and held in reserve, sometimes fired upon but not returning the fire.

July 4. Withdrew about 8 A.M. and marched to Cashtown to reinforce the cavalry escorting the wagon train. Losses not reported in detail.

COMMENTARY

This marker shows the position occupied by the battery on July 2. On July 1 it was engaged against the Union First Corps from a position on Herr Ridge 1¾ mile northwest of this marker (see No. A-13). On

July 3 it was held in reserve one mile south of this marker on Seminary Ridge. The battery had an engaged strength of about 114.[1]

25. LOUISIANA GUARD ARTILLERY (JULY 1 AND 2) (GREEN'S BATTERY)

Cast iron tablet.
Located .3 mile east of Harrisburg Road, .5 mile north of Rock Creek.
Erected 1907.

TEXT

Army of Northern Virginia. Ewell's Corps, Early's Division. Jones's Artillery Battalion, Green's Battery. Louisiana Guard Artillery. Two 10 pounder Parrotts, two 3 inch rifles.

July 1. Arrived on the field with Early's Division. Placed in position to the right of Tanner's Battery on the north side of Rock Creek and opened fire on Union troops on south side of creek; continued firing with effect until the Confederate Infantry was in position and advancing.

July 2. Occupied the position of the previous day; before sunset was ordered to General Hampton at Hunterstown with a section of Parrott Guns. Engaged Battery M 2d U.S. Fell back a mile and remained for the night.

July 3. Moved forward with the Cavalry about 2 P.M. Guns placed in position and opened on a column of advancing Cavalry. Received a severe fire and ordered to be withdrawn. Again engaged in the afternoon.

Casualties. Killed 2, wounded 5. Ammunition expended 161 rounds.

COMMENTARY

This marker shows the position held by the battery from 3 P.M. on July 1 until sunset on July 2. The battery then reported to Stuart's cavalry, and fought on July 3 in the cavalry engagement east of Gettysburg (see No. 26). Its estimated battle strength was 60.[1]

26. LOUISIANA GUARD ARTILLERY (JULY 3) (GREEN'S BATTERY)

Cast iron tablet.
Located east of Confederate Cavalry Avenue, .56 mile north of intersection of
Confederate Cavalry Avenue and Gregg Avenue.
Erected 1906.

TEXT

Army of Northern Virginia. Ewell's Corps, Early's Division. Jones's Battalion, Green's Battery. Louisiana Guard Artillery. Two 10 pounder Parrotts and two 3 inch rifles.

July 3. After taking part in the fighting on the previous two days at Gettysburg and Hunterstown, this Battery being detached from its

Battalion brought its Parrott guns here and rendered important service in the cavalry battle, not withdrawing until after dark. Losses. Killed 2, wounded 5. Total 7. Horses disabled 2.

COMMENTARY

This marker shows the position held by the battery from 2 to 3 P.M. on July 3. For its strength and movements on July 1 and 2, see No. 25.

27. MADISON (LA.) LIGHT ARTILLERY (MOODY'S BATTERY)

Cast iron tablet.
Located east of West Confederate Avenue, .01 mile north of intersection of West Confederate Avenue and Millerstown Road.
Erected 1901-1902.

TEXT

Army of Northern Virginia. Longstreet's Corps, Artillery Reserve. Alexander's Battalion. Moody's Battery. The Madison Light Artillery. Four 24 pounder howitzers.

July 2. Arrived here and opened fire at 4 P.M. Following the infantry charge upon the Peach Orchard took position near there and with other batteries supported the infantry in its further advance. Aided in so harassing the retiring Union forces as to compel the temporary abandonment of several guns. Kept up a spirited fire until nightfall and prevented pursuit of the Confederate advanced lines when they fell back shortly before dark.

July 3. In position at dawn in the artillery line on the ridge running north from the Peach Orchard and on duty there all day. Took part in the cannonade preceding Longstreet's assault and retired from the front after night.

July 4. Remained near here until 4 P.M. and then withdrew to Marsh Creek on the Fairfield Road.

Losses heavy but not reported in detail.

COMMENTARY

This marker shows the general position held by the battery from 4 to 7 P.M. on July 2; it was also posted near here on July 4. At 7 P.M. on the 2nd the battery moved with its battalion $5/8$ mile to the northeast to a position northeast of the Peach Orchard. On July 3 the battery was posted $1/4$ mile north of the Peach Orchard along the Emmitsburg Road. The battery had a battle strength of about 135.[1]

28. 1ST COMPANY WASHINGTON (LA.) ARTILLERY (SQUIRES'S BATTERY)

Cast iron tablet.
Located east of West Confederate Avenue, .11 mile north of intersection of West Confederate Avenue and Millerstown Road.
Erected 1901-1902.

TEXT
Army of Northern Virginia. Longstreet's Corps, Artillery Reserve.
Eshleman's Battalion, Squires's Battery. One Napoleon.
July 3. Having but one gun it co-operated all day with Miller's Battery.
Advanced before daylight into position about 100 yards north of the
Peach Orchard; assisted in repelling skirmishers and took part in the
cannonade preceding Longstreet's assault. Moved several hundred
yards to the left after the repulse of that assault to aid in resisting a
countercharge if attempted. Withdrew soon afterward to the rear.
July 4. At 9 A.M. marched with the Battalion to Cashtown to reinforce
the cavalry escorting the wagon train. Losses not reported in detail.

COMMENTARY
   This battery was not engaged at the position of this marker, but
fought ⅝ mile to the northeast, where it was posted on the Emmitsburg
Road near the Smith house. It had a battle strength of about 77.[1]

29. 2ND COMPANY WASHINGTON (LA.) ARTILLERY (RICHARDSON'S BATTERY)
Cast iron tablet.
*Located east of West Confederate Avenue, .13 mile north of intersection of West
Confederate Avenue and Millerstown Road.*
Erected 1901-1902.

TEXT
Army of Northern Virginia. Longstreet's Corps, Artillery Reserve.
Eshleman's Battalion, Richardson's Battery. Two Napoleons and one 12
pounder howitzer. July 3. The Napoleons took position before daylight
north of the Peach Orchard but moved at dawn further northward and
west of the Emmitsburg Road. A Union 3 inch Rifle left the day before
between the lines was brought in under a heavy fire of skirmishers and
served with this battery, which took part in the cannonade preceding
Longstreet's assault. After the repulse of that assault was joined by the
Howitzer and made preparations to assist in repelling a countercharge
if attempted. Withdrew from the front after dark.
July 4. At 9 A.M. marched with the Battalion to Cashtown to reinforce
the cavalry escorting the wagon train. Losses not reported in detail.

COMMENTARY
   This battery was not engaged at the position of this marker, but
fought ¾ mile to the northeast, where it was posted on the Emmitsburg
Road near the Rogers house. The captured 3 inch rifle had been left
behind by Thompson's Battery C&F Pennsylvania Artillery.[1] It was
pulled in by two drivers from this battery.[2] The battery had a battle
strength of about 80.[3]

30.   3RD COMPANY WASHINGTON (LA.) ARTILLERY (MILLER'S BATTERY)

Cast iron tablet.
Located east of West Confederate Avenue, .1 mile north of intersection of West
Confederate Avenue and Millerstown Road.
Erected 1901-1902.

TEXT

Army of Northern Virginia. Longstreet's Corps, Artillery Reserve. Eshleman's Battalion, Miller's Battery. Three Napoleons.

July 3. Advanced before daylight into position about 100 yards north of the Peach Orchard. This Battery fired the signal guns for the cannonade preceding Longstreet's assault; took part therein and supported the charge of the infantry by advancing 450 yards and keeping up a vigorous fire. After the repulse of the assault moved to the left and west of the Emmitsburg Road ready to aid in resisting a countercharge if attempted. From loss of horses but one gun could then be used. The others were sent to the rear and that gun was withdrawn after dark.

July 4. At 9 A.M. marched with the Battalion to Cashtown to reinforce the cavalry escorting the wagon train. Losses heay but not reported in detail.

COMMENTARY

This battery was not engaged at the position of this marker, but fought ⅝ mile to the northeast, where it was posted on the Emmitsburg Road near the Smith house (see No. A-6). The signal guns for the cannonade preceding Longstreet's assault were fired by this battery shortly after 1 P.M. on July 3. The battery had a battle strength of about 92.[1]

31.   4th COMPANY WASHINGTON (LA.) ARTILLERY (NORCOM'S BATTERY)

Cast iron tablet.
Located east of West Confederate Avenue, .15 mile north of intersection of West
Confederate Avenue and Millerstown Road.
Erected 1901-1902.

TEXT

Army of Northern Virginia. Longstreet's Corps, Artillery Reserve. Eshleman's Battalion, Norcom's Battery. Two Napoleons and one 12 pounder howitzer.

July 3. The Napoleons advanced before daylight into position 150 yards north of Peach Orchard near the Emmitsburg Road, but their fire in the forenoon was desultory. Took active part in the cannonade preceding Longstreet's assault and one of the guns supported the infantry attack by pushing forward 450 yards and keeping up a vigorous fire. After the assault was repulsed the Napoleons were moved several hundred yards to the left but soon disabled and sent to the rear. The Howitzer was brought forward and did effective service until withdrawn after dark.

July 4. At 9 A.M. marched with the Battalion to Cash town to reinforce the cavalry guarding the wagon train. Losses not reported in detail.

COMMENTARY

This battery was not engaged at the position of this marker, but fought ⅝ mile to the northeast, where it was posted on the Emmitsburg Road between the Smith house and the Rogers house. It had a battle strength of about 80.[1]

32. 1ST MARYLAND INFANTRY

Granite monument surmounted by granite ball.
Located east of Slocum Avenue, .06 mile southeast of southern junction of Slocum Avenue and Williams Avenue.
Dedicated November 19, 1886.

TEXT

The First Maryland Battalion Infantry. Lieut. Col. Jas. R. Herbert. Steuart's Brigade, Johnson's Division, Ewell's Corps, Army of Northern Virginia. Advancing from Rock Creek about 7 P.M. July 2 occupied the line of works at this point and held its position until next morning. On the morning of July 3rd the Battalion moving by the left flank, formed at right angles with and inside the works, and charged under a fire in front, flank and rear, to a stone planted 100 yards west from this monument. 400 strength in battle. 52 killed, 140 wounded. 1st Md. changed to 2d Md. Infantry C.S.A.

33. (32-L) 1ST MARYLAND INFANTRY, LEFT FLANK

Located 200 feet southeast of Regiment monument (No. 32).

TEXT

Left flank 1st Md. C.S.A.

34. (32-R) 1ST MARYLAND INFANTRY, RIGHT FLANK

Located 30 feet northwest of Regiment monument (No. 32).

TEXT:

Right flank 1st Md. C.S.A.

COMMENTARY

This marker was the first Confederate marker erected on the battlefield. It was erected by the regimental reunion association, and was dedicated on November 19, 1886. Captain George Thomas gave the dedicatory speech, and former brigade commander General George

"Maryland" Steuart was among the crowd of over 1500 attending the ceremony.[1]

The marker shows the position occupied by the regiment about dusk on July 2 when it held the right flank of the brigade. At this point the regiment's commander, Lieutenant Col. James R. Herbert, was mortally wounded. For the position the regiment reached in its charge on the morning of July 3, see No. 35. The regiment had a battle strength of 400.[2] Its losses were reported by the army's Medical Director to be 144—25 killed and 119 wounded.[3]

As the marker's text and flank markers show, there was some confusion about the regiment's nomenclature. The regiment was technically called the "2nd Infantry," but many of its members called it the "1st Battalion" because it was formed in September 1862 as the successor to the disbanded 1st Infantry. When the regimental association wanted to label its marker "1st Maryland Infantry," the Battlefield Association's Superintendent of Tablets and Legends, John Bachelder, insisted that the name be changed because it might be confused with two Union 1st Maryland infantry regiments present at the battle—the 1st Infantry (Potomac Home Brigade) and the 1st Infantry (Eastern Shore). For these reasons the inscription on the monument now reads "1st Md. changed to 2d Md. Infantry C.S.A." However, for some reason this change was not made on the monument's two flank markers (which read "1st Md. C.S.A.") or advanced position marker (No. 35, which reads "1st Md. Battalion C.S.A.").

The monument is 9 feet 6 inches tall and consists of a base (5 feet 4 inches square), plinth, die (2 feet 8 inches square), fascia and capstone supporting a gray granite sphere. On the west face of the die is a bas relief of the Maryland state seal, and on the same face of the fascia is a Baltimore Cross, commemorating the fact that most of the regiment was raised in Baltimore. The two flank markers are 1 foot square and 1 foot 6 inches tall.

35. 1ST MARYLAND INFANTRY (ADVANCE POSITION)
Marker.
Located 30 feet east of Geary Avenue, 50 feet southwest of northern junction of Geary Avenue and Slocum Avenue; it is about 350 feet west of its Regimental monument (No. 32).
Dedicated November 19, 1886.

TEXT
Point reached by 1st Md. Battalion C.S.A. July 3d, 1863.

COMMENTARY
This marker shows the farthest point reached by the regiment during its charge made about 8 A.M. on July 3. The regiment held the right

flank of the brigade during this advance, and had to retire when the regiments to its left refused to press the attack. For a time during this fighting the regiment faced Federal troops from Maryland. For the regiment's position before this attack, see No. 32.

36. CHESAPEAKE (MD.) ARTILLERY (BROWN'S BATTERY)
Cast iron tablet.
Located on Benner's Hill, 350 feet south of Hanover Road.
Erected 1905.

TEXT
Army of Northern Virginia. Ewell's Corps, Johnson's Division. Latimer's Battalion, Brown's Battery. The Chesapeake Md. Artillery. Four 10 pounder Parrotts.

July 2. Took position here about 4 P.M. and was engaged for over two hours in a severe conflict with the Union Batteries on East Cemetery Hill and Stevens Knoll. Capt. Brown being severely wounded, one of his guns disabled and his ammunition almost exhausted, the Battery was withdrawn by order of Gen. Johnson.

July 3. Remained in reserve and not engaged.

July 4. Withdrew from the field with the Battalion. Losses. Killed 4. Wounded 12. Horses killed 9.

COMMENTARY
This marker shows the position held by the battery from 4 to 6:30 P.M. on July 2. It then withdrew to a new position one mile to the northeast. The battery had an estimated battle strength of 76.[1]

37. FIRST MARYLAND BATTERY (DEMENT'S BATTERY)
Cast iron tablet.
Located on Benner's Hill, .13 mile south of Hanover Road.
Erected 1905.

TEXT
Army of Northern Virginia. Ewell's Corps, Johnson's Division. Latimer's Battalion, Dement's Battery. First Maryland Battery. Four Napoleons.

July 2. In position here about 4 P.M. and took part in the cannonade against the Union batteries on East Cemetery Hill and Culp's Hill which continued over two hours. When the Battalion was withdrawn, two guns of the Battery were left here to aid in repelling any attack. Soon afterward they reopened fire in support of the attack of Johnson's Infantry on Culp's Hill, which drew from the Union guns a heavy responsive fire by which Maj. Latimer was mortally wounded.

July 3. Remained in reserve and was not engaged.

July 4. Withdrew from the field with the Battalion.

Losses. Killed 1. Wounded 4. Horses killed 9. One caisson exploded and one disabled.

COMMENTARY

This marker shows the position held by the battery from 4 to 6:30 P.M. on July 2. It then withdrew to a new position one mile to the northeast. The battery had an estimated battle strength of 90.[1]

38. MADISON (MISS.) LIGHT ARTILLERY (WARD'S BATTERY)
Cast iron tablet.
Located east of West Confederate Avenue, just north of Virginia Monument.
Erected 1901-1902.

TEXT

Army of Northern Virginia. Hill's Corps, Pender's Division. Poague's Battalion, Ward's Battery. The Madison (Miss.) Light Artillery. Three Napoleons, one 12 pounder.

July 2. Late in the evening the Napoleons were placed in position about 400 yards eastward from this point.

July 3. The Napoleons participated actively in all the operations of the artillery during the day including the cannonade preceding Longstreet's assault, withdrawing afterward to a position near here. The Howitzer was kept in the rear and took no part in the battle but was held in readiness to resist any advance of the Union forces.

July 4. In the evening about dusk began the march to Hagerstown. Losses not reported in detail.

COMMENTARY

This marker shows the position held by the battery's Napoleon guns from late on the evening of July 2 until dusk on July 4. During this time the battery's howitzer was detached to a reserve position just to the north of this marker (see No. 184). From the morning to the evening of July 2 the whole battery was at a reserve position ⅛ mile southwest of this marker. The battery had a battle strength of about 91.[1]

39.   26TH NORTH CAROLINA INFANTRY
Bronze tablet on granite marker.
Located west of Meredith Avenue, .29 mile west of South Reynolds Avenue.
Dedicated October 5, 1985.

TEXT

North Carolina.

Twenty-Sixth North Carolina Regiment. Pettigrew's Brigade, Heth's Division, Hill's Corps, Army of Northern Virginia. Henry King Burgwyn, Jr., Colonel. John Thomas Jones, Major. John Randolph Lane, Lieutenant Colonel. Pettigrew's Brigade moved toward Gettysburg early on the morning of July 1 and shortly after noon deployed in line of battle on the ridge 600 yards west of here. The 26th North Carolina stood on the Brigade's left flank, facing these woods and the 24th Michigan of Meredith's Iron Brigade. The order to advance was made about 2:30 P.M. On nearing Willoughby Run the regiment received a galling fire from the opposite bank. By Maj. Jones' account the "fighting was terrible" with the forces "pouring volleys into each ether at a distance not greater than 20 paces." After about an hour the regiment had incurred very heavy losses; Col. Burgwyn had been mortally wounded and Lieutenant Col. Lane injured. The attack continued until the Union troops fell back through the streets of Gettysburg and took up positions south of town.

On July 9 Brigadier General James Johnston Pettigrew wrote that the regiment had "covered itself with glory . . . it fell to the lot of the 26th to charge one of the strongest positions possible . . . with a gallantry unsurpassed." Addressing his remarks to Zebulon Baird Vance, who had served as colonel of the 26th until his election as Governor in August 1862, Pettigrew concluded that "your old comrades did honor to your association with them, and to the state they represented." Erected by the State of North Carolina, 1985.

COMMENTARY

This monument was the third Confederate regimental marker erected on the battlefield.[1] It is located at the position at which the regiment made its flnal attack against the 24th Michigan of the "Iron Brigade" at about 3:30 P.M. on July 1. In this area the regiment lost most of its 588 casualties (86 killed and 502 wounded)[2] who fell during the battle, a number that was the highest suffered by any Confederate Regiment in any battle.[3] Its combat strength during the battle was about 840.[4]

At about 4 P.M. on July 1st the regiment was relieved in the general area of this marker by the left of Perrin's brigade. It encamped for the night in the woods $5/8$ mile to the west of here, and was held in reserve there all day on the 2nd. On July 3rd, the regiment participated in Pickett's Charge with its brigade (see No. 176).

The monument was erected largely through the efforts of Archie K. Davis, the President of the North Caroliniana Society. It was sponsored by the North Caroliniana Society in conjunction with the North Carolina Historical Commission and the North Carolina Department of Cultural Resources. It consists of a bronze plaque set on the beveled top of a granite marker. The bronze plaque was cast by Karkadoulias Bronze Art, Inc., and measures 30 by 36 inches. The marker is made of Salisbury Pink granite and consists of a shaft and plinth on a cement base. It was made by Keystone Memorials of Elverton, Georgia, and measures 54 inches in width, 48 inches in depth and 58 inches in height.

The monument was erected on September 7, 1985, and was dedicated on October 5, 1985. Archie K. Davis presided over the dedication ceremonies, and the day's speakers included William C. Friday (President of the University of North Carolina), and Civil War historians John G. Barrett and Warren W. Hassler, Jr.

40. BRANCH (N.C.) ARTILLERY (LATHAM'S BATTERY)
Cast iron tablet.
Located east of South Confederate Avenue, 300 feet south of intersection of South Confederate Avenue and Emmitsburg Road.
Erected 1898-1899.

TEXT
Army of Northern Virginia. Longstreet's Corps, Hood's Division, Henry's Battalion. Latham's Battery. The Branch Artillery. Three Napoleons, one 12 pounder howitzer, one 6 pounder bronze gun.
July 2. Took position here 4 P.M. and was actively engaged until night. The Howitzer and the Bronze gun were disabled and two captured 10 pounder Parrotts substituted.
July 3. Engaged in firing upon the Union lines within range. About 5 P.M. aided in repelling cavalry under Brig. Gen. Farnsworth which had charged into the valley between this point and Round Top.
July 4. Occupied position near by and west of this until 6 P.M. Then withdrew from the field.
Losses not reported in detail.

COMMENTARY
This marker shows the position held by the battery from 4 P.M. on July 2 until 5 P.M. on July 3. After it helped repel Farnsworth's cavalry attack on the late afternoon of the 3rd, the battery moved northwest from here to the Emmitsburg Road, where it formed facing east. The battery had an estimated battle strength of 112.[1] The two Federal 10 pounder Parrotts mentioned on the marker were captured at Devil's Den from Smith's 4th New York battery.[2]

41. CHARLOTTE (N.C.) ARTILLERY (J. GRAHAM'S BATTERY)
Cast iron tablet.
Located east of West Confederate Avenue, .33 mile north-east of Virginia Monument.
Erected 1901-1902.

TEXT
Army of Northern Virginia. Hill's Corps, Pender's Division. Poague's Battalion, Graham's Battery. The Charlotte N.C. Artillery. Two Napoleons, two 12 pounder howitzers.
July 2. Late in the evening the Napoleons were placed in position here.
July 3. At 7 A.M. they opened on the Union position but were soon ordered to cease firing as they drew concentrated fire of several

batteries. They afterward took part in all the operations of the Artillery during the day including the cannonade which preceded Longstreet's assault. The Howitzers remained in the rear and were not engaged in the battle but held in readiness to resist any advance of the Union forces. July 4. In the evening about dusk began the march to Hagerstown. Losses not reported in detail.

COMMENTARY

This marker shows the position held by the battery's Napoleon guns from late on the evening of July 2 until dusk on July 4. During this time the battery's howitzers were detached to a reserve position ¼ mile to the southwest (see No. 184). From the morning to the evening of July 2 the whole battery was at a reserve position .4 mile southwest of this marker. The battery had a battle strength of about 125.[1]

42. BATTERY "A" FIRST NORTH CAROLINA ARTILLERY (MANLY'S BATTERY)

Cast iron tablet.
Located west of West Confederate Avenue, .25 mile south of intersection of West Confederate Avenue and Millerstown Road.
Erected 1898-1899.

TEXT

Army of Northern Virginia. Longstreet's Corps, McLaws's Division, Cabell's Battalion. Manly's Battery. First North Carolina Artillery. Two Napoleons, two 3 inch rifles.
July 2. Took position here 3:30 P.M. and became active ly engaged. At 5 P.M. advanced to Peach Orchard and continued firing until dark. Returned here after night.
July 3. The Napoleons remained here. The two rifles with the two rifles of Fraser's Battery took position at 5 A.M. under Capt. Manly on crest beyond Emmitsburg Road and north of Peach Orchard; were engaged in the great cannonade and after Longstreet's assault aided in checking pursuit. Continued firing at intervals until 7:30 P.M. Then resumed this position.
July 4. At 10 A.M. aided in checking an advance of three regiments. After night withdrew from the field. Ammunition expended 1146 rounds. Losses. Killed 3, wounded 4, missing 4. Horses killed or disabled 20.

COMMENTARY

This marker shows the general position held by the battery from 3:30 to 5 P.M. on July 2, from dusk on July 2 to 5 A.M. on July 3, and from 7:30 P.M. on July 3 to the night of July 4. From 5 P.M. to dusk on July 2 the battery held a position at the Peach Orchard, ½ mile to the northeast. The position of its rifles on July 3 was on the right end of the corps artillery line, on the Emmitsburg Road about ⅛ mile north of the Peach Orchard. The battery had an estimated battle strength of 131; [1] its casualties were reported by the army's Medical Director as 1 killed and 6 wounded.[2]

43.   ROWAN (N.C.) ARTILLERY (REILLY'S BATTERY)
Cast iron tablet.
Located west of South Confederate Avenue, .3 mile south of intersection of South Confederate Avenue and Emmitsburg Road.
Erected 1898-1899.

TEXT
Army of Northern Virginia. Longstreet's Corps, Hood's Division, Henry's Battalion. Reilly's Battery. The Rowan Artillery. Two Napoleons, two 10 pounder Parrotts, two 3 inch rifles.
July 2. Took position here 4 P.M. and was actively engaged until night. One rifle burst and a captured 10 pounder Parrott was substituted.
July 3. Two Parrotts moved to right. The other guns engaged in firing upon the Union lines within range. About 5 P.M. aided in repelling cavalry under Brig. Gen. Farnsworth which had charged into the valley between this point and Round Top.
July 4. Occupied position near by and west of this until 6 P.M. Then withdrew from the field.
Losses not reported in detail.

COMMENTARY
This marker shows the position held by the battery from 4 P.M. on July 2 until 6 P.M. on July 4. On the 2nd, it faced the Union lines on the Round Tops; on the 3rd and 4th it turned to face the Union cavalry lines ¼ mile to the south. For the position held by the Parrott rifles on July 3, see No. 44. Colonel Alexander in his memoirs says that some guns of this battery were advanced to support Pickett's Charge when it was faltering about 3:30 P.M. on July 3. [1] The battery had an estimated battle strength of 148.[2] The captured Federal 10 pounder Parrott mentioned on the marker was captured at Devil's Den from Smith's 4th New York battery.[3]

44.   ROWAN (N.C.) ARTILLERY (SECTION) (REILLY'S BATTERY)
Cast iron tablet.
Located west of South Confederate Avenue, .51 mile south of intersection of Emmitsburg Road and South Confederate Avenue.

TEXT
Army of Northern Virginia. Longstreet's Corps, Hood's Division, Henry's Battalion. Reilly's Battery. The Rowan Artillery. A section: two 10 pounder Parrotts.
July 3. These guns were detached and first occupied position 300 yards

west of this, hotly engaged with the artillery of the Union Cavalry Division down the Emmitsburg Road. When the Cavalry under Brig. Gen. Farnsworth charged into the valley of Plum Run they were placed here; aided in repelling that charge and guarded this flank until night. July 4. Rejoined the Battery and shared in all its movements.

COMMENTARY

This marker shows the position of one section of this battery from 5 P.M. until dark on July 3rd. For the position held by this section during the remaining portion of the battle, see No. 43.

45. BROOKS (S.C.) ARTILLERY (RHETT'S BATTERY)

Cast iron tablet.
Located east of West Confederate Avenue, .03 mile north of intersection of West Confederate Avenue and Millerstown Road.
Erected 1901-1902.

TEXT

Army of Northern Virginia. Longstreet's Corps, Artillery Reserve, Alexander's Battalion. Rhett's Battery. The Brooks Artillery. Four 12 pounder howitzers.

July 2. Took position here at 4 P.M. and opened fire. When the charge was made on the Peach Orchard, moved to a point near there and with other batteries supported the infantry in its further advance. Assisted in harassing the retiring Union forces, causing them to abandon temporarily several guns. Continued firing until night and aided in preventing pursuit of the Confederate advanced lines when they fell back shortly before dark.

July 3. In position at dawn in the artillery line on the ridge running north from the Peach Orchard and on duty there all day. Took part in the cannonade preceding Longstreet's assault and retired from the front after night.

July 4. Remained near here until 4 P.M. and then withdrew to Marsh Creek on the Fairfield Road.

Losses heavy but not reported in detail.

COMMENTARY

This marker shows the general position held by the battery from 4 to 7 P.M. on July 2; it was also posted near here on July 4. At 7 P.M. on the 2nd the battery moved with its battalion 5/8 mile to the northeast to a position northeast of the Peach Orchard. On July 3 the battery was posted along the Emmitsburg Road 3/8 mile northeast of the Peach Orchard. The battery had a battle strength of about 71.[1]

46. GERMAN (S.C.) ARTILLERY (BACHMAN'S BATTERY)

Cast iron tablet.

Located east of South Confederate Avenue, .11 mile south of intersection of South Confederate Avenue and Emmitsburg Road.
Erected 1898-1899.

TEXT

Army of Northern Virginia. Longstreet's Corps, Hood's Division, Henry's Battalion. Bachman's Battery. The German Artillery. Four Napoleons.

July 2. In reserve near here but not engaged.

July 3. In position here and actively engaged in firing upon the Union lines within range. About 5 P.M. aided in repelling cavalry under Brig. Gen. Farnsworth which had charged into the valley between this point and Round Top.

July 4. Occupied position near by and west of this until 6 P.M. Then withdrew from the field.

Losses not reported in detail.

COMMENTARY

This marker shows the position held by the battery on July 3 and most of July 4. It spent part of the time facing the Union position on the Round Tops and part of the time facing the Union cavalry lines ¼ mile to the south. The battery had a battle strength of about 71.[1]

47. PALMETTO (S.C.) LIGHT ARTILLERY (GARDEN'S BATTERY)
Cast iron tablet.
Located east of South Confederate Avenue, .23 mile south of intersection of South Confederate Avenue and Emmitsburg Road.
Erected 1898-1899.

TEXT

Army of Northern Virginia. Longstreet's Corps, Hood's Division, Henry's Battalion. Garden's Battery. The Palmetto Light Artillery. Two Napoleons, two 10 pounder Parrotts.

July 2. In reserve near here but not engaged.

July 3. In position here and actively engaged in firing upon the Union lines within range. About 5 P.M. aided in repelling cavalry under Brig. Gen. Farnsworth which had charged into the valley between this point and Round Top.

July 4. Occupied position near by and west of this until 6 P.M. Then withdrew from the field.

Losses not reported in detail.

COMMENTARY

This marker shows the general position held by part of the battery on July 3. Colonel Alexander in his memoirs states that some guns from this battery were advanced to support Pickett's charge when it was faltering about 3:30 P.M. on the 3rd.[1] The battery had a battle strength of about 63.[2]

48.   PEE DEE (S.C.) ARTILLERY (ZIMMERMAN'S BATTERY)
Cast iron tablet.
Located east of West Confederate Avenue, .55 mile northeast of Virginia Monument.
Erected 1901-1902.

TEXT
Army of Northern Virginia. Hill's Corps, Artillery Reserve, Pegram's Battalion. Zimmerman's Battery. The Pee Dee Artillery. Four 3 inch rifles.

July 1. Three guns were in position on the ridge west of Herr's Tavern actively engaged and did effective service. The other was disabled for the day by accident while hastening into action.

July 2. Early in the morning took position here and at intervals was engaged with the Union batteries endeavoring especially to enfilade them when they sought to concentrate their fire upon the Confederate right.

July 3. Took an active part in all the operations of the artillery including the cannonade preceding Longstreet's assault.

July 4. Withdrew about sunset and began the march to Hagerstown.

Losses not reported in detail.

COMMENTARY
This marker shows the position held by the battery on July 2, 3 and 4. For its position on July 1, see No. A-10. The battery had a battle strength of about 65.[1]

49.   ALBEMARLE (VA.) ARTILLERY (WYATT'S BATTERY)
Cast iron tablet.
Located east of West Confederate Avenue, .3 mile northeast of Virginia Monument.
Erected 1901-1902.

TEXT
Army of Northern Virginia. Hill's Corps, Pender's Division. Poague's Battalion. Wyatt's Battery. The Albemarle Va. Artillery. One 10 pounder Parrott, two 3 inch rifles and one 12 pounder howitzer.

July 2. Late in the evening the Parrott and Rifles took position here.

July 3. At 7 A.M. they opened on the Union position but were soon ordered to cease firing as they drew the concentrated fire of several batteries. They afterward took part in all the operations of the artillery during the day including the cannonade which preceded Longstreet's assault. The Howitzer remained in the rear and was not engaged in the battle but held in readiness to resist any advance of the Union forces.

July 4. In the evening about dusk began the march to Hagerstown.

Losses not reported in detail.

COMMENTARY

This marker shows the position held by the battery's Parrott and rifled guns from late on the evening of July 2 to dusk on July 4. During this time the battery's howitzer was detached to a reserve position ¼ mile southwest of this marker (see No. 184). From the morning to the evening of July 2 the whole battery was at a reserve position .4 mile southwest of this marker. The battery had a battle strength of about 94.[1]

50. ALLEGHANY (VA.) ARTILLERY (CARPENTER'S BATTERY)
Cast iron tablet.
Located on Benner's Hill, .08 mile south of Hanover Road.
Erected 1905.

TEXT

Army of Northern Virginia. Ewell's Corps, Johnson's Division. Latimer's Battalion, Carpenter's Battery. The Alleghany Artillery. Two Napoleons and two 3 inch rifles.

July 2. The Battery took a prominent part in the cannonade against the Union Artillery on East Cemetery Hill and other points which began about 4 P.M. and continued over two hours. Some of the Union guns on the left enfiladed the Battalion and caused the Battery to suffer severely, and having exhausted its ammunition it was ordered to withdraw.

July 3. Remained in reserve and not engaged.

July 4. Withdrew from the field with the Battalion.

Losses. Killed 5, Wounded 24. Horses killed 9.

COMMENTARY

This marker shows the position held by the battery from 4 to 6:30 P.M. on July 2. It then withdrew to a new position one mile to the northeast. The battery had an estimated battle strength of 91.[1]

51. AMHERST (VA.) ARTILLERY (KIRKPATRICK'S BATTERY)
Cast iron tablet.
Located on Benner's Hill, 260 feet north of Hanover Road.
Erected 1905.

TEXT

Army of Northern Virginia. Ewell's Corps, Artillery Reserve. Nelson's Battalion, Kirkpatrick's Battery. Amherst Va. Artillery. One 3 inch rifle, three Napoleons.

July 1. The Battery arrived on the field too late to participate in the engagement of the day. July 2. Took position on the Seminary Ridge ¼ mile north of Chambersburg Pike. About 11 A.M. moved to the rear of Pennsylvania College and remained until night when the Battery returned to the position of the morning.

July 3. Ordered to the extreme left of Confederate line. At midnight moved with Johnson's Division to Seminary Ridge.

July 4. Took position on the ridge west of town and at midnight took up the line of march to Hagerstown. No report of casualties or ammunition expended.

COMMENTARY

On July 3 this battery held a position ¼ mile north of this marker. The battery had a battle strength of about 105.[1]

52. ASHLAND (VA.) ARTILLERY (WOOLFOLK'S BATTERY)

Cast iron tablet.
Located east of West Confederate Avenue, 200 yards south of intersection of West Confederate Avenue and Millerstown Road.
Erected 1898-1899.

TEXT

Army of Northern Virginia. Longstreet's Corps. Artillery Reserve, Alexander's Battalion. Woolfolk's Battery. The Ashland Virginia Artillery. Two 20 pounder Parrotts and two Napoleons.

July 2. Took position here 4:30 P.M. and opened fire. Joined soon in the advance of the infantry. During remainder of the day occupied position on the crest near Peach Orchard and was actively engaged in firing upon the new line of the Union forces.

July 3. In position near N.E. corner of Spangler's Woods on left of the artillery line which occupied the ridge from Peach Orchard to that point. Took part in the cannonade preceding Longstreet's assault; followed and supported it. Aided then in repelling sharpshooters and withdrew at midnight.

July 4. In position near here until 4 P.M. Then withdrew to Marsh Creek on Fairfield Road.

Losses heavy but not reported in detail.

COMMENTARY

This marker shows the general position held by the battery at about 4:30 P.M. on July 2; it was also posted near here on July 4. About 5 P.M. on the 2nd the battery moved up to support the infantry attacking the Peach Orchard. At 7 P.M. the battery joined its battalion ⅝ mile northeast of this marker at a position northeast of the Peach Orchard. On July 3 the battery was posted along the Emmitsburg Road one mile northeast of this marker. It had a battle strength of about 103.[1]

53. BEDFORD (VA.) ARTILLERY (JORDAN'S BATTERY)

Cast iron tablet.
Located east of West Confederate Avenue, .06 mile south of intersection of West Confederate Avenue and Millerstown Road.
Erected 1898-1899.

TEXT

Army of Northern Virginia. Longstreet's Corps. Artillery Reserve, Alexander's Battalion. Jordan's Battery. The Bedford Virginia Artillery. Four 3 inch rifles.

July 2. Took position here 4:30 P.M. Fired a few rounds at the Peach Orchard. Joined in the infantry charge and afterwards occupied position on crest near the Peach Orchard and was actively engaged until night.

July 3. Remained near the same position which was on the main artillery line. Took part in the cannonade preceding Longstreet's final assault and aided in supporting that assault. Retired from the front after night.

July 4. In position near here until 4 P.M. Then withdrew to Marsh Creek on Fairfield Road.

Losses serious but not reported in detail.

COMMENTARY

This marker shows the general position held by the battery at about 4:30 P.M. on July 2; it was also posted near here on July 4. About 5 P.M. on the 2nd the battery moved up to support the infantry attacking the Peach Orchard. At 7 P.M. the battery rejoined its battalion on a line ¼ mile northeast of the Peach Orchard. On July 3 the battery was posted on the Emmitsburg Road ¼ mile north of the Peach Orchard on the left flank of the battalion. The battery had a battle strength of about 78.[1]

54.   BLOUNT'S (VA.) BATTERY

Cast iron tablet.
Located east of West Confederate Avenue, .3 mile north of intersection of West Confederate Avenue and Millerstown Road.
Erected 1901-1902.

TEXT

Army of Northern Virginia. Longstreet's Corps, Pickett's Division. Dearing's Battalion, Blount's Battery. Four Napoleons.

July 3. Advanced to the front about daybreak. Later in the morning took position on the ridge west of the Emmitsburg Road 200 yards from the Rogers House and remained there for hours unengaged. When the signal guns were fired about 1 P.M., moved forward to the crest of the hill and took an active part in the cannonade. But its ammunition being exhausted as Longstreet's infantry was advancing and all efforts to procure a fresh supply proving fruitless, the Battery was withdrawn.

July 4. In line of battle all day with the left wing of McLaws's Division. Marched at sunset to Black Horse Tavern.

Losses not reported in detail.

COMMENTARY

This marker shows the general position held by the battery on July

4. During the great artillery bombardment from 1 to 3 P.M. on July 3, the battery was at a position ¼ mile north of the Rogers house, about ¾ mile northeast of this marker. The battery had an estimated battle strength of 96.[1]

55. 1ST STUART (VA.) HORSE ARTILLERY (BREATHED'S BATTERY)
Cast iron tablet.
Located east of Confederate Cavalry Avenue, .62 mile north of Gregg Avenue.
Erected 1906.

TEXT
Army of Northern Virginia. Stuart's Horse Artillery, Beckham's Battalion. Breathed's Battery. Four 3 inch rifles.
July 3. The Battery arrived here about 2 P.M. and took an active part in the fight until its ample supply of ammunition received in the forenoon was exhausted. It was withdrawn from the field about dark.
Losses. Killed 6. Wounded 8. Total 14. Horses killed or disabled 10.

COMMENTARY
This marker shows the position held by the battery from 2 P.M. until dusk on July 3. It had a battle strength of about 106.[1]

56. BROOKE'S (VA.) BATTERY
Cast iron tablet.
Located east of West Confederate Avenue, .03 mile northeast of Virginia Monument.
Erected 1901-1902.

TEXT
Army of Northern Virginia. Hill's Corps, Pender's Division. Poague's Battalion. Brooke's Battery. Two Napoleons, two 12 pounder howitzers.
July 2. Late in the evening the Napoleons were placed in position about 400 yards eastward from this point.
July 3. The Napoleons participated actively in all the operations of the artillery during the day including the cannonade preceding Longstreet's assault, withdrawing afterward to a position near here. The Howitzers were kept in the rear and took no part in the battle but were held in readiness to resist any advance of the Union forces.
July 4. In the evening about dusk began the march to Hagerstown.
Losses not reported in detail.

COMMENTARY
This marker shows the position held by the battery's Napoleons from late on the evening of July 2 to dusk on July 4. During this time the battery's howitzers were detached to a reserve position west of this marker (see No. 184). From the morning to the evening of July 2 the

73

whole battery was at a reserve position .2 mile southwest of this marker. The battery had a battle strength of about 58.[1]

57. CHARLOTTESVILLE (VA.) ARTILLERY (CARRINGTON'S BATTERY)

Cast iron tablet.
Located .05 mile east of Harrisburg Road, .5 mile north of Rock Creek.
Erected 1907.

TEXT

Army of Northern Virginia. Ewell's Corps, Early's Division. Jones's Artillery Battalion. Carrington's Battery. Charlottesville (Virginia) Artillery. Four Napoleons.

July 1. Arrived on the field with Early's Division in the afternoon. Was ordered to cross Rock Creek and move in rear of Gordon's Brigade, then advancing. Went into battery on a street in suburbs of the town and remained until near dark when ordered to a position near the railroad.

July 2. Remained near the Railroad. Not engaged.

July 3. Occupied the same position. Not engaged.

July 4. Moved in the rear of Early's Division.

Casualties not reported.

COMMENTARY

About 3 P.M. on July 1 the battery passed by the location indicated by this marker on its way to support the infantry attacking Barlow Knoll ½ mile to the southwest. It then formed ¼ mile north of town, where it remained until it withdrew to northern Seminary Ridge early on July 4. The battery had an estimated battle strength of 71.[1]

58. COURTNEY (VA.) ARTILLERY (TANNER'S BATTERY)

Cast iron tablet.
Located .28 mile east of Harrisburg Road, .5 mile north of Rock Creek.
Erected 1907.

TEXT

Army of Northern Virginia. Ewell's Corps, Early's Division. Jones's Artillery Battalion. Tanner's Battery. Courtney (Virginia) Artillery. Four 3 inch rifles.

July 1. Arrived on the field with Early's Division. Moved into battery on north side of Rock Creek. Opened an effective fire on Union Infantry on south side of the creek. Ceased firing as the Confederate Infantry advanced.

July 2. Took position of the day before; remained until 3 P.M. Ordered to report on the York Road and remained until the morning of the 3d. Not engaged.

July 3. Moved nearer the town and remained until night. Ordered to the Wagon Park to move with train to the rear. Casualties not reported. Ammunition expended 595 rounds.

COMMENTARY

This marker shows the position held by the battery from 3 P.M. on July 1 to 3 P.M. on July 2. It was then moved to a position 1⅛ mile east on the York Pike. On July 3 the battery rejoined its battalion on the northern edge of Gettysburg, one mile southwest of this marker. The battery had an estimated battle strength of 90.[1]

59.   CRENSHAW'S (VA.) BATTERY

Cast iron tablet.
Located east of West Confederate Avenue, .52 mile northeast of Virginia Monument (opposite McMillan Woods).
Erected 1901-1902.

TEXT

Army of Northern Virginia. Hill's Corps, Artillery Reserve. Pegram's Battalion, Crenshaw's Battery. Two Napoleons, two 12 pounder howitzers.

July 1. The Napoleons occupied the ridge west of Herr's Tavern and took an active part in the battle. The Howitzers were not engaged.

July 2. Early in the morning all the guns took position here and were actively engaged throughout the day. Sometimes annoyed by sharpshooters which the Howitzers aided in silencing.

July 3. Remained here and participated in all the operations of the Artillery.

July 4. About sunset withdrew and began the march to Hagerstown. Losses not reported in detail.

COMMENTARY

This marker shows the position held by the battery on July 2, 3 and 4. For its position on July 1, see No. A-10. It had a battle strength of about 76.[1]

60.   DANVILLE (VA.) ARTILLERY (WEST POSITION) (RICE'S BATTERY)

Cast iron tablet.
Located 100 feet west of West Confederate Avenue, .12 mile south of Fairfield Road.
Erected 1898-1899.

TEXT

Army of Northern Virginia. Hill's Corps, Artillery Reserve. McIntosh's Battalion, Rice's Battery. Danville Virginia Artillery. Four Napoleons.

July 1. In position near Chambersburg Pike west of Herr's Tavern and firing when Union forces were visable. Enfiladed their line at one time in and near railroad cut.

July 2. Two guns took position here and were actively engaged under heavy fire of sharpshooters and artillery. The other two guns in reserve.

July 3. All the guns were actively engaged in this position.

July 4. Withdrew at evening to Marsh Creek on Fairfield Road.

Losses not reported in detail.

COMMENTARY

This marker shows the position occupied by the battery on July 2, 3 and 4. For its position on July 1 see No. A-9. It had an estimated battle strength of 71.[1]

61. DANVILLE (VA.) ARTILLERY (EAST POSITION) (RICE'S BATTERY)

Cast iron tablet.
Located east of West Confederate Avenue, .12 mile south of Fairfield Road.
Erected 1898-1899.

TEXT

Army of Northern Virginia. Hill's Corps, Artillery Reserve. McIntosh's Battalion, Rice's Battery. Danville Virginia Artillery. Four Napoleons.

July 2. Two guns took position here and were actively engaged under the heavy fire of Union Sharpshooters and artillery. Two guns of the Battery were in reserve.

July 3. All the guns were actively engaged in this position.

July 4. Withdrew in the night to Marsh Creek on the Fairfield Road.

Losses not reported in detail.

COMMENTARY

This marker is basically a duplicate in text and position to No. 60, which is located 130 feet to the west on the other side of West Confederate Avenue.

62. FAUQUIER (VA.) ARTILLERY (STRIBLING'S BATTERY)

Cast iron tablet.
Located east of West Confederate Avenue, .2 mile north of intersection of West Confederate Avenue and Millerstown Road.
Erected 1901-1902.

TEXT

Army of Northern Virginia. Longstreet's Corps, Pickett's Division. Dearing's Battalion, Stribling's Battery. The Fauquier Artillery. Two 20 pounder Parrotts and four Napoleons.

July 3. Advanced to the front about daybreak. Later in the morning took position on the crest of ridge west of Emmitsburg Road and near the Rogers House. Drove back with a dozen well directed rounds a strong line of skirmishers whose fire wounded a few men and horses. Bore a conspicuous part in the cannonade preceding Longstreet's assault. But its ammunition being exhausted about the time the assault began and repeated efforts to obtain a fresh supply proving fruitless, the Battery was withdrawn.

July 4. In line of battle all day with the left wing of McLaws's Division. Marched about sunset to Black Horse Tavern.

Losses not reported in detail.

COMMENTARY

This marker shows the general position held by the battery on July 4. During the great artillery bombardment from 1 to 3 P.M. on July 3, the battery was at a position just north of the Rogers house, about ¾ mile northeast of this marker. The battery had an estimated battle strength of 134.[1]

63. FLUVANNA (VA.) ARTILLERY (MASSIE'S BATTERY)

Cast iron tablet.
Located on Benner's Hill, 400 feet north of Hanover Road.
Erected 1905.

TEXT

Army of Northern Virginia. Ewell's Corps, Artillery Reserve. Nelson's Battalion, Massie's Battery. Fluvanna Virginia Artillery. One 3 inch rifle, three Napoleons.

July 1. The Battery arrived on the field too late to participate in the engagement of the day.

July 2. Took position on the Seminary Ridge   mile north of Chambersburg Pike. About 11 A.M. moved to the rear of Pennsylvania College and remained until night when the Battery returned to the position of the morning. July 3. Ordered to the extreme left of Confederate line. At midnight moved with Johnson's Division to Seminary Ridge.

July 4. Took position on the ridge west of town and at midnight moved on the march to Hagerstown. No report of casualties or ammunition expended.

COMMENTARY

On July 3 this battery held a position ¼ mile north of this marker. The battery had a battle strength of about 90.[1]

64. FREDERICKSBURG (VA.) ARTILLERY (MARYE'S BATTERY)

Cast iron tablet.
Located east of West Confederate Avenue, .48 mile northeast of Virginia Monument.
Erected 1901-1902.

TEXT

Army of Northern Virginia. Hill's Corps, Artillery Reserve. Pegram's

Battalion, Marye's Battery. The Fredericksburg Artillery. Two Napoleons, two 10 pounder Parrotts.

July 1. This Battery fired the first cannon-shot of the battle from a point near the south side of the Chambersburg Pike on the ridge west of Herr's Tavern and was actively engaged until the close of the day's conflict.

July 2. Early in the morning took position here. Opened at intervals upon the Union lines and enfiladed their batteries when they sought to concentrate their fire upon the Confederate right.

July 3. Participated actively in all the operations of the artillery including the cannonade which preceded Longstreet's assault.

July 4. About sunset withdrew and began the march to Hagerstown. Losses not reported in detail.

COMMENTARY

This marker shows the position held by the battery on July 2, 3 and 4. For its position on July 1, see No. A-10. It had a battle strength of about 71.[1]

65. HAMPDEN (VA.) ARTILLERY (CASKIE'S BATTERY)

Cast iron tablet.
Located east of West Confederate Avenue, .23 mile north of intersection of West Confederate Avenue and Millerstown Road.
Erected 1901-1902.

TEXT

Army of Northern Virginia. Longstreet's Corps, Pickett's Division. Dearing's Battalion, Caskie's Battery. The Hampden Artillery. One 10 pounder Parrott, one 3 inch rifle and two Napoleons.

July 3. Advanced to the front about daylight. Later in the morning took position on the ridge west of the Emmitsburg Road and near the Rogers House, remaining for hours unengaged. When the signal guns were fired about 1 P.M. moved forward to the crest of the hill and took an active part in the cannonade. Ammunition was exhausted while Longstreet's column was advancing, the last rounds being fired at the Union infantry which assailed his right flank. Efforts to procure a fresh supply of ammunition proving unsuccessful, the Battery was withdrawn.

July 4. In line of battle all day with the left wing of McLaws's Division. Marched at sunset to Black Horse Tavern.

Losses not reported in detail.

COMMENTARY

This marker shows the general position held by the battery on July 4. During the great artillery bombardment from 1 to 3 P.M. on July 3, the battery held a position ⅛ mile north of the Rogers house, about

⅞ mile northeast of this marker. The battery had an estimated battle strength of 90.[1]

66.   HUGER (VA.) ARTILLERY (MOORE'S BATTERY)
Cast iron tablet.
Located east of West Confederate Avenue, .47 mile south of Fairfield Road.
Erected 1901-1902.

TEXT
Army of Northern Virginia. Hill's Corps, Heth's Division. Garnett's Battalion, Moore's Battery. The Huger Artillery. One 10 pounder Parrott, one 3 inch rifle, and two Napoleons.

July 1. The Parrott and Rifle about 3:30 P.M. relieved some of Pegram's guns on the ridge west of Herr's Tavern, their ammunition being exhausted, and from that time took part in the conflict.

July 2. Opened fire here at 3 P.M. on East Cemetery Hill and kept it up for some hours. Renewed it at dusk in support of Early's assault.

July 3. Moved under orders to position south of McMillan's Woods and remained inactive all day though sometimes under fire.

July 4. At 8 A.M. marched to Cashtown to reinforce the cavalry escorting the wagon train. The Napoleons took no part in the battle but were in position here on this day and at evening began the march to Hagerstown.

Losses not reported in detail.

COMMENTARY
This marker shows the position occupied on July 2 by the battery's two rifled guns; the Napoleons were held in reserve ¼ mile to the west. On July 3 the whole battery was held in reserve one mile to the south. The Napoleons were returned to the position indicated by this marker on July 4. The battery had a battle strength of about 77.[1]

67.   JACKSON'S (VA.) BATTERY
Cast iron tablet.
Located east of Confederate Cavalry Avenue, .4 mile north of Gregg Avenue.
Erected 1906.

TEXT
Army of Northern Virginia. Stuart's Horse Artillery. Captain Thomas E. Jackson's Battery. Two 3 inch rifles and two howitzers.

July 3. The Battery was attached to Jenkins' Cavalry Brigade and took part in the fight here on the right wing of the Confederates not far from the Rummel barn but its limited supply of ammunition was soon exhausted and it was withdrawn.

Losses not reported.

COMMENTARY

This marker shows the position held by the battery from noon until about 4 P.M. on July 3. It had a battle strength of about 107.[1]

68.   M. JOHNSON'S (VA.) BATTERY (WEST POSITION)
Cast iron tablet.
Located 130 feet west of West Confederate Avenue, .16 mile south of Fairfield Road.
Erected 1898-1899.

TEXT

Army of Northern Virginia. Hill's Corps, Artillery Reserve. McIntosh's Battalion, Johnson's Virginia Battery. Two Napoleons and two 3 inch rifles.

July 1. In position on hill near Fairfield Road west of Willoughby Run. Not engaged though under fire and losing one man killed.

July 2. In position here and actively engaged under a heavy fire of sharpshooters and artillery.

July 3. Remained in this position and was actively engaged.

July 4. Withdrew at evening to Marsh Creek on Fairfield Road.

Losses not reported in detail.

COMMENTARY

This marker shows the general position held by the battery on July 2, 3 and 4. On July 1 it was posted one mile to the west-northwest of this marker (see No. A-9). The battery had an estimated battle strength of 96.[1]

69.   M. JOHNSON'S (VA.) BATTERY (EAST POSITION)
Cast iron tablet.
Located east of West Confederate Avenue, .16 mile south of Fairfield Road.
Erected 1898-1899.

TEXT

Army of Northern Virginia. Hill's Corps, Artillery Reserve. McIntosh's Battalion, Johnson's Virginia Battery. Two Napoleons and two 3 inch rifles.

July 2. In position here and actively engaged under the heavy fire of Union sharpshooters and artillery.

July 3. Remained in this position all day and actively engaged.

July 4. Withdrew in the night to Marsh Creek on the Fairfield Road.

Losses not reported in detail.

COMMENTARY

This marker is basically a duplicate in text and position to No. 68, which is located 150 feet to the west on the other side of West Confederate Avenue.

70. KING WILLIAM (VA.) ARTILLERY (W.CARTER'S BATTERY)
Cast iron tablet.
Located on Oak Hill, 120 feet west-northwest of Peace Memorial.
Erected 1906.

TEXT
Army of Northern Virginia. Ewell's Corps, Rodes's Division. T.H. Carter's Battalion, W.P. Carter's Battery. The King William Artillery. Two 10 pounder Parrotts and two Napoleons.

July 1. Soon after arriving here it opened an enfilading fire on the Union forces near the Chambersburg Pike causing some to seek shelter in the railroad cuts. Their guns replied slowly but not without inflicting some losses on the Battery in its exposed position. Later in the day it moved to the foot of this ridge to aid Doles's Brigade in repelling the Eleventh Corps and rendered effective service. When the fight ended by the withdrawal of the First Corps, it pursued the Union forces to the edge of the town.

July 2. In position but was not engaged.

July 3. The Parrott guns on Seminary Ridge near the railroad cut took part in the cannonade preceding Longstreet's assault.

July 4. After nightfall began the march to Hagerstown.

Losses. Killed 4. Wounded 7. Ammunition expended 572 rounds.

COMMENTARY
This marker shows the position held by the battery from noon to 2 P.M. on July 1. It then moved ⅜ mile southeast to a position on the east slope of Oak Ridge near that marked by No. 75. For the battery's positions on July 2 and 3, see No. 155. The battery had an estimated battle strength of 103.[1]

71. LEE (VA.) ARTILLERY (RAINE'S BATTERY)
Cast iron tablet.
Located on Benner's Hill, .2 mile south of Hanover Road.
Erected 1905.

TEXT
Army of Northern Virginia. Ewell's Corps, Johnson's Division. Latimer's Battalion, Raine's Battery. The Lee Battery. Two 20 pounder Parrotts, one 10 pounder Parrott and one 3 inch rifle.

July 2. The 10 pounder Parrott and 3 inch Rifle took position here about 4 P.M. and were engaged in the severe cannonade that lasted over two hours. They also aided in supporting the attack of Johnson's Infantry on Culp's Hill and did not retire to the rear until dark. The 20 pounder Parrotts took an active part in the cannonade from their position some distance in the rear of the other guns.

July 3. The 20 pounder Parrotts were actively engaged in the great cannonade.
July 4. Withdrew from the field with the Battalion.
Losses. Wounded 8. Horses killed 3.

COMMENTARY

This marker shows the position held by two guns of the battery from 4 to 8 P.M. on July 2. They then withdrew to a new position one mile to the northeast. The battery's two 20 pounder Parrotts were posted ¾ mile northeast of this marker from 4 P.M. on July 2 until the evening of July 3. The battery had an estimated battle strength of 90.[1]

72. LETCHER (VA.) ARTILLERY (BRANDER'S BATTERY)

Cast iron tablet.
Located east of West Confederate Avenue, .62 mile northeast of Virginia Monument.
Erected 1901-1902.

TEXT

Army of Northern Virginia. Hill's Corps, Artillery Reserve. Pegram's Battalion, Brander's Battery. The Letcher Artillery. Two Napoleons, two 10 pounder Parrotts.
July 1. In position at first on the ridge west of Herr's Tavern, but moved later to a hill east of Willoughby Run about 500 yards from the Union batteries and from that point fired upon the Union infantry with much effect although itself exposed to a heavy fire of canister.
July 2. Occupied this position early in the morning and was engaged at intervals in firing upon the Union lines and batteries.
July 3. Actively participated in all the operations of the artillery including the cannonade preceding Longstreet's assault.
July 4. Withdrew about sunset and began the march to Hagerstown.
Losses not reported in detail.

COMMENTARY

This marker shows the position held by the battery on July 2, 3 and 4. For its position on July 1, see No. A-10. It had a battle strength of about 65.[1]

73. LEWIS (VA.) ARTILLERY (LEWIS'S BATTERY)

Cast iron tablet.
Located east of West Confederate Avenue, .3 mile south of Fairfield Road.
Erected 1901-1902.

TEXT

Army of Northern Virginia. Hill's Corps, Heth's Division. Garnett's Battalion, Lewis's Battery. The Lewis Artillery. Two 3 inch rifles and two Napoleons.

July 1. One of the Rifles at 3:30 P.M. relieved one of Pegram's guns on the ridge west of Herr's Tavern and was engaged until the fight ended.

July 2. Both Rifles were in position here and took an active part in the artillery duel in the afternoon and evening with the Union batteries on Cemetery Hill.

July 3. Moved under orders to a point south of McMillan's Woods but not engaged at any time although from time to time under fire.

July 4. The Napoleons were never actively engaged in the battle but on this day were placed in position here. At night they rejoined the Rifles and with them began the march to Hagerstown.

Losses not reported in detail.

COMMENTARY

This marker shows the position occupied on July 2 by the battery's rifled guns; its Napoleons were held in reserve ¼ mile to the west. On July 3 the whole battery was held in reserve one mile to the south. The Napoleons were returned to the position indicated by this marker on July 4. The battery had a battle strength of about 90.[1]

74. 2ND STUART (VA.) HORSE ARTILLERY (MCGREGOR'S BATTERY)

Cast iron tablet.
Located east of Confederate Cavalry Avenue, .5 mile north of Gregg Avenue.
Erected 1906.

TEXT

Army of Northern Virginia. Stuart's Horse Artillery, Beckham's Battalion. McGregor's Battery. Two Napoleons and two 3 inch rifles.

July 3. The Battery took an active part in the fight, arriving about 2 P.M. and keeping up its fire until the ample supply of ammunition furnished on its way here in the forenoon was exhausted. It withdrew from the field under orders about nightfall.

Losses. Killed 5. Wounded 7. Total 12.

Horses killed and disabled 11.

COMMENTARY

This marker shows the position held by the battery's Napoleons from 2 P.M. until dusk on July 2. Its rifled guns were posted one mile to the north. The battery had a battle strength of about 106.[1]

75. MORRIS (VA.) ARTILLERY (PAGE'S BATTERY)

Cast iron tablet.
Located on Oak Hill, 60 feet north of North Confederate Avenue and .1 mile east of Peace Memorial.
Erected 1906.

TEXT

Army of Northern Virginia. Ewell's Corps, Rodes's Division. Carter's Battalion, Page's Battery. The Morris Artillery. Four Napoleons.

July 1. Not engaged until the Union forces on Seminary Ridge extended their line to the right, when it opened upon then with a rapid enfilading fire in support of the Infantry in the conflict which ensued. Meanwhile it suffered from the fire of Union Artillery in the valley north of the town. Afterward moved to the foot of the ridge and aided in dislodging both the Artillery and Infantry of the Eleventh Corps.

July 2. Held in readiness to move into position but was not engaged.

July 3. On Seminary Ridge in reserve.

July 4. After nightfall began the march to Hagerstown.

Losses. Killed and mortally wounded 4, Wounded 26. Ammunition expended 215 rounds. Horses killed or disabled 17.

COMMENTARY

This marker shows the position held by the battery from 2 P.M. on July 1 until the end of the day. From noon to 2 P.M. on the 1st it was located ⅜ mile to the northwest near the position marked by No. 70. For the battery's positions on July 2 and 3 see No. 155. The battery had an estimated battle strength of 114.[1]

76. NORFOLK (VA.) LIGHT ARTILLERY BLUES (GRANDY'S BATTERY)

Cast iron tablet.
Located east of West Confederate Avenue, .5 mile south of Fairfield Road.
Erected 1901-1902.

TEXT

Army of Northern Virginia. Hill's Corps, Heth's Division. Garnett's Battalion, Grandy's Battery. The Norfolk Light Artillery Blues. Two 3 inch rifles, two 12 pounder howitzers.

July 1. Arrived on the field in the afternoon but was not engaged.

July 2. The Rifles took position here in the morning and participated during the afternoon and evening in the artillery duel with the Union batteries on Cemetery Hill.

July 3. Ordered to the south side of McMillan's Woods and held all day in reserve without firing a shot though sometimes under fire.

July 4. The Howitzers were never actively engaged in the battle but on this day were placed in position here. At night they rejoined the Rifles and with them began the march to Hagerstown.

Losses not reported in detail.

COMMENTARY

This marker shows the position occupied on July 2 by the battery's rifled guns; its howitzers were held in reserve ¼ mile to the west. On

July 3 the whole battery was held in reserve one mile to the south. The howitzers were returned to the position indicated by this marker on July 4. The battery had a battle strength of about 106.[1]

77. ORANGE (VA.) ARTILLERY (FRY'S BATTERY)

Cast iron tablet.
Located on Oak Hill, 100 feet southeast of Peace Memorial.
Erected 1906.

TEXT

Army of Northern Virginia. Ewell's Corps, Rodes's Division. Carter's Battalion, Fry's Battery. The Orange Artillery. Two 10 pounder Parrotts and two 3 inch rifles.

July 1. Opened fire soon after arriving here upon the Union troops near the Chambersburg Pike, to which their Artillery replied with a heavy fire that caused some loss. Soon afterward the Union forces extended their line northward to the Mummasburg Road and this Battery by its enfilading fire aided our Infantry in the severe conflict which ended with the withdrawal of the First Corps from Seminary Ridge.

July 2. In position but was not engaged.

July 3. All its guns were on Seminary Ridge near the Railroad cut and took part in the cannonade preceding Longstreet's assault.

July 4. After nightfall began the march to Hagerstown. Losses not reported. Ammunition expended 882 rounds.

COMMENTARY

This marker shows the position held by the battery from noon on July 1 to the end of the day. For the positions it held on July 2 and 3, see No. 155. The battery had an estimated battle strength of 80.[1]

78. PARKER'S (VA.) BATTERY

Cast iron tablet.
Located east of West Confederate Avenue, .03 mile south of intersection of West Confederate Avenue and Millerstown Road.
Erected 1898-1899.

TEXT

Army of Northern Virginia. Longstreet's Corps, Artillery Reserve. Alexander's Battalion, Parker's Battery. One 10 pounder Parrott and three 3 inch rifles.

July 2. Took position here 4 P.M. and opened fire on Peach Orchard. Joined at 5 P.M. in the infantry charge advancing to position east of Emmitsburg Road and 200 feet north of Peach Orchard continuing actively engaged until night.

July 3. Remained near the same position which was on the main artillery line; took part in the cannonade preceding Longstreet's assault and aided in supporting that assault. Retired from the front after night.

July 4. In position near here until 4 P.M. Then withdrew to Marsh Creek on Fairfield Road.

Losses heavy but not reported in detail.

COMMENTARY

This marker shows the position held by the battery from 4 to 7 P.M. on July 2; it was also posted near here on July 4. At 7 P.M. (not 5 P.M. as the marker states) the battery moved with its battalion ⅝ mile to the northeast to a position northeast of the Peach Orchard. On July 3 the battery was posted along the Emmitsburg Road ¼ mile northeast of the Peach Orchard. It had a battle strength of about 90.[1]

79. POWHATEN (VA.) ARTILLERY (CUNNINGHAM'S BATTERY)

Cast iron tablet.
Located west of Seminary Avenue, just north of Fairfield Road.
Erected 1898-1899.

TEXT

Army of Northern Virginia. Ewell's Corps, Artillery Reserve. Dance's Battalion, Cunningham's Battery. The Powhaten Artillery. Four 3 inch rifles.

July 1. Reached the field in evening too late to take part in the Battle.

July 2. Early in morning took position here. Opened fire about 4 P.M. upon the batteries on Cemetery Hill and continued firing until dark.

July 3. Remained here all day. Took part in the great cannonade preceding Longstreet's final assault. At night withdrew to camp in rear.

July 4. After nightfall began the march to Hagerstown. Ammunition expended 308 rounds. Losses not reported in detail.

COMMENTARY

This marker shows the position held by the battery from the morning of July 2 to the night of July 4. It had an estimated battle strength of 78.[1]

80. PURCELL (VA.) ARTILLERY (MCGRAW'S BATTERY)

Cast iron tablet.
Located east of West Confederate Avenue, .58 mile north of Virginia Monument.
Erected 1901-1902.

TEXT

Army of Northern Virginia. Hill's Corps, Artillery Reserve. Pegram's Battalion, McGraw's Battery. The Purcell Artillery. Four Napoleons.

July 1. In position south of the Chambersburg Pike on the ridge west of Herr's Tavern and actively engaged.

July 2. Early in the morning occupied this position and took part in the day's conflict with the Union Batteries and now and then dropped a shell among the busy sharpshooters.

July 3. Remained here and actively participated in all the operations of the artillery.

July 4. Withdrew about sunset and began the march to Hagerstown. Losses not reported in detail.

COMMENTARY

This marker shows the position held by the battery on July 2, 3 and 4. For its position on July 1, see No. A-10. The battery had a battle strength of about 89.[1]

81. RICHMOND (VA.) FAYETTE ARTILLERY (MACON'S BATTERY)

Cast iron tablet.
Located east of West Confederate Avenue, .28 mile north of intersection of West Confederate Avenue and Millerstown Road.
Erected 1901-1902.

TEXT

Army of Northern Virginia. Longstreet's Corps, Pickett's Division. Dearing's Battalion, Macon's Battery. The Richmond Fayette Artillery. Two Napoleons and two 10 pounder Parrotts.

July 3. Advanced to the front about daybreak. Later in the morning took position on the ridge west of the Emmitsburg Road and near the Rogers House but remained inactive until the signal guns were fired some time after noon. Moved forward then to the crest of the hill and took a prominent part in the cannonade. Ammunition was exhausted while Longstreet's column was advancing, the last rounds being fired at the Union infantry assailing his right flank. Efforts to procure a fresh supply of ammunition proving unsuccessful, the Battery was withdrawn.

July 4. In line of battle all day with the left wing of McLaws's Division. Marched at sunset to Black Horse Tavern.

Losses not reported in detail.

COMMENTARY

This marker shows the general position held by the battery on July 4. During the great artillery bombardment from 1 to 3 P.M. on July 3, the battery held a position just north of the Rogers house, about ¾ mile northeast of this marker. The battery had an estimated battle strength of 90.[1]

82. FIRST RICHMOND (VA.) HOWITZERS (MCCARTHY'S BATTERY)

Cast iron tablet.
Located east of West Confederate Avenue, .3 mile north of intersection of West Confederate Avenue and Emmitsburg Road.
Erected 1898-1899.

TEXT

Army of Northern Virginia. Longstreet's Corps, McLaws's Division. Cabell's Battalion, McCarthy's Battery. First Richmond Howitzers. Two Napoleons, two 3 inch rifles.

July 2. At 3:30 P.M. placed in reserve near here. The rifled guns advanced to this position at 4 P.M. and engaged in severe artillery fight until dark. The men of the Napoleon section sometimes relieved those of the rifle section.

July 3. Advanced and formed part of the main artillery line, the rifle section near Emmitsburg Road, the Napoleons further to the left, all hotly engaged, sometimes changing positions. Retired from the front after dark.

July 4. In position near here. One Napoleon aided in checking a hostile advance. All withdrew from the field at night.

Ammunition expended about 850 rounds. One rifle was disabled.

Losses. Killed 2, wounded 8. Horses killed or disabled 25.

COMMENTARY

This marker shows the position held by the battery's rifled guns from 2:30 P.M. on July 2 to the morning of July 3; in addition, the entire battery held this position on July 4. On the morning of the 3rd the battery was posted on the left end of the Corps artillery line about one mile north-northeast of the Peach Orchard. The battery's estimated battle strength was 90;[1] its casualties as reported by the army's Medical Director were 2 killed and 3 wounded.[2]

83. SECOND RICHMOND (VA.) HOWITZERS (WEST POSITION) (WATSON'S BATTERY)

Cast iron tablet.
Located 150 feet west of West Confederate Avenue, .2 mile south of Fairfield Road.
Erected 1898-1899.

TEXT

Army of Northern Virginia. Ewell's Corps, Artillery Reserve. Dance's Battalion, Watson's Battery. Second Richmond Howitzers. Four 10 pounder Parrotts.

July 1. Reached the field in evening too late to take part in the battle.

July 2. Early in the morning took position on this ridge just north of Western Maryland R.R. Cut. Opened fire about 4 P.M. upon the batteries on Cemetery Hill and continued firing until dark.

July 3. Moved to this position. Took part in the great cannonade preceding Longstreet's final assault and kept firing for some time afterwards. Withdrew at night to camp in rear.

July 4. After nightfall began the march to Hagerstown. Ammunition expended 661 rounds. Losses not reported in detail.

COMMENTARY

This marker shows the position held by the battery for most of July 3. On July 2 it was posted on Seminary Ridge about ⅞ mile north of this marker, near No. 89. The battery had a battle strength of about 64.[1]

84. SECOND RICHMOND (VA.) HOWITZERS (EAST POSITION) (WATSON'S BATTERY)

Cast iron tablet.
Located east of West Confederate Avenue, .2 mile south of Fairfield Road.
Erected 1898-1899.

TEXT

Army of Northern Virginia. Ewell's Corps, Artillery Reserve. Dance's Battalion, Watson's Battery. Second Richmond Howitzers. Four 10 pounder Parrotts.

July 3. Moved to this position. Took part in the cannonade preceding Longstreet's final assault and continued firing for some time afterwards. Moved at night to rear of this line.

July 4. In the night withdrew and began the march to Hagerstown. Ammunition expended 661 rounds. Losses not reported in detail.

COMMENTARY

This marker is substantially the same in location and text as No. 83, which is located 180 feet to the west on the other side of West Confederate Avenue.

85. THIRD RICHMOND (VA.) HOWITZERS (SMITH'S BATTERY)

Cast iron tablet.
Located west of Seminary Avenue, .1 mile north of Fairfield Road. Erected 1898-1899.

TEXT

Army of Northern Virginia. Ewell's Corps, Artillery Reserve. Dance's Battalion, Smith's Battery. Third Richmond Howitzers. Four 3 inch rifles.

July 1. Reached the field in evening too late to take part in the Battle.

July 2. Early in the morning took position here. About 4 P.M. opened fire upon the batteries on Cemetery Hill and continued firing until dark.

July 3. Moved to position south of Fairfield Road. Took part in the great cannonade preceding Longstreet's final assault and kept firing for some time afterwards. Withdrew at night to camp in rear.

July 4. After nightfall began the march to Hagerstown. Ammunition expended 314 rounds. Losses killed 1, wounded not reported.

COMMENTARY

This marker shows the position held by the battery from early morning until dark on July 2. On July 3 and 4 it was posted on Seminary

Ridge ½ mile south of this marker. The battery had an estimated battle strength of 62.[1]

86. FIRST ROCKBRIDGE (VA.) ARTILLERY (A. GRAHAM'S BATTERY)

Cast iron tablet.
Located on Benner's Hill, 180 feet south of Hanover Road.
Erected 1905.

TEXT

Army of Northern Virginia. Ewell's Corps, Artillery Reserve. Dance's Battalion, Graham's Battery. Rockbridge Artillery. Four 20 pounder Parrotts.

July 1. The battery arrived on the field too late to participate in the engagement of the day. Was ordered to report to Lieut. Colonel H.P. Jones commanding Artillery, Early's Division, and moved into position on the left, to the south and east of town.

July 2. Remained in position on the left, firing occasionally.

July 3. Remained in position during the day and rejoined the Battalion during the night.

July 4. Took up line of march to Hagerstown. Ammunition expended 439 rounds. Losses not reported in detail.

COMMENTARY

On July 2 and 3 this battery was detached from its battalion and was posted ⅝ mile north of this marker on this ridge. It had an estimated battle strength of 85.[1]

87. SECOND ROCKBRIDGE (VA.) ARTILLERY (WALLACE'S BATTERY)

Cast iron tablet.
Located 70 feet west of West Confederate Avenue, .1 mile south of Fairfield Road.
Erected 1898-1899.

TEXT

Army of Northern Virginia. Hill's Corps, Artillery Reserve. McIntosh's Battalion, Wallace's Battery. Second Rockbridge Artillery. Four 3 inch rifles.

July 1. In position near Chambersburg Pike west of Herr's Tavern and actively engaged in the evening.

July 2. Occupied this position and was actively engaged. Had one gun disabled.

July 3. Remained here and was actively engaged.

July 4. Withdrew at evening to Marsh Creek on Fairfield Road.

Losses not reported in detail.

COMMENTARY

This marker shows the general position held by the battery on July 2, 3 and 4. For its position on July 1, see No. A-9. The battery had an estimated battle strength of 67.[1]

88. SALEM (VA.) ARTILLERY (JULY 2) (C. GRIFFIN'S BATTERY)

Cast iron tablet.
Located in Sheads' Woods on Seminary Ridge, 120 feet north of Railroad Cut, 1100 feet east of North Reynolds Avenue bridge over Railroad Cut.
Erected ca. 1906.

TEXT

Army of Northern Virginia. Ewell's Corps, Artillery Reserve. 1st Virginia Artillery, Hupp's Battery. Salem Virginia Artillery. Two 3 inch rifles, two Napoleons.

July 1. The Battery reached the field too late to participate in the engagement of the day.

July 2. Held in reserve near the W.M. Railroad cut.

July 3. The Rifle guns were in position near Fairfield Road. The Napoleons were placed at the Railroad cut and remained until night but were not engaged.

July 4. At midnight began the march to Hagerstown. Casualties not reported. Ammunition expended 154 rounds.

COMMENTARY

This marker shows the position held by the battery on July 2. On July 3 the Napoleons remained here while the rifled guns were moved to the position marked by No. 89. The battery had an estimated battle strength of 69.[1]

89. SALEM (VA.) ARTILLERY (JULY 3) (C. GRIFFIN'S BATTERY)

Cast iron tablet.
Located east of West Confederate Avenue, .22 mile south of Fairfield Road.
Erected 1901-1902.

TEXT

Army of Northern Virginia. Ewell's Corps, Artillery Reserve. Dance's Battalion, Griffin's Battery. The Salem Artillery. Two 3 inch rifles, two Napoleons.

July 1. Reached the field too late to take part in the battle.

July 2. Remained in reserve on this Ridge north of the Railroad.

July 3. The Rifles were moved to this position early in the morning and took part in the cannonade preceding Longstreet's assault and continued firing for some time afterward. Withdrew at night to camp in rear.

July 4. The Napoleons occupied a position on this Ridge south of the

Railroad cut but did no firing. After nightfall they joined the Rifles and with them began the march to Hagerstown.

No losses reported. Ammunition expended 154 rounds.

COMMENTARY

This marker shows the position held by the rifled section of this battery on July 3. On July 2 it was posted at the position marked by No. 88. The battery had an estimated battle strength of 69.[1]

90. STAUNT0N (VA.) ARTILLERY (GARBER'S BATTERY)

Cast iron tablet.
Located .25 mile east of Harrisburg Road, .5 mile north of Rock Creek.
Erected 1907.

TEXT

Army of Northern Virginia. Ewell's Corps, Early's Division. Jones's Artillery Battalion, Garber's Battery. Staunton (Virginia) Artillery. Four Napoleons.

July 1. Reached the field with Early's Division and immediately went into battery near this position. Fired with effect on Howard's 11th Corps and on Infantry retiring from Seminary Ridge. Ceased firing as the Confederate Infantry advanced.

July 2. Occupied the same position. Not engaged.

July 3. Remained in the same position. Not engaged. Casualties, wounded 1. Ammunition expended 106 rounds.

COMMENTARY

This marker shows the position held by the battery from 3 P.M. on July 1 to the close of July 2. It then moved one mile to the southwest to a reserve position ¼ mile north of town near the Carlisle Road. The battery had an estimated battle strength of 60.[1]

91. TAYLOR'S (VA.) BATTERY

Cast iron tablet.
Located east of West Confederate Avenue, .02 mile south of intersection of West Confederate Avenue and Millerstown Road.
Erected 1898-1899.

TEXT

Army of Northern Virginia. Longstreet's Corps, Artillery Reserve. Alexander's Battalion, Taylor's Battery. Four Napoleons.

July 2. Took position here 4 P.M. and opened fire on Peach Orchard. Advanced at 5 P.M. with the infantry to a position about 400 feet north of Peach Orchard and east of Emmitsburg Road, continuing actively engaged until night.

July 3. Took position 3 A.M. in main artillery line near Smith House northeast of Sherfy House on Emmitsburg Road and held it all day.

Took part in cannonade preceding Longstreet's final assault, supported that assault and aided in repelling sharpshooters afterwards. Retired from the front after night.

July 4. In position near here until 4 P.M. Then withdrew to Marsh Creek on Fairfield Road.

Losses. Killed 2, wounded 10.

COMMENTARY

This marker shows the general position held by the battery from 4 to 7 P.M. on July 2; it was also posted near here on July 4. At 7 P.M. on the 2nd (not 5 P.M. as the marker states) the battery moved with its battalion ⅝ mile to the northeast to a position northeast of the Peach Orchard. At 9 P.M. it withdrew one mile to get fresh ammunition and feed its horses, returning at 2:30 A.M. on the 3rd to the Emmitsburg Road ½ mile northeast of the Peach Orchard. Captain Taylor in his battle report states that he withdrew at 10 P.M. on the 3rd, not at 4 P.M. on the 4th as the marker's text states.[1] The battery had a battle strength of about 90.[2]

92. ARMY OF NORTHERN VIRGINIA

Tablet on granite marker.
Located west of West Confederate Avenue, opposite Virginia Monument.
Erected Summer 1908.

TEXT

Army of Northern Virginia. General Robert E. Lee Commanding. The Army consisted of Three Army Corps. First Corps. Lieutenant General James Longstreet. Second Corps. Lieutenant General Richard S. Ewell. Third Corps. Lieutenant General Ambrose P. Hill. Cavalry Division. Major General J.E.B. Stuart.

July 1. Heth's and Pender's Divisions, Hill's Corps, and Early's and Rodes's Divisions, Ewell's Corps, reached the field about 1 P.M. and were soon engaged on the North and West of town with the First and Eleventh Corps of the Army of the Potomac. Johnson's Division, Ewell's Corps, and Anderson's Division, Hill's Corps, reaching the field about dark, were not engaged; Longstreet's Corps on the march. Stuart's Cavalry Division marching from Dover to Carlisle.

July 2. McLaws's and Hood's Divisions, Longstreet's Corps, arrived on the field about 3 P.M. and formed facing the Union left. An assault was made by the two Divisions assisted by Anderson's Division, Hill's Corps. The Union troops were dislodged from Emmitsburg Road and Peach Orchard, engagement lasting until night; losses heavy. Pickett's Division, Longstreet's Corps, on the march. Johnson's Division, Ewell's Corps, about dusk advanced to the assault of Culp's Hill in connection with Early's Division, Ewell's Corps. Rodes's Division, Ewell's Corps, held position in valley west of town; not engaged. Heth's and Pender's Divisions, Hill's Corps, occupied Seminary Ridge facing Union line; not engaged. Stuart's Cavalry on left flank of Confederate Army.

July 3. Pickett's Division, Longstreet's Corps, reached the field in the morning. Assaulted the Union line on Cemetery Ridge about 3 P.M. assisted by Hill's Corps. The assault failed with great loss. An attack made on the left by Johnson's Division, Ewell's Corps, reinforced by three Brigades of the Corps, failed. Stuart's Cavalry Division engaged with 2d Union Cavalry Division and 2d Brigade 3d Cavalry Division on the Confederate left about 1 P.M.

July 4. The Army took up the line of march during the night.

COMMENTARY

This marker is located near the center of the Confederate line of battle on July 2, 3 and 4. From near this position General Lee watched some of the fighting on July 2 and 3, though his actual headquarters were one mile to the north (see No. 94). The army had a battle strength of 70,274[1] and suffered 20, 451 reported casualties—2592 killed, 12, 709 wounded and 5150 captured or missing.[2]

The marker's text errs on the arrival times of the different divisions on July 1. Heth's division was in action by 8 A.M., Rodes and Pender were on the field by noon, and Early was forming for battle before 1 P.M. The July 2 text errs by stating that McLaws and Hood arrived on the field at 3 P.M. This was actually the time when they began forming their battle lines; they had been on the field since early morning. In addition, Pickett's division reached the battlefield area late on the afternoon of the 2nd, not on the morning of the 3rd as the marker's text states. On July 3, Johnson's division was reinforced by four brigades of Ewell's Corps (Daniel's, O'Neal's, Walker's and Smith's), not three as the marker's text states.

93.   RIGHT OF THE ARMY OF NORTHERN VIRGINIA

Tablet.
Located west of South Confederate Avenue, .52 mile south of intersection of South Confederate Avenue and Emmitsburg Road.
Erected November 1, 1900.

TEXT

Right of the Army of Northern Virginia.

COMMENTARY

This marker is symbolic of the right flank of the Army of Northern Virginia, but does not show the actual position of any units. Part of Law's brigade was posted nearby at the Slyder farm on July 3, and one section of Reilly's battery was posted slightly to the west of this marker on the late afternoon of July 3 (see No. 44). The primary purpose of this marker is probably to show the boundary between the Union and Confederate lines to those traveling along South Confederate Avenue.

94. LEE'S HEADQUARTERS

Bronze cannon barrel in concrete base.
Located south of Chambersburg Pike, 200 feet west of Seminary Avenue.
Erected 1920-1921.

TEXT

C.S.A. In this field was located Head Quarters of the Army of Northern Virginia, July 1, 2, 3, 4, 1863. "My Head Quarters were in an apple orchard back of the Seminary along the Chambersburg Pike." Robt. E. Lee.

COMMENTARY

This marker shows the location occupied by General Lee's field headquarters on July 2, 3 and 4. On July 1, and occasionally during the rest of the battle, he held meetings in the Thompson house on the north side of the Chambersburg Pike near this marker. It was but a short ride from here to the Lutheran Seminary 1000 feet to the south, whose cupola offered the best observation post in the area. On July 2 and 3 Lee at times observed the fighting from the position now marked by the Virginia Monument (see Nos. 11 and 92).

95. LONGSTREET'S CORPS

Tablet on granite marker.
Located west of West Confederate Avenue, .02 mile south of intersection of West Confederate Avenue and Millerstown Road.
Erected 1907.

TEXT

Army of Northern Virginia. First Army Corps. Lieutenant General James Longstreet. McLaws's Division. Major General Lafayette McLaws. Pickett's Division. Major General George E. Pickett. Hood's Division. Major General John B. Hood, Brigadier General E.M. Law. Artillery Reserve. Ten Batteries. Colonel J.B. Walton.
July 1. McLaws's Division encamped about four miles from Gettysburg a little after dark. Hood's Division reached the same distance about 12 P.M. Law's Brigade on picket at New Guilford. Pickett's Division guarding trains at Chambersburg.
July 2. Moved that portion of the Command which was up to gain the Emmitsburg Road on Union left. Delayed attack until 3:30 P.M. when Law's Brigade joined from New Guilford. McLaws's Division in position facing Union left. About 4 P.M. Hood's Division moved further to the right and took position partially enveloping Union left. The Batteries opened about 4 P.M. upon Union troops on Emmitsburg Road, Hood's Division pressing on left and McLaws's in front; the Union

troops were dislodged. The engagement lasted until nearly night with heavy losses. The ground gained on the front was held. The left was withdrawn to first Union position at Peach Orchard.

July 3. Pickett's Division reached the field at 9 A.M. Pickett's, Heth's and part of Pender's Division were ordered to form column of assault on Union centre on Cemetery Hill. The Batteries opened about 1 P.M. About 3 P.M. Pickett advanced in good order under a severe fire and was repulsed at the stone wall losing heavily. McLaws's and Hood's Divisions were not seriously engaged and after rectifying their lines remained on the field during the day and night.

July 4. The Corps took up the line of march during the night.

Casualties. Killed 910, wounded 4339, captured or missing 2290. Total 7539.

COMMENTARY

This marker is located on the left of the position held by McLaws' division from 4 to 6:30 P.M. oN July 2. The corps had a battle strength of 20, 935[1] and reported 7539 casualties—910 killed, 4339 wounded, and 2290 captured or missing.[2] The July 2 text is in error by stating that "The ground gained on the front was held." The corps did hold onto gains at the Peach Orchard, Rose Woods, and Devil's Den, but counterattacks drove it back from the Round Tops and the Wheatfield. The July 3 text errs at two points. Firstly, Pickett's division arrived in the battle area on the afternoon of the 2nd, not the morning of the 3rd. Secondly, no mention is made of the Union cavalry attack against Hood's division late on the afternoon of the 3rd.

96. LONGSTREET'S HEADQUARTERS

Cannon barrel in granite base.
Located west of West Confederate Avenue, .08 mile south of intersection of West Confederate Avenue and Millerstown Road.
Erected 1920-1921.

TEXT

C.S.A. Army of Northern Virginia. 1st Corps Headquarters. Lieut. Gen. James Longstreet. Divisions. Major Gen. Lafayette McLaws. Major Gen. George E. Pickett. Major Gen. John B. Hood. July 1, 2, 3, 4, 5, 1863. These headquarters were located at a schoolhouse 900 yards westerly.

COMMENTARY

As the marker states, Longstreet's headquarters were located some 900 yards west of the marker at a schoolhouse. This schoolhouse was adjacent to Willoughby Run, about 300 yards south of the S. Pitzer farm. Longstreet had his headquarters there for only three days (July 2, 3, and 4), not the five days stated on the marker. The First Corps did not begin to form on this flank until the afternoon of July 2, and it retreated from this area about midnight on July 4/5. For the proposed monument to General Longstreet, see No. A-5.

97.   ALEXANDER'S BATTALION
Tablet on granite pedestal.
Located east of West Confederate Avenue, .03 mile south of intersection of West Confederate Avenue and Millers-town Road.
Erected 1910-1911, replacing earlier tablet erected ca. 1903.

TEXT
C.S.A. Army of Northern Virginia. Longstreet's Corps, Artillery Reserve, Alexander's Battalion. Woolfolk's, Jordan's, Parker's, Taylor's, Moody's and Rhett's Batteries. Two 20 pounder Parrotts, one 10 pounder Parrott, seven 3 inch rifles, six Napoleons, four 24 pounder howitzers, four 12 pounder howitzers.
July 2. Came into position on this line about 4 P.M. Advanced soon after with the Infantry and occupied a line on the crest near the Peach Orchard.
July 3. In the line on ridge from Peach Orchard to N.E. corner of Spangler's Woods. Aided in the cannonade and supported Longstreet's assault.
July 4. In position near here until 4 P.M. Then withdrew to Marsh Creek on Fairfield Road.
Losses. Killed 19, wounded 114, missing 6. Horses killed or disabled 116.

COMMENTARY
This marker shows the position taken by the battalion at 4 P.M. on July 2 and held until 7 P.M.; the battalion was also on this line most of July 4. It reached the battlefield about 9 A.M. on July 2, and remained in the rear until it took this position. From here Parker's, Taylor's, Moody's and Rhett's batteries bombarded the enemy position at the Peach Orchard from 4 to 4:30 P.M. Jordan's and Woolfolk's batteries advanced with the infantry as they charged the enemy position. At 7 P.M. the entire battalion formed northeast of the Peach Orchard, ¾ mile northeast of this marker. Its position on July 3 was along the Emmitsburg Road from the Sherfy house to Smith's apple orchard (see No. A-6). The battalion had a battle strength of 576.[1] For the individual positions held by the batteries of the battalion, see Nos. 27 (Moody), 45 (Rhett), 52 (Woolfolk), 53 (Jordan), 78 (Parker) and 91 (Taylor).

98.   ESHLEMAN'S BATTALION
Tablet on granite pedestal.
Located east of West Confederate Avenue, .12 mile north of intersection of West Confederate Avenue and Millerstown Road.
Erected 1910-1911, replacing earlier tablet erected ca. 1903.

TEXT

C.S.A. Army of Northern Virginia. Longstreet's Corps, Artillery Reserve, Eshleman's Battalion. The Washington Louisiana Artillery. Miller's, Squires's, Richardson's and Norcom's Batteries. Eight Napoleons and two 12 pounder howitzers.

July 3. Arrived on the field before daylight and was engaged all day. Captured one 3 inch rifle.

July 4. At 9 A.M. ordered to Cashtown to reinforce the Cavalry escorting the wagon train.

Losses. Killed 3, wounded 26, missing 16. Total 45. Horses killed and disabled 37. Guns disabled 3.

COMMENTARY

Eshleman's battalion was not engaged at the position of this marker, but was posted in line 5/8 mile east of here, along the Emmitsburg Road between the Smith and Rogers houses (see No. A-6). The 3 inch rifle captured was actually found abandoned between the opposing lines early in the morning of the 3rd. It had been left behind the previous evening by Thompson's Battery C&F Pennsylvania Artillery.[1] It was pulled in by two drivers from Captain Richardson's battery.[2] The signal shots for the great cannonade that preceded Pickett's Charge were fired by two guns from Miller's battery. The battalion had a battle strength of about 338.[3] For the positions held by the battalion's individual batteries, see Nos. 28 (squires), 29 (Richardson), 30 (Miller) and 31 (Norcom). On June 6, 1917, veterans of the battalion requested the War Department to change the unit's designation from "Eshleman's Battalion" to "Battalion of Washington Artillery of New Orleans, Louisiana, Commanded by Lieut. Col. B.F. Eshleman." This change was approved on June 15, 1917, but was never implemented.

99. HOOD'S DIVISION

Tablet on granite marker.
Located west of South Confederate Avenue, 400 feet south of intersection of South Confederate Avenue and Emmitsburg Road. Erected 1909.

TEXT

C.S.A. Army of Northern Virginia. First Army Corps, Hood's Division. Maj. Gen. J.B. Hood, Brig. Gen. E.M. Law. Law's Brigade. Brig. Gen. E.M. Law, Col. James L. Sheffield. Robertson's Brigade. Brig. Gen. J.B. Robertson. Anderson's Brigade. Brig. Gen. George T. Anderson, Lieut. Col. William Luffman. Benning's Brigade. Brig. Gen. Henry L. Benning. Artillery Battalion. Four Batteries. Major M.W. Henry.

July 1. On the march to Gettysburg. Encamped about four miles from the field with the exception of Law's Brigade left on picket at New Guilford.

July 2. Law's Brigade joined from New Guilford about noon. The

Division was formed on extreme right of the Army and then directed to drive in and envelop the Union left. About 4 P.M. the Batteries opened and soon after the Division moved forward. After a severe struggle the Union line retired to the ridge in rear. The ground fought over was obstructed by stone fences and very difficult. The movement was partially successful, the battle continuing until nearly dark. The advance gained was held.

July 3. Occupied the ground gained and with the exception of resisting a Cavalry charge and heavy skirmishing was not engaged.

July 4. The Division took up the line of march during the night.

Casualties. Killed 343, wounded 1504, missing 442. Total 2289.

COMMENTARY

This marker is located at the center of the line formed by the division at 4 P.M. on July 2 prior to its attack on the Union left flank. The division formed in two lines of two brigades each, though this is not clearly indicated by the brigade markers. G.T. Anderson formed behind J.B. Robertson (see No. 100) and Benning formed behind Law (see No. 102). About 4:30 P.M. Hood was badly wounded in the left arm by a shell fragment about ¼ mile east of this marker. The text of the marker is in error by stating that on July 2, "The advance gained was held." The division did hold Devil's Den, but was repulsed from the Round Tops. It had a battle strength of 7375.[1]

100. G.T. ANDERSON'S BRIGADE

Tablet on granite pedestal.
Located west of West Confederate Avenue, .05 mile north of intersection of West Confederate Avenue and Emmitsburg Road.
Erected 1910-1911, replacing earlier tablet erected 1899.

TEXT

C.S.A. Army of Northern Virginia. Longstreet's Corps, Hood's Division, Anderson's Brigade. 7th, 8th, 9th, 11th, 59th Georgia Infantry.

July 2. After march of several miles formed line about 4 P.M. 100 yards west of this. The Seventh Regiment was sent southward to watch Union Cavalry. The others charged into the woods south of Wheatfield and dislodged the Union line from stone fence there but flanked on the left retired to crest of Rose Hill. Reinforced later by parts of other Brigades they again advanced. The wounding of Gen. G.T. Anderson caused a brief halt and some confusion but they advanced a third time and after a struggle occupied the woodland to its border on Plum Run Valley.

July 3. The Brigade was sent down Emmitsburg Road and assisted in repulsing and holding in check Union Cavalry which sought to flank the Division.

July 4. Assisted in constructing works to protect the flank.

July 5. About 5 A.M. began the march to Hagerstown, Md. Present about 1800. Losses 671.

COMMENTARY

This marker shows the position held by the brigade from 4:30 to 5:30 P.M. on July 2 before its attack against the Union line in the woods south of the Wheatfield. It first formed at 4 P.M. in the rear of this position, which was occupied by Robertson's brigade. When Robertson moved forward to attack at 4:30, this brigade moved forward to this line. At 5:30 it attacked east across the Timber farm with its regiments formed in the following order from north to south: 8-9-11-59; the 7th regiment was detached to the right. For the route of the brigade's attack on the 2nd, see No. 101. The brigade had a battle strength of about 1874,[1] and reported losses of 105 killed, 512 wounded and 54 captured or missing.[2]

101. G.T. ANDERSON'S BRIGADE (ADVANCE POSITION)
Cast iron tablet.
Located north of Cross Avenue, about .15 mile west of intersection of Brooke Avenue and Sickles Avenue.
Erected 1907-1908.

TEXT

Army of Northern Virginia. Longstreet's Corps, Hood's Division, Anderson's Brigade. 7th, 8th, 9th, 11th, 59th Georgia Infantry.
July 2. Reached the Field about 4 P.M. and formed line. The 7th Regiment was sent southward to watch the Union Cavalry. The others charged into the woods south of Wheatfield and dislodged the Union line from the stone fence. Being outflanked on left retired to crest of Rose Hill. Reinforced by parts of other Brigades they again advanced. The Brigades advanced a third time and after a struggle occupied the Woodland to its border in Plum Run Valley.

COMMENTARY

About 5:45 P.M. on July 2 the brigade passed by this position on its way from the position marked by No. 100 to attack the stone wall at the southern edge of the Wheatfield, about ¼ mile north of this marker.

102. BENNING'S BRIGADE
Tablet on granite pedestal.
Located west of South Confederate Avenue, .1 mile south of intersection of South Confederate Avenue and Emmitsburg Road.
Erected 1910-1911, replacing earlier tablet erected 1899.

TEXT

C.S.A. Army of Northern Virginia. Longstreet's Corps, Hood's Division, Benning's Brigade. 2nd, 15th, 17th, 20th Georgia Infantry.
July 2. Arrived and formed line about 4 P.M. in rear of Law's and Robertson's Brigades, and moving forward in support of these took

prominent part in the severe conflict which resulted in the capture of Devil's Den together with a number of prisoners and three guns of the 4th New York Battery.

July 3. Held Devil's Den and the adjacent crest of Rocky Ridge until late in the evening when under orders the Brigade retired to position near here. Through mistake of orders the 15th Georgia did not retire directly but moved northward; encountered a superior Union force and suffered considerable loss.

July 4. Occupied breastworks near here facing southward until midnight.

July 5. About 5 A.M. began the march to Hagerstown, Md. Present about 1500. Losses 509.

COMMENTARY

About 4 P.M. on July 2 this brigade formed .1 mile west of this marker in the rear of Law's brigade, which was then in position along the line of this marker. Around 4:45 P.M. the brigade moved past this location as it advanced to attack Devil's Den. Its regiments were then in the following order from north to south: 2-20-17-15. The position at which Devil's Den was attacked is marked by No. 103. Late on the afternoon of the 3rd the brigade withdrew to the position indicated by this marker and remained here on the 4th. The brigade had a battle strength of 1420[1] and, according to the report of the army's Medical Director, suffered 497 casualties—76 killed, 299 wounded, and 122 captured or missing.[2]

103. BENNING'S BRIGADE (ADVANCE POSITION)
Cast iron tablet.
Located west of Sickles Avenue on western side of Devil's Den.
Erected 1907-1908.

TEXT

Army of Northern Virginia. Longstreet's Corps, Hood's Division, Benning's Brigade. 2d, 15th, 17th, 20th Georgia Infantry.

July 2. Formed in line about 4 P.M. in rear of Law's and Robertson's Brigade and moving forward in support took active part in the conflict that resulted in the capture of Devil's Den together with a number of prisoners and 3 guns of Smith's 4th New York Battery.

COMMENTARY

This marker shows the position at which the brigade assaulted Devil's Den from 5:15 to 6 P.M. on July 2. After capturing Devil's Den, the brigade remained in line here until late on the afternoon of the 3rd, when it withdrew to the position marked by No. 102.

104. LAW'S BRIGADE
Tablet on granite pedestal.

Located west of South Confederate Avenue, .18 mile south of intersection of South Confederate Avenue and Emmitsburg Road.
Erected 1910-1911, replacing earlier tablet erected 1899.

TEXT

C.S.A. Army of Northern Virginia. Longstreet's Corps, Hood's Division, Law's Brigade. 4th, 15th, 44th, 47th, 48th Alabama Infantry.

July 2. Left New Guilford 25 miles distant at 3 A.M. Arrived and formed line 50 yards west of this about 4 P.M. and advanced against the Union positions. The 4th, 15th and 47th Regiments attacked Little Round Top and continued the assault until dark. The 44th and 48th assisted in capturing Devil's Den and 3 guns of the 4th New York Battery.

July 3. Occupied the breastworks on west slope of Round Top. The 4th and 15th Regiments assisted at 5 P.M. in repulsing cavalry led by Brig. Gen. E.J. Farnsworth in Plum Run Valley.

July 5. About 5 A.M. began the march to Hagerstown, Md. Present about 1500. Losses about 550.

COMMENTARY

This marker designates the right flank of the line formed by the brigade at 4 P.M. on July 2nd prior to its attack against the Round Tops. The brigade's regiments extended north from this point to the Emmitsburg Road in the following order: 15-48-47-4-44. For the position held during the attack on Little Round Top, see No. 105. The movements of the 4th Alabama regiment are narrated on No. 13. See pages 13-14 for a discussion of the controversy surrounding the proposed erection of a marker to the 15th Alabama. The brigade had a battle strength of about 1933[1] and had 496 casualties according to the army's Medical Director—74 killed, 276 wounded, and 146 captured or missing.[2]

105. LAW'S BRIGADE (ADVANCE POSITION)

Cast iron tablet.
Located south of Warren Avenue, 200 feet west of intersection of Warren Avenue and Sykes Avenue.
Erected 1907-1908.

TEXT

Army of Northern Virginia. Longstreet's Corps, Hood's Division, Law's Brigade. 4th, 15th, 44th, 47th, 48th Alabama Infantry.

July 2. Arrived on the field about 4 P.M. and advanced against the Union positions. The 4th, 15th and 47th Regiments attacked Little Round Top and continued the assault until dark. The 44th and 48th assisted in capturing Devil's Den and 3 guns of Smith's 4th New York Battery.

COMMENTARY

This marker shows the center of the line held by the brigade when it was attacking Little Round Top and Plum Run Valley from 4:30 to

7:30 P.M. on July 2. At dusk the brigade moved 1/4 mile to the south to face Big Round Top. For the brigade's strength and other movements in the battle, see No. 104.

106.   J.B. ROBERTSON'S BRIGADE
Tablet on granite pedestal.
Located west of South Confederate Avenue, 300 feet south of intersection of South Confederate Avenue and Emmitsburg Road.
Erected 1910-1911, replacing earlier tablet erected 1899.

TEXT
C.S.A. Army of Northern Virginia. Longstreet's Corps, Hood's Division, Robertson's Brigade. 1st, 4th, 5th Texas and 3rd Arkansas Infantry.
July 2. Arrived after a march of several miles and formed line 50 yards west of this at 4 P.M. Advanced against the Union positions. The 4th and 5th Texas joined in the attack on Little Round Top, which continued until dark. The 1st Texas and 3rd Arkansas attacked and assisted in taking Devil's Den and Rocky Ridge with a number of prisoners and 3 guns of the 4th New York Battery.
July 3. At 2 A.M. the 1st Texas and 3rd Arkansas were moved to the right and joined the 4th and 5th Texas on the northwest spur of Big Round Top. Three Regiments occupied the breastworks there all day skirmishing hotly with Union sharpshooters. Early in the day the 1st Texas was sent to confront the Union Cavalry threatening the right flank. After night the Brigade took position near here.
July 5. About 5 A.M. began the march to Hagerstown, Md. Present about 1100. Losses about 540.

COMMENTARY
This tablet is 50 yards south of the right flank of the line held by the brigade from 4 to 4:15 P.M. on July 2 prior to its attack on Devil's Den and Little Round Top. The brigade line began at Emmitsburg Road and extended north along the ridge for 3/8 mile with its regiments in the following order from south to north: 5, 4 and 1 Texas, 3 Arkansas. See No. 107 for the position at which the left of the brigade assaulted Devil's Den. The brigade had a battle strength of about 1734[1] and reported losses of 597 (84 killed, 393 wounded and 120 captured or missing) in the army Medical Director's report.[2]

107.   J.B. ROBERTSON'S BRIGADE (ADVANCE POSITION)
Cast iron tablet.
Located west of Sickles Avenue on the western side of Devil's Den.
Erected 1907-1908.

TEXT
Army of Northern Virginia. Longstreet's Corps, Hood's Division, Robertson's Brigade. 1st, 4th, 5th Texas and 3d Arkansas Infantry.

July 2. Arrived on the field about 4 P.M. Advanced against the Union positions. The 4th and 5th Texas joined in the attack on Little Round Top, which continued until dark. The 1st Texas and 3d Arkansas attacked and assisted in taking the Devil's Den and Rocky Ridge with a number of prisoners and 3 guns of Smith's 4th New York Battery.

COMMENTARY

This marker shows the position at which the 1st Texas and 3rd Arkansas regiments assaulted Devil's Den from 5 to 6 P.M. on July 2. After the capture of Devil's Den, these two regiments remained in this area until dusk. They then moved ¼ mile to the southeast to rejoin the rest of the brigade in Plum Run Valley facing Big Round Top. The brigade's position from 4 to 4:15 P.M. on July 2 is indicated by No. 106.

108. HOOD'S TEXAS BRIGADE MONUMENT

Granite monument.
Located west of South Confederate Avenue, 250 feet south of intersection of South Confederate Avenue and Emmitsburg Road.
Dedicated September 27, 1913.

TEXT

C.S.A. Hood's Texas Brigade. Brig. General J.B. Robertson, Commanding. 1, 4, 5 Texas and 3 Arkansas Infantry Regiments. July 2nd and 3rd, 1863.

COMMENTARY

This monument is one of the few Confederate markers on the battlefield erected by private individuals not connected with a veterans' or state organization. It was donated to the Park in 1913 by a committee of Texas citizens headed by Mrs. Mabel M. Bates of San Antonio. The monument's site was selected in July of 1913 and it was dedicated on September 27, 1913. It stands 6 feet 5 inches tall and consists of a base measuring 1 foot 10 inches by 1 foot 8 inches, a plinth, and a granite shaft with an apex top. The monument is located near the position from which Hood's old Texas Brigade began its attack against Devil's Den and Little Round Top about 4:30 P.M. on July 2nd (see Nos. 2, 10 and 106). The advanced position held by the brigade near Devil's Den' is marked by No. 107.

109. HENRY'S BATTALION

Tablet on granite pedestal.
Located east of South Confederate Avenue, .12 mile south of intersection of South Confederate Avenue and Emmitsburg Road.
Erected 1910-1911, replacing earlier tablet erected ca. 1903.

TEXT

C.S.A. Army of Northern Virginia. Longstreet's Corps, Hood's Division, Henry's Battalion. Reilly's, Bachman's, Garden's and Latham's

Batteries. Eleven Napoleons, four 10 pounder Parrotts, two 3 inch rifles, one 12 pounder howitzer and one 6 pounder bronze gun.

July 2-3. Occupied this line and took active part in the battle as described on the tablets of the several batteries. The Howitzer, the Bronze gun and one 3 inch Rifle were disabled and three captured 10 pounder Parrotts substituted.

July 4. On a line a little west of this until 6 P.M.; then withdrew from the field.

Ammunition expended 1500 rounds. Losses. Killed 4, wounded 23.

COMMENTARY

This marker shows the position at which Latham's and Reilly's batteries were posted at 4 P.M. on July 2 when they began shelling the Union positions ¾ mile to the northeast; Garden's and Bachman's batteries were not engaged on the 2nd. On July 3 Reilly's, Bachman's and Garden's batteries were positioned near this marker facing the Union cavalry line some ¼ mile to the south; Latham's battery was formed ¼ mile northwest of this marker along the Emmitsburg Road, facing east. For the movements and positions of each battery, see Nos. 40 (Latham), 43 and 44 (Reilly), 46 (Bachman) and 47 (Garden). Major Henry in his official battle report states that the bronze 6 pounder gun mentioned on the tablet was withdrawn on the 4th.[1] The three Federal 10 pounder Parrotts mentioned on the tablet were captured at Devil's Den from Smith's 4th New York Battery.[2] The battalion had a battle strength of about 403.[3]

110. MCLAWS' DIVISION

Tablet on granite marker.
Located west of West Confederate Avenue, .17 mile south of intersection of West Confederate Avenue and Millerstown Road.
Erected 1907.

TEXT

Army of Northern Virginia. First Army Corps, McLaws's Division. Maj. Gen. Lafayette McLaws. Kershaw's Brigade. Brig. Gen. J.B. Kershaw. Barksdale's Brigade. Brig. Gen. William Barksdale, Col. B.G. Humphreys. Semmes's Brigade. Brig. Gen. P.J. Semmes, Col. George Bryan. Wofford's Brigade. Brig. Gen. W.T. Wofford. Artillery Battalion. Four Batteries. Col. H.C. Cabell.

July 1. The Division reached Marsh Creek four miles from Gettysburg after dark.

July 2. The Division was placed in position facing the Union line on the Emmitsburg Road. About 4 P.M. the Batteries opened on the position, the Division pressing to the front and the Union troops retiring to the hill in rear. The battle continued until nearly night when a strong Union force met the supporting Division which was co-operating on the left

and drove one Brigade back and checked the support of the other Brigade exposing the left. It was thought prudent not to push farther until other troops of the Corps came up. The Division was withdrawn to the first position of Union troops resting at the Peach Orchard, the conflict to be renewed in the morning when other orders were received.
July 3. With the exception of severe skirmishing the Division was not engaged and after night dispositions were made to withdraw.
July 4. The Division took up the line of march during the night.
Casualties. Killed 313, wounded 1538, captured or missing 327. Total 2178.

COMMENTARY

This marker is located at the center of the line formed by the division at 4 P.M. on July 2 and held until the several brigades began their attacks against the Union line ½ mile to the east. The division was formed in two lines, as explained on the brigade markers. In the first line, Kershaw attacked at 5:30 and Barksdale about 6 P.M.; in the second line, Semmes attacked at 5:40 and Wofford at 6:30. The "supporting Division which was co-operating on the left" was R.H. Anderson's. For the route taken by McLaws' division to the front on the 2nd, see No. 111. McLaws' division had a battle strength of about 7153.[1]

111. MCLAWS' AND PICKETT'S DIVISIONS

Cast iron tablet.
Located north of Fairfield Road at Black Horse Tavern, three miles west of Gettysburg Town Square.
Erected ca. 1903.

TEXT

Army of Northern Virginia. Longstreet's Corps. McLaws's and Pickett's Divisions.
July 1. McLaws's Division arrived late in the day and camped in this vicinity.
July 2. In the morning McLaws's Division moved on the road towards Gettysburg but turning to the right half mile this side of Willoughby Run and crossing that stream lower down formed line as marked on the battlefield. Pickett's Division marched by this place in the afternoon but followed the other road with some deflections to avoid being seen by the Union Signal Corps and crossing Willoughby Run lay that night on the west side of Spangler's Woods.

COMMENTARY

This marker is located near Black Horse Tavern and shows part of the route taken to the front by McLaws' division on July 2 and Pickett's division on July 3. On July 2nd, McLaws was ordered to march to the army's right without being detected by Union observers McLaws began at his camp along Marsh Creek north of this marker, and marched by here about noon on July 2. He proceeded ¾ mile to the southeast along a farm lane until he reached a crest visable from the Union lines. He then backtracked from there to this position in order to march north on a lengthy detour. This countermarch and circuitous route delayed the Confederate attack several hours that afternoon. For the position McLaws' division took before its late afternoon assault on July 2, see No. 110. For the battle position taken by Pickett's division on July 3, see No. 122.

112. BARKSDALE'S BRIGADE
Tablet on granite pedestal.
Located west of West Confederate Avenue, .1 mile north of intersection of West Confederate Avenue and Millerstown Road.
Erected 1910-1911, replacing earlier tablet erected 1901-1902.

TEXT
C.S.A. Army of Northern Virginia. Longstreet's Corps, McLaws' Division, Barksdale's Brigade. 13th, 17th, 18th, 21st Mississippi Infantry.
July 2. Arrived about 3 P.M. and formed line here. Advanced at 5 P.M. and took part in the assault on the Peach Orchard and adjacent positions vigorously pursuing the Union forces as they retired. The 21st Regiment pushed on past the Trostle House and captured but were unable to bring off 9th Mass. Battery and I Battery 5th U. States. The other Regiments inclining more to the left pressed forward to Plum Run where they encountered fresh troops and a fierce conflict ensued in which Brig. Gen. Wm. Barksdale fell mortally wounded.
July 3. Supported artillery on Peach Orchard Ridge. Withdrew from the front late in the afternoon.
July 4. In position near here all day. About midnight began the march to Hagerstown. Present 1598. Killed 105, wounded 550, missing 92. Total 747.

COMMENTARY
This marker shows the position held by the brigade from 3 to 6 P.M. on July 2 before it began its attack on the Union line ½ mile east at the Peach Orchard. No. 113 marks the route taken by this attack. The brigade's regiments were then in the following order from north to south: 18-13-17-21. The brigade's position on July 3 was just' north of No. 113. Its battle strength was about 1620.[1]

113. BARKSDALE'S BRIGADE (ADVANCE POSITION)
Cast iron tablet.
Located west of Emmitsburg Road, 80 feet southwest of intersection of Emmitsburg Road and Wheatfield Road.

Erected 1907-1908.

TEXT

Army of Northern Virginia. Longstreet's Corps, McLaws's Division, Barksdales's Brigade. 13th, 17th, 18th, 21st Mississippi Infantry.

July 2. Arrived about 3 P.M. and formed in line. Advanced at 5 o'clock and took part in the assault on the Peach Orchard and adjacent positions pursuing the Union forces as they retired. The 21st Regiment pushed beyond the Trostle House and captured but were unable to bring off Bigelow's and Watson's Batteries. The other Regiments inclining to the left pressed forward to Plum Run where they encountered Union troops and a fierce conflict ensued in which Brig. Gen. Wm. Barksdale fell mortally wounded.

COMMENTARY

This marker shows the right flank of the 21st Mississippi from 6 to 6:30 P.M. on July 2. During this time this regiment formed the right of Barksdale's brigade during its attack on the Peach Orchard. After carrying the Union line here, the brigade continued to advance ⅝ mile to the east-northeast until it was stopped by Union counterattacks. At that point General Barksdale was mortally wounded about 7:30 P.M. The brigade then retired to the Peach Orchard, where on July 3 it supported artillery posted along the Emmitsburg Road north of this marker. See No. 112 for the brigade's position from 3 to 6 P.M. on July 2.

114. KERSHAW'S BRIGADE

Tablet on granite pedestal.
Located west of West Confederate Avenue, .22 mile south of intersection of West Confederate Avenue and Millerstown Road.
Erected 1910-1911, replacing earlier tablet erected 1899.

TEXT

C.S.A. Army of Northern Virginia. Longstreet's Corps, McLaws's Division, Kershaw's Brigade. 2nd, 3rd, 7th, 8th, 15th Regiments and 3rd Battalion South Carolina Infantry.

July 2. Arrived at 3:30 P.M. and formed line here. Advanced about 4:30 P.M. to battle. The 8th and 2nd Regiments and 3rd Battalion shared in the attack on Peach Orchard and Batteries near there on Wheatfield Road. The 7th and 3rd Regiments were engaged in the long and severe conflict at and around the Loop. The 15th Regiment fought on Rose Hill and in the ravine and forest beyond. Late in the evening the Brigade took part in the general advance by which the Union forces were forced from Wheatfield and across Plum Run Valley. At dark under orders it retired to Peach Orchard.

July 3. At Peach Orchard until noon. Then sent farther to front. At 1

P.M. under orders resumed position here extending line to right and keeping in touch with Hood's Division on the left.

July 4. About midnight began the march to Hagerstown, Md. Present about 1800. Losses 630.

COMMENTARY

This marker shows the position held by the brigade from 3:30 to 5:30 P.M. on July 2 before it began its attack on the Union line at and near the Peach Orchard. During the attack the regiments were in the following order from north to south: 8-3 Battalion-2-7-3-15. No. 116 shows the point at which the brigade crossed the Emmitsburg Road and No. 114 shows where the 15th regiment struck the Union line in the Rose Woods. This marker's text errs at the end of the July 3 entry—Hood's division was then on McLaws's right, not left. It also misrepresents what happened at the close of the action on July 2. After forcing the Union lines back across Plum Run Valley, the Confederates were in turn pushed back by Union counterattacks led by Crawford's division and three brigades of the Sixth Corps. The brigade had an estimated battle strength of 2183;[1] its 630 battle losses included 115 killed, 483 wounded, and 32 captured or missing.[2]

115. KERSHAW'S BRIGADE (ADVANCE POSITION)

Cast iron tablet.
Located south of Brooke Avenue, 47 mile west by road from intersection of Brooke Avenue and Sickles Avenue.
Erected 1907-1908.

TEXT

Army of Northern Virginia. Longstreet's Corps, McLaws's Division, Kershaw's Brigade. 2d, 3d, 7th, 8th, 15th Regiments and 3d Battalion South Carolina Infantry.

July 2. Arrived on the Field at 3:30 P.M. Formed line and advanced about 4:30 o'clock. The 8th and 2d Regiments and 3d Battalion shared in the attack on the Peach Orchard and Batteries near there on Wheatfield Road. The 7th and 3d Regiments were engaged at and around the Loop. The 15th Regiment fought on Rose Hill and in the ravine and forest beyond. Late in the evening the Brigade took part in the advance by which the Union forces were forced from the Wheatfield and across Plum Run Valley. At dark under orders the Brigade retired to and occupied the Peach Orchard.

COMMENTARY

This tablet marks the ground in Rose Woods over which the 15th South Carolina advanced on the right of the brigade line as it attacked the Union position south of the Wheatfield about 5:45 P.M. on July 2. The center of the brigade's line during this attack was about $\frac{3}{8}$ mile to the north. The brigade began its attack from the position occupied by No. 114, about ½ mile west of this marker, and crossed the Emmitsburg Road at the point marked by No. 116. This attack started at 5:30 P.M., not 4:30 as stated on the marker. For the brigade's movements in the remainder of the battle, see No. 114.

116.   KERSHAW'S BRIGADE MARKER
Bronze tablet on granite monolith.
Located west of Emmitsburg Road, .22 mile southwest of Peach Orchard and just north of junction of Emmitsburg Road and Rose Farm lane.
Erected 1970.

TEXT
Kershaw's Brigade. Brigadier General Joseph B. Kershaw's South Carolina Brigade of McLaws' Division, ordered on the afternoon of July 2, 1863, to attack the Union battle line north and east of the Rose Farm, 100 yards eastward, crossed the Emmitsburg Road in this area. By nightfall their attack, joined with those of other Confederate Brigades, had forced the Union troops from the Peach Orchard and Wheatfield. Late on July 3 the Brigade withdrew and went into position in the woods a quarter mile west. Erected by "Project Southland" in cooperation with the Gettysburg Battlefield Preservation Association, 1970.

COMMENTARY
This is one of only three markers erected by private citizens to show Confederate advanced battle positions. The marker was commissioned by "Project Southland" as represented by John Kershaw, a descendant of Joseph B. Kershaw, the brigade's commander during the battle. It was erected in 1970 to show the point at which Kershaw's brigade crossed the Emmitsburg Road at approximately 5:30 P.M. on July 2. The brigade was advancing to attack the left of Sickles' Union line from a starting position marked by No. 114. After passing the position of this marker (No. 116), the brigade's regiments advanced to the Rose Farm and then divided into two wings. The 2nd, 3rd and 15th regiments attacked eastward as noted by No. 115; the rest of the brigade moved north against the Peach Orchard. For the brigade's composition, strength and losses, see No. 114.

The monument was set up in 1970 by Codori Memorials of Gettysburg. The bronze tablet measures 25 by 30 inches, and the granite monolith by which it is supported is 48 inches high, 40 inches wide, and 9 inches thick.

117.   SEMMES' BRIGADE
Tablet on granite pedestal.

Located west of West Confederate Avenue, .21 mile south of intersection of West Confederate Avenue and Millerstown Road.
Erected 1910-1911, replacing earlier tablet erected 1899.

TEXT

C.S.A. Army of Northern Virginia. Longstreet's Corps, McLaws's Division, Semmes's Brigade. 10th, 50th, 51st, 53rd Georgia Infantry. July 2. Arrived about 3:30 P.M. and formed line 50 yards west of this. Advanced about 5 P.M. in support of Kershaw and Anderson and took a prominent part in the severe and protracted conflict on Rose Hill and in the ravine and forest east of there and in the vicinity of the Loop. Participated also in the general advance late in the evening by which the Union forces were forced out of the Wheatfield and across Plum Run Valley. Brig. Gen. Paul J. Semmes fell mortally wounded in the ravine near the Loop.

July 3. During the forenoon Anderson's Brigade being withdrawn for duty elsewhere, the Brigade was left in occupancy of the woodland south of the Wheatfield. At 1 P.M. under orders it resumed its original position near here.

July 4. About midnight began the march to Hagerstown, Md. Present about 1200. Losses 430.

COMMENTARY

On July 2 this brigade formed about ¼ mile south of this marker, some ⅛ mile behind Kershaw's brigade. From there it advanced about 5:40 P.M. and not 5 P.M. as stated on the marker. During its advance the brigade's regiments were in the following order from north to south: 50-10-51-53. The course of its advance is noted by No. 118. The brigade had an estimated battle strength of 1334;[1] its losses included 55 killed, 284 wounded and 91 captured or missing.[2]

118. SEMMES' BRIGADE (ADVANCE POSITION)

Cast iron tablet.
Located south of Brooke Avenue, about .26 mile by road west of intersection of Brooke Avenue and Sickles Avenue.
Erected 1907-1908.

TEXT

Army of Northern Virginia. Longstreet's Corps, McLaws's Division, Semmes's Brigade. 10th, 50th, 51st, 53d Georgia Infantry.

July 2. Arrived on the Field about 3:30 P.M. Advanced about 5 o'clock in support of Kershaw's and Anderson's Brigades and took an active part in the conflict on Rose Hill and in the ravine and forest East of there and in the vicinity of the Loop. Participated in the general advance late in the evening by which the Union forces were forced out of the Wheatfield and across the Plum Run Valley. Brig. Gen. Paul J. Semmes fell mortally wounded in the ravine near the Loop.

COMMENTARY

This marker describes the advance of Semmes' brigade against the Union line at the Loop about 6 P.M. on July 2. The brigade began its attack from the position marked by No. 117 at about 5:40 P.M., not 5 P.M. as stated on the marker. It struck the Union line at the Loop about ¼ mile north of this marker. General Semmes was mortally wounded about ¼ mile northwest of this marker. For the brigade's strength and movements in the rest of the battle, see No. 117.

119. WOFFORD'S BRIGADE

Tablet on granite pedestal.
Located west of West Confederate Avenue, .11 mile north of intersection of West Confederate Avenue and Millerstown Road.
Erected 1910-1911, replacing earlier tablet erected 1901-1902.

TEXT

C.S.A. Army of Northern Virginia. Longstreet's Corps, McLaws's Division, Wofford's Brigade. 16th, 18th, 24th Regiments, Cobb's and Phillips's Legions Georgia Infantry.

July 2. Arrived at 4 P.M. and formed line 100 yards west of this. Ordered to the front about 6 P.M. and advanced soon afterward along the Wheatfield Road, flanked the Union force assailing the Loop, and aided the Confederates, thereby relieved in forcing them back through the Wheatfield to the foot of Little Round Top. Assailed there by a strong body of fresh troops and receiving at the same moment an order to withdraw the Brigade fell back at sunset to the grove west of the Wheatfield.

July 3. One regiment was left on outpost duty in that grove. The others supported artillery on Peach Orchard Ridge. All withdrew late in the afternoon.

July 4. In line here all day. At midnight began the march to Hagerstown. Present about 1350. Killed 36, wounded 207, missing 112. Total 355.

COMMENTARY

This marker shows the general position held by the brigade from 4 to 6:30 P.M. on July 2, and from late on July 3 through the end of July 4. On the afternoon of July 2 the brigade was formed behind Barksdale's brigade about ¼ mile south of this marker. When it advanced about 6:30 P.M. (not 6 P.M. as stated on the marker), its regiments were in the following order from north to south: Phillips' Legion, Cobb's Legion, 24th, 18th, 16th. For the route of its advance towards the Wheatfield, see No. 120. The brigade had an estimated battle strength of 1627.[1] Its casualties as reported by the army's Medical Director totaled 334—30 killed, 192 wounded, and 112 captured or missing.[2]

120. WOFFORD'S BRIGADE (ADVANCE POSITION)

Cast iron tablet.
Located west of Emmitsburg Road, 360 feet southwest of intersection of Emmitsburg
Road and Wheatfield Road.
Erected 1907-1908.

TEXT

Army of Northern Virginia. Longstreet's Corps, McLaws's Division, Wofford's Brigade. 16th, 18th, 24th Regiments, Cobb's and Phillips' Legions Georgia Infantry.

July 2. Arrived at 4 P.M. and formed line 500 yards west of here; ordered to the front about 6 o'clock. Advanced soon afterwards along Wheatfield Road; struck the Union line near the Loop, and joined Kershaw's brigade in driving the Union forces through the Wheatfield to the base of Little Round Top. Assailed by Union reinforcements and receiving orders to withdraw, the brigade fell back at sunset to the cover of the woods west of the Wheatfield.

July 3. One regiment was left on outpost duty in that grove. The others supported artillery on Peach Orchard Ridge. All withdrew late in the afternoon.

July 4. In line 500 yards west of here all day. At midnight began the march to Hagerstown.

Present about 1,355. Killed 36. Wounded 207. Missing 112. Total 355.

COMMENTARY

This marker shows the route taken by the brigade about 6:40 P.M. on July 2 as it moved to attack the Union position ⅜ mile southwest of here in the woods west of the Wheatfield. This attack began at 6:30 P.M. (not 6 P.M. as the marker states) from the position indicated by No. 119 about 500 yards west of here. At the close of the fighting on July 2, the brigade formed in the woods ½ mile southeast of this marker. On the morning of the 3rd, the brigade was ordered to the support of the batteries posted at the Peach Orchard. It formed north of this marker with its right at the position of this marker. The estimated battle strength of the brigade was 1627.[1]

121. CABELL'S BATTALION

Tablet on granite pedestal.
Located west of West Confederate Avenue, .36 mile north of intersection of West
Confederate Avenue and Emmitsburg Road.
Erected 1910-1911, replacing earlier tablet erected ca. 1903.

TEXT

C.S.A. Army of Northern Virginia. Longstreet's Corps, McLaws's Division, Cabell's Battalion. Fraser's, McCarthy's, Carlton's and Manly's Batteries. Four Napoleons, four 10 pounder Parrotts, six 3 inch rifles, two 12 pounder howitzers.

July 2-3. Took an active part in the battle.

July 4. Remained in position near here and withdrew from the field after night.

Ammunition expended about 3300 rounds.

Losses. Killed 12, wounded 30, missing 4. Horses killed or disabled 80.

COMMENTARY

This marker shows the left flank of the position held by the battalion from 3:30 P.M. on July 2 to the morning of July 3. The line on July 2 stretched south from this marker to the P. Snyder farm near the Emmitsburg Road with the batteries in the following order from north to south: Manly–McCarthy–Fraser–Carlton. On the morning of July 3, the battalion moved ¾ mile to the northeast to a line along the Emmitsburg Road at the Peach Orchard. There McCarthy and Carlton formed the far left of the Corps' artillery line, while Fraser and Manly were on the far right at the Peach Orchard. For the positions held during the battle by the individual batteries, see Nos. 18 (Fraser), 22 and 23 (Carlton), 42 (Manly) and 82 (McCarthy). The battalion had a battle strength of 378.[1] According to the report of the army's Medical Director it lost 37 casualties—8 killed and 29 wounded.[2]

122. PICKETT'S DIVISION

Tablet on granite marker.
Located west of West Confederate Avenue, .08 mile southwest of Virginia Monument. Erected 1909.

TEXT

Army of Northern Virginia. First Army Corps, Pickett's Division. Maj. Gen. Geo. E. Pickett. Garnett's Brigade. Brig. Gen. R.B. Garnett, Major C.S. Peyton. Armistead's Brigade. Brig. Gen. L.A. Armistead, Lieut. Col. William White. Kemper's Brigade. Brig. Gen. J.L. Kemper, Col. Joseph Mayo Jr. Artillery Battalion. Four Batteries. Major James Dearing.

July 1. Guarding trains at Chambersburg.

July 2. On march to Gettysburg.

July 3. Reached the field about 9 A.M. Near 12 M. took position beyond crest of hill on which the artillery was placed. About 1:30 P.M. Division was formed in an open field east of Spangler's Woods, the right near a barn facing the Union line on Cemetery Ridge. At 3 P.M. moved forward to assault across the field about three fourths of a mile under a severe fire losing many officers and men, only a few reaching the salient. The Division being separated from its support on the right and left and the assault having failed returned to its former position on the ridge.

July 4. The Division took up the line of march during the night.

Casualties. Killed 232, wounded 1157, missing 1499. Total 2888.

COMMENTARY

This marker is located about ⅜ mile north of where the division formed for its famous charge on July 3. R.B. Garnett's and Kemper's brigades were formed in the first line immediately behind the artillery, and Armistead's brigade formed in the rear near the H. Spangler farmhouse. For part of the route that the division took to reach the front, see No. 111. General Pickett probably watched the course of the assault from a position ⅝ mile to the east at the Codori farmhouse. The division had a battle strength of about 5473.[1] Its listed battle casualties are probably incomplete because of the nature of the assault and the heavy losses incurred.

123. ARMISTEAD'S BRIGADE

Tablet on granite pedestal.
Located west of West Confederate Avenue, .1 mile southwest of Virginia Monument.
Erected 1910-1911, replacing earlier tablet erected 1901-1902.

TEXT

C.S.A. Army of Northern Virginia. Longstreet's Corps, Pickett's Division, Armistead's Brigade. 9th, 14th, 38th, 53rd, 57th Virginia Infantry.

July 2. Arrived about sunset and bivouacked on the Western border of Spangler's Woods.

July 3. In the forenoon formed line behind Kemper and Garnett east of the Woods. When the cannonade ceased, advanced to support Kemper's and Garnett's Brigades, forming the right of Longstreet's Corps. Its losses being less at first than those of the other Brigades, it passed the Emmitsburg Road in compact ranks and as the front line was going to pieces near the stone wall pushed forward and many of its men and some from other commands responding to the call and following Gen. L.A. Armistead sprang over the wall into the Angle and continued the desperate struggle until he fell mortally wounded beyond the stone wall.

July 4. Spent the day in reorganization and during the night began the march to Hagerstown.

Present 1650. Killed 88, wounded 460, missing 643. Total 1191.

COMMENTARY

This marker is ¼ mile north of the position where the brigade formed before Pickett's Charge on July 3. During the charge, which began about 3 P.M., the brigade's regiments were in the following order from north to south: 38-57-53-9-14. General Armistead was mortally wounded at the position of No. 124, about ⅞ mile east of here. The brigade had an estimated battle strength of 1950.[1]

124. ARMISTEAD MARKER
Granite marker.
Located 120 feet west of Hancock Avenue in the Angle, 220 feet northwest of High Water Mark.
Erected early 1888.

TEXT
Brigadier General Lewis A. Armistead C.S.A. fell here July 3, 1863.

COMMENTARY
This marker was erected to mark the spot where Brigadier General Lewis A. Armistead was mortally wounded about 3:30 P.M. on July 3 while leading his brigade in its assault on the center of the Union line on Cemetery Ridge. He reportedly had his hand on a captured cannon when he was shot. He was then captured and died two days later in a Federal field hospital (see also No. 202). He was buried in Baltimore. The General was born in New Bern, North Carolina, on February 18, 1817, and was 46 years old when he died. He had attended West Point, but was dismissed before he graduated. At the beginning of the Civil War he was appointed Colonel of the 57th Virginia Infantry. He was promoted to Brigadier General on April 1, 1862.

This marker was the second Confederate tablet to be erected on the battlefield. It was first proposed on May 5, 1887, when some friends of the General asked permission from the Gettysburg Battlefield Memorial Association to mark the spot where he fell. The directors of the GBMA at first refused the request because it violated their rule that all monuments had to be in battle lines. However, the directors of the GBMA said that if a marker were erected at Armistead's pre-attack position, the spot where he fell could then be marked with an "advance position" tablet. When Armistead's friends objected to this technicality because numerous markers to Union commanders had already been erected without regard to the position of related unit monuments, the GBMA reconsidered and approved this marker on July 12, 1887. It was erected by Thomas Nawn Company of Concord, New Hampshire, in early 1888. The marker is 4 feet 6 inches tall and consists of a tablet in the form of a scroll resting on a pedestal and a base 2 feet square.

125. R.B. GARNETT'S BRIGADE
Tablet on granite pedestal.
Located west of West Confederate Avenue, .03 mile southwest of Virginia Monument.
Erected 1910-1911, replacing earlier tablet erected 1901-1902.

TEXT
C.S.A. Army of Northern Virginia. Longstreet's Corps, Pickett's Division, Garnett's Brigade. 8th, 18th, 19th, 28th, 56th Virginia Infantry.

July 2. Arrived about sunset and bivouacked on the Western border of Spangler's Woods.

July 3. In the forenoon formed line on Kemper's left in the field east of the Woods. At the cessation of the cannonade advanced and took part in Longstreet's assault on the Union position in the vicinity of the Angle. This advance was made in good order under a storm of shells and grape and a deadly fire of musketry after passing the Emmitsburg Road. The lines were much broken in crossing the post and rail fences on both sides of that road but with shattered ranks the Brigade pushed on and took part in the final struggle at the Angle. Gen. R.B. Garnett fell dead from his saddle in front of the stone wall.

July 4. Spent the day in reorganization and during the night began the march to Hagerstown.

Present 1480. Killed 78, wounded 324, missing 539. Total 941.

COMMENTARY

This marker is ⅜ mile northwest of the position where the brigade formed before Pickett's Charge on July 3. During the charge, which began about 3 P.M., the brigade's regiments were in the following order from north to south: 56-28-19-18-8. General R.B. Garnett was killed in front of the stone wall ¾ mile to the east of this marker. Because he was dressed in a captured Federal overcoat, his body was not properly identified and was probably buried in an "unknown" plot in the Union cemetery established on Cemetery Hill after the battle. The brigade had a battle strength of about 1459.[1]

126.   KEMPER'S BRIGADE

Tablet on granite pedestal.
Located west of West Confederate Avenue, .17 mile southwest of Virginia Monument.
Erected 1910-1911, replacing earlier tablet erected 1901-1902.

TEXT

C.S.A. Army of Northern Virginia. Longstreet's Corps, Pickett's Division, Kemper's Brigade. 1st, 3rd, 7th, 11th, 24th Virginia Infantry.

July 2. Arrived about sunset and bivouacked on the Western border of Spangler's Woods.

July 3. In the forenoon formed line in the field east of the woods with right flank near Spangler's Barn. At the close of the cannonade advanced and took part in Longstreet's assault upon the Union position in the vicinity of the Angle. Exposed to a severe fire of Artillery and vigorously assailed beyond the Emmitsburg Road by Infantry on the right flank, with ranks thinned and much disorganized by its losses, especially of officers, it pressed on against the Union line at the stone wall where after a fierce encounter the struggle ended. Gen. J.L. Kemper fell wounded in front of the stone wall.

July 4. Spent the day in reorganization and during the night began the march to Hagerstown.

Present 1575. Killed 58, wounded 356, missing 717. Total 731.

COMMENTARY

This marker is ½ mile north of the position where the brigade formed before Pickett's Charge on July 3. During the charge, which began about 3 P.M., the brigade's regiments were in the following order from north to south: 3-7-1-11-24. General Kemper was badly wounded in front of the Union position ¾ mile east of this marker, and was captured there. The brigade had a battle strength of about 1634.[1]

127. DEARING'S BATTALION

Tablet on granite pedestal.
Located east of West Confederate Avenue, .26 mile north of intersection of West Confederate Avenue and Millerstown Road.
Erected 1910-1911, replacing earlier tablet erected ca. 1903.

TEXT

C.S.A. Army of Northern Virginia. Longstreet's Corps, Pickett's Division, Dearing's Battalion. Stribling's, Caskie's, Macon's and Blount's Batteries. Two 20 pounder Parrotts, three ten pounder Parrotts, one 3 inch rifle and twelve Napoleons.

July 3. Advanced to the front about daybreak and took a conspicuous part in the battle. In the cannonade preceding Longstreet's assault it fired by Battery and very effectively. Having exhausted its ammunition and being unable to obtain a fresh supply it was withdrawn from the field about 4 P.M.

July 4. In line of battle all day with McLaws's Division. Marched at sunset to Black Horse Tavern.

Losses. Killed 8, wounded 17. Total 25. Horses killed and disabled 37.

COMMENTARY

This marker shows the general position held by the battalion on July 4. During the great artillery bombardment from 1 to 3 P.M. on July 3, the battalion was at a position along the Emmitsburg Road north of the Rogers farmhouse about ¾ mile northeast of this marker. For the positions held by the individual batteries of the battalion, see Nos. 54 (Blount), 62 (Stribling), 65 (Caskie) and 81 (Macon). The battalion had a battle strength of about 419.[1]

128. EWELL'S CORPS

Tablet on granite marker.
Located southwest of Peace Memorial, on west side of North Confederate Avenue, 50 feet north of Mummasburg Road.
Erected 1907.

TEXT

Army of Northern Virginia. Second Army Corps. Lieutenant General Richard S. Ewell. Early's Division. Major General Jubal A. Early. Johnson's Division. Major General Edward Johnson. Rodes's Division. Major General R.E. Rodes. Artillery Reserve. Eight Batteries. Colonel J. Thompson Brown.

July 1. The Corps occupied the left of the Confederate line and reached the field in the following order: Rodes's Division by Newville Road about noon and deploying along Oak Ridge soon became engaged; Early's Division on the Harrisburg Road about 1 P.M. and united with Rodes's left in an attack on the First and Eleventh Corps Union troops and drove them through the town to Cemetery Ridge. The two Divisions occupied the town. Johnson's Division reached the field about night and not engaged. Late in the night moved along the Railroad and took position on the left of Corps and northeast of town.

July 2. In the early morning Johnson's Division was ordered to take possession of a wooded hill on the left. Skirmishers were advanced and a desultory fire kept up until 4 P.M. when the Artillery from Benner's Hill opened; the firing continued for two hours. The Batteries were withdrawn much crippled. The Division about dusk was advanced to the assault in connection with Early's Division on the right, the battle continuing until after dark. A partial success was made by a portion of each Division, but not being supported on the right was withdrawn to the former positions.

July 3. Early in the morning an attack was made by Johnson's Division, having been reinforced by three Brigades from the Corps; two other assaults were made but failed. Early's Division was withdrawn and occupied its former position in the town and not engaged. At night the Corps fell back to the range of hills west of the town.

July 4. The Corps took up the line of march during the night.

Casualties. Killed 809, wounded 3823, missing 1305. Total 5937.

COMMENTARY

This marker is located at the position held by the right of Rodes' division on July 1, and is 1 ¼ mile north of the right flank of the position held by the Corps on July 2 and 3. For the position held by the Corps on July 4, see No. 129. The "wooded hill on the left" mentioned on the marker's inscription is Culp's Hill. On July 3 Johnson's division was reinforced by four brigades from the Corps, not three as the marker states. The Corps had an estimated battle strength of 20,503.[1]

129.   EWELL'S CORPS (JULY 4)

Cast iron tablet.
Located west of Seminary Avenue, .04 mile south of Chambersburg Pike.
Erected ca. 1903.

TEXT

Army of Northern Virginia. Ewell's Corps. Rodes's, Early's and Johnson's Divisions.

July 4. Having withdrawn under orders from its previous positions, the Corps formed line about daybreak on this ridge with its right a short distance south of the Hagerstown Road, its left near the Mummasburg Road and its center near here. Rodes was on the right, Johnson on the left and Early on a supporting line in their rear. The breastwork of stone here and the old earthworks beyond the railroad are remains of defenses then thrown up and indicate the position of the front line.

July 5. The three Divisions left here at different hours but all were on the march to Hagerstown early in the morning of this day.

COMMENTARY

For the breastworks erected by Rodes' division on July 4, see No. 147.

130. EWELL'S HEADQUARTERS

Bronze cannon barrel in granite base.
Located north of Hanover Road, .1 mile west of Rock Creek.
Erected 1920-1921.

TEXT

Army of Northern Virginia. 2nd Corps Headquarters. Lieut. Gen. Richard S. Ewell. Divisions. Maj. Genl. Jubal A. Early. Maj. Genl. Edward Johnson. Maj. Genl. R.E. Rodes. July 1, 2, 3, 4, 5, 1863.

COMMENTARY

This marker shows the approximate location of the headquarters established by General Ewell late on July 1. This headquarters location was occupied for two days, until the Corps withdrew to northern Seminary Ridge late on July 3; the marker's text errs in placing the headquarters here on July 4 and 5.

131. DANCE'S BATTALION

Tablet on granite pedestal.
Located west of Seminary Avenue, 160 feet north of intersection of Fairfield Road and Seminary Avenue.
Erected 1910-1911, replacing earlier tablet erected ca. 1903.

TEXT

C.S.A. Army of Northern Virginia. Ewell's Corps, Artillery Reserve. Dance's Battalion, First Virginia Artillery. Cunningham's, Smith's, Watson's, Griffin's and Graham's Batteries. Four 20 pounder Parrotts, four 10 pounder Parrotts, two 3 inch rifles, two Napoleons.

July 1. The Battalion reached the field in evening too late to take part in the battle.

July 2 & 3. The four first named Batteries occupied positions at various points on this ridge. Graham's Battery of 20 pounder Parrotts served east of Rock Creek. All were actively engaged.

July 4. At nightfall began the march to Hagerstown. Ammunition expended 1888 rounds. Losses. Killed 3, wounded 19.

COMMENTARY

This marker is located at the position held by Smith's and Cunningham's batteries on July 2, and by Cunningham alone on July 3. Watson and C. Griffin were posted along this ridge ½ mile to the north of this marker on July 2. On July 3, Watson, Smith and C. Griffin were posted along this ridge ½ mile south of this marker. A. Graham's battery on July 2 and 3 was detached to the left flank and fought on Benner's Hill. All the guns of the battalion were withdrawn to the rear on the night of July 3. On the morning of the 4th two Napoleons from C. Griffin's battery were posted at the position of No. 89, and remained there until dark. For the specific movements of each battery, see Nos. 79 (Cunningham), 83 and 84 (Watson), 85 (Smith), 86 (A. Graham), and 88 and 89 (C. Griffin). The battalion had a battle strength of about 367.[1]

132. NELSON'S BATTALION
Tablet on granite pedestal.
Located on Benner's Hill, 170 feet north of Hanover Road.
Erected 1910-1911, replacing earlier tablet erected ca. 1903.

TEXT

C.S.A. Army of Northern Virginia. Ewell's Corps, Artillery Reserve, Nelson's Battalion. Kirkpatrick's, Massie's and Milledge's Batteries. One 10 pounder Parrott, four 3 inch rifles, six Napoleons.

July 1. The Battalion arrived on the field too late to participate in the engagement of the day; was ordered to report to the chief of Artillery, Rodes's Division.

July 2. Took position on Seminary Ridge ¼ mile north of Chambersburg Pike. About 11 A.M. moved to the rear of Pennsylvania College and remained until night when the Battalion returned to the position of the morning.

July 3. Ordered to the extreme left of the Confederate line to find a position to withdraw the fire from the Confederate Infantry. Opened about 12 M. firing 20 to 25 rounds. At midnight moved with Johnson's Division to Seminary Ridge.

July 4. Was ordered to take position on the ridge west of town. At night took up the line of march to Hagerstown.

Ammunition expended 48 rounds. Casualties not reported.

COMMENTARY

This marker is ¼ mile south of the position held by the battalion on Benner's Hill on July 3. For the specific positions held by the individual batteries of the battalion, see Nos. 17 (Milledge), 51 (Kirkpatrick), and 63 (Massie). The battalion had an estimated battle strength of 277.[1]

133. EARLY'S DIVISION

Tablet on granite marker.
Located east of East Confederate Avenue, .05 mile south of East Middle Street.
Erected 1909.

TEXT

C.S.A. Army of Northern Virginia. Second Army Corps, Early's Division. Maj. Gen. Jubal A. Early. Hays's Brigade. Brig. Gen. Harry T. Hays. Smith's Brigade. Brig. Gen. William Smith. Hoke's Brigade. Col. Isaac E. Avery, col. A.C. Godwin. Gordon's Brigade. Brig. Gen. John B. Gordon. Artillery Battalion. Four Batteries. Col. H.P. Jones.

July 1. The Division arrived about noon within two miles of Gettysburg by Harrisburg Road. Formed line across road north of Rock Creek. Gordon's Brigade ordered to support of a Brigade of Rodes's Division engaged with a Division of Eleventh Corps which had advanced to a wooded hill in front of town. The remainder of the Division was ordered forward as Gordon's Brigade was engaged. After a short and severe contest the Union troops were forced through the town losing many prisoners. Later in the day Gordon's Brigade ordered to the York Road in support of Smith's Brigade. Hays's and Hoke's Brigades occupied the town.

July 2. In the early morning Hays's and Hoke's Brigades took position to front and left of town. Gordon's Brigade in reserve moved to rear of the Brigades. Smith's Brigade remained in this position until nearly dusk when Hays's and Hoke's Brigades advanced on Cemetery Hill. The Brigades reached the crest of hill but not being supported on the right were forced to retire. Gordon's Brigade advanced to support the attack.

July 3. At daylight Smith's Brigade was ordered to support of Johnson's Division on the left. Hays's and Hoke's Brigades formed line in town holding the position of previous day. Gordon's Brigade held the line of the day before. The Division not further engaged.

July 4. In the morning the Division was withdrawn to Cashtown Road to west of town.

Casualties. Killed 156, wounded 806, missing 226. Total 1188.

COMMENTARY

This marker shows the position at which Hays', Hoke's and Gordon's brigades massed on the evening of July 2 before their attack on East Cemetery Hill. The marker's text fails to mention that Hays' and Hoke's brigades were engaged in the fighting on July 1. The division had an engaged strength of about 5460.[1]

134. GORDON'S BRIGADE (JULY 1)
Cast iron tablet.
Located north of East Howard Avenue, .2 mile west of Harrisburg Road.
Erected 1906.

TEXT
Army of Northern Virginia. Ewell's Corps, Early's Division, Gordon's Brigade. 13th, 26th, 31st, 38th, 60th, 61st Georgia Infantry.

July 1. Arrived on the field from Harrisburg Road in the early afternoon and formed line on North side of Rock Creek. About 3 P.M. moved across the creek to support of Rodes's left which was attacked from Barlow Knoll. Charged the Union Forces upon this hill and after a most obstinate resistance succeeded in breaking the line. The Brigade was afterwards moved to the support of Smith's Brigade on the York Road. The Brigade captured a large number of prisoners during the day.

July 2. Moved to the railroad in support of Hays's and Avery's Brigades in their attack on Cemetery Ridge.

July 3. Occupied the position at foot of Cemetery Ridge and not engaged.

July 4. At 2 A.M. the Brigade was withdrawn and moved to Cashtown Road.

Casualties. Killed 71, Wounded 270, Missing 39, Total 380.

COMMENTARY
This marker is located at the center of the brigade's line when it was attacking the Union position on Barlow Knoll from 3 to 4 P.M. on July 1. During this attack the regiments of the brigade were in the following order from east to west: 38-61-60-13-31; the 26th regiment remained in reserve along the Harrisburg Road ½ mile to the northeast. For the brigade's position on July 3, see No. 135. The marker's text twice incorrectly reads "Cemetery Ridge" instead of "East Cemetery Hill" The brigade had an estimated battle strength of 1813.[1]

135. GORDON'S BRIGADE (JULY 2 AND 3)
Tablet on granite pedestal.
Located east of East Confederate Avenue, .13 mile southeast of East Middle Street.
Erected 1910-1911, replacing earlier tablet erected 1899.

TEXT
C.S.A. Army of Northern Virginia. Ewell's Corps, Early's Division, Gordon's Brigade. 13th, 26th, 31st, 38th, 60th, 61st Georgia Infantry.

July 2. After participating in the operations of July 1st at Barlow Knoll and elsewhere, it took position in the afternoon on the railroad between the town and Rock Creek. When the assault was made at 8 P.M. on East Cemetery Hill, the Brigade advanced to its support but was halted here because the expected re-enforcements were unable to cooperate and it was evident that the assault would fail.

July 3. Remained here skirmishing with sharpshooters and exposed to Artillery fire.

July 4. The Brigade was withdrawn and moved to Seminary Ridge. After midnight began the march to Hagerstown.

Present about 1500. Killed 71, wounded 270, missing 39. Total 380.

COMMENTARY

This marker shows the general position held by the brigade from the afternoon of July 2 to the early morning of July 4. At dusk on July 2 it advanced from this position to support the unsuccessful assault on East Cemetery Hill. For the brigade's position on July 1, see No. 134. On the morning of July 2 the brigade was posted on York Road 1½ miles northeast of this marker. The brigade had an estimated battle strength of 1813.[1]

136. HAYS' BRIGADE

Tablet on granite pedestal.
Located east of East Confederate Avenue, .1 mile southeast of East Middle Street.
Erected 1910-1911, replacing earlier tablet erected 1899.

TEXT

C.S.A. Army of Northern Virginia. Ewell's Corps, Early's Division, Hays's Brigade. 5th, 6th, 7th, 8th, 9th Louisiana Infantry.

July 1. Advancing at 3 P.M. with Hokes's Brigade flanked Eleventh Corps, aided in taking two guns, pursued retreating Union troops into town, capturing many and late in evening halting on East High St.

July 2. Moved forward early into the low ground here with its right flank resting on Baltimore St. and skirmished all day. Enfiladed by Artillery and exposed to musketry fire in front, it pushed forward over all obstacles, scaled the hill, and planted its colors on the lunettes, capturing several guns. Assailed by fresh troops and with no supports it was forced to retire but brought off 75 prisoners and 4 stands of colors.

July 3. Occupied a position on High St. in the town.

July 4. At 2 A.M. moved to Seminary Ridge. After midnight began the march to Hagerstown.

Present about 1200. Killed 26, wounded 201, missing 95. Total 332.

COMMENTARY

This marker shows the position held all day July 2 until the assault began on East Cemetery Hill at 8 P.M. During this unsuccessful attack the brigade's regiments were in the following order from east to west: 8-7-9-6-5. On July 3 the brigade was posted in town along High Street, ¼ mile to the northwest. For the brigade's position on July 1, see No. A-7. The brigade had a battle strength of about 1295.[1] The army's

Medical Director reported the brigade's losses to be 303—36 killed, 201 wounded, and 76 captured or missing.[2]

137. HOKE'S BRIGADE

Tablet on granite pedestal.
Located east of East Confederate Avenue, .18 mile southeast of East Middle Street.
Erected 1910-1911, replacing earlier tablet erected 1899.

TEXT

C.S.A. Army of Northern Virginia. Ewell's Corps, Early's Division, Hoke's Brigade. 6th, 21st, 57th North Carolina Infantry.

July 1. Advanced at 3 P.M. with Hays's Brigade; flanked Eleventh Corps; aided in taking two guns; repulsed First Brigade Second Division and captured many prisoners. Late in evening took position here.

July 2. Skirmished all day; at 8 P.M. with Hays's Brigade charged East Cemetery Hill. Severely enfiladed on the left by artillery and musketry, it pushed on over infantry line in front, scaled the Hill, planted its colors on the lunettes and captured several guns. But assailed by fresh forces and having no supports it was soon compelled to relinquish what it had gained and withdraw. Its commander Col. Isaac E. Avery was mortally wounded leading the charge.

July 3. Ordered to railroad cut in rear and later to High Street in town.

July 4. At 2 A.M. moved to Seminary Ridge. After midnight began the march to Hagerstown.

Present about 900. Killed 35, wounded 216, missing 94. Total 345.

COMMENTARY

This marker shows the position held by the brigade all day July 2 until its attack on East Cemetery Hill at 8 P.M. During this attack the brigade's regiments were in the following order from east to west: 59-21-6. Colonel Avery, who commanded the brigade, was wounded $\frac{3}{8}$ mile south of this marker. On July 3 the brigade was posted in town $\frac{1}{4}$ mile north of this marker. For the brigade's position on July 1, see No. A-8. The brigade had an estimated battle strength of 1244.[1]

138. SMITH'S BRIGADE

Tablet on granite pedestal.
Located east of East Confederate Avenue, .05 mile north of Spangler Meadow.
Erected 1910-1911, replacing earlier tablet erected 1899.

TEXT

C.S.A. Army of Northern Virginia. Ewell's Corps, Early's Division, Smith's Brigade. 31st, 49th, 52nd Virginia Infantry.

July 3. The Brigade having been detached two days guarding York Pike and other roads against the reported approach of Union Cavalry, was ordered to Culp's Hill to reinforce Johnson's Division. Arriving early formed in line along this stone wall, receiving and returning fire of

Infantry and sharpshooters in the woods opposite and being also subjected to heavy fire of Artillery. It repulsed the charge of the 2nd Massachusetts and 27th Indiana Regiments against this line and held its ground until the Union forces regained their works on the Hill. It then moved to a position further up the Creek and during the night marched to Seminary Ridge where it rejoined Early's Division.

July 4. Occupied Seminary Ridge. After midnight began the march to Hagerstown.

Present about 800. Killed 12, wounded 113, missing 17. Total 142.

COMMENTARY

This marker shows the position held by the brigade during the fighting on the morning of July 3. It was formed along the nearby stone wall, facing south across Spangler's meadow. On July 2 the brigade was posted along the York Pike two miles northeast of Gettysburg. The brigade had an estimated battle strength of 806.[1]

139. H. JONES' BATTALION
Tablet on granite pedestal.
Located 60 feet east of Harrisburg Road, .5 mile north of Rock Creek.
Erected 1910-1911, replacing earlier tablet erected 1907.

TEXT

C.S.A. Army of Northern Virginia. Ewell's Corps, Early's Division, Jones's Artillery Battalion. Carrington's, Tanner's, Green's, Garber's Batteries. Two 10 pounder Parrotts, six 3 inch rifles, eight Napoleons.

July 1. Arrived on the field with Early's Division about 2:45 P.M. Moved into battery 400 yards east of this position; opened an effective enfilading fire on Infantry retiring from Seminary Ridge. Ceased firing as the Confederate Infantry advanced.

July 2. The Battalion remained in the same position. Not actively engaged.

July 3. Occupied same position. Not actively engaged.

COMMENTARY

This marker shows the position held by most of the battalion from 2:45 P.M. on July 1 until the evening of July 2. From 2:45 to 4 P.M. on July 1 Garber's, Green's and Tanner's batteries engaged the Union forces on Barlow Knoll from this position. The three batteries then remained here on July 2. At 3 P.M. on the 2nd Tanner's battery was sent to the York Road, and at sunset Green's battery was sent to join Stuart, with whom it remained on the 3rd; these movements are not noted in the text of the marker. The marker also fails to mention that Garber's and Carrington's batteries were moved late on July 2 to a reserve position between the Harrisburg and Carlisle Roads about ¼ mile north of Gettysburg. They remained at this new reserve position on the 3rd, being joined by Tanner's battery. For the specific positions held by the individual batteries of the battalion, see Nos. 25 and 26 (Green), 57 (Carrington), 58 (Tanner) and 90 (Garber). The battalion had an estimated battle strength of 290.[1] Its losses were reported to be 2 killed and 8 wounded.[2]

140. JOHNSON'S DIVISION
Tablet on granite marker.
Located east of East Confederate Avenue, .52 mile north of Spangler Meadow,
opposite Culp's Hill.
Erected 1909.

TEXT
Army of Northern Virginia. Second Army Corps, Johnson's Division. Maj. Gen. Edward Johnson. Steuart's Brigade. Brig. Gen. Geo. H. Steuart. Stonewall Brigade. Brig. Gen. James A. Walker. Nicholl's Brigade. Col. J.M.Wllliams. Jones's Brigade. Brig Gen. John M. Jones, Lieut. Col. R.H. Duncan. Artillery Battalion. Four Batteries. Major J.W. Latimer, Captain C.L. Raine.
July 1. The Division arrived on the field too late to participate in the engagement of the day. Moved to the northeast of town during the night to take possession of wooded hill that commanded Cemetery Ridge.
July 2. Early in the morning skirmishers advanced and a desultory fire kept up. The Artillery was posted on hill in rear of line and opened fire about 4 P.M. The Infantry advanced to assault at dusk up the steep hill. Steuart's Brigade captured a line of works on the left. Firing continued at close range during night.
July 3. The assault was renewed in early morning. An attempt was made by the Union forces to retake the works occupied the night before and was repulsed. The Division being reinforced by four Brigades, two other assaults were made and repulsed. Retired at 10:30 A.M. to former position of July 2, which was held until 10 P.M. when the Division was withdrawn to the ridge northwest of town.
July 4. The Division took up the line of march during the day.
Casualties. Killed 229, wounded 1269, missing 375. Total 1873.

COMMENTARY
This marker is at the center of the line held by the division when it was attacking the Union right flank from the evening of July 2 until noon on July 3. Before it moved to this position, the division was posted one mile to the northeast between York Pike and Hanover Road. The marker's text neglects to mention that on July 2 Walker's brigade was sent to the army's far left flank two miles east of Gettysburg. The division's battle strength was about 6380.[1]

141. J. JONES' BRIGADE
Tablet on granite pedestal.
Located east of East Confederate Avenue, .75 mile north of Spangler Meadow,
opposite Culp's Hill.
Erected 1910-1911, replacing earlier tablet erected 1899.

TEXT
C.S.A. Army of Northern Virginia. Ewell's Corps, Johnson's Division, Jones's Brigade. 21st, 25th, 42nd, 44th, 48th, 50th Virginia Infantry.

July 1. Arrived near nightfall and took position east of Rock Creek and north of Hanover Road with pickets advanced to the front.

July 2. About 4 P.M. moved forward to support Artillery on Benner's Hill. Crossed Rock Creek at 6 P.M. and assailed the Union position on the summit of Culp's Hill, charging up to the Union breastworks and continuing the struggle until dark.

July 3. In line near here all day sometimes skirmishing heavily. About midnight moved with the Division and Corps to Seminary Ridge northwest of the town.

July 4. Occupied Seminary Ridge. About 10 P.M. began the march to Hagerstown.

Present 1600. Killed 58, wounded 302, missing 61. Total 421.

COMMENTARY
This marker is located ¼ mile south of the position held by the brigade when it was attacking Culp's Hill from the evening of July 2 until about noon on July 3. Its position early on July 2 was one mile to the northeast of this marker. The brigade's battle strength was about 1467.[1]

142. NICHOLLS' BRIGADE
Tablet on granite pedestal.
Located east of East Confederate Avenue, .57 mile north of Spangler Meadow,
opposite Culp's Hill.
Erected 1910-1911, replacing earlier tablet erected 1899.

TEXT
C.S.A. Army of Northern Virginia. Ewell's Corps, Johnson's Division, Nicholl's Brigade. 1st, 2nd, 10th, 14th, 15th Louisiana Infantry.

July 1. Arrived near nightfall and took position east of Rock Creek north of Hanover Road and on the right of the Division.

July 2. About 6 P.M. changing to left of Jones's Brigade crossed the Creek; attacked Union forces on Culp's Hill; drove in their outposts and reached and held a line about 100 yards from their breastworks against which a steady fire was maintained for hours and some vigorous but unsuccessful assaults made.

July 3. At dawn the Brigade reopened fire and continued it for many hours, then retired to line near the Creek whence about midnight it moved with the Division and Corps to Seminary Ridge.

July 4. Occupied Seminary Ridge. About 10 P.M. began the march to Hagerstown.

Present about 1100. Killed 43, wounded 309, missing 36. Total 388.

COMMENTARY

This marker shows the general position held by the brigade during its attacks against Culp's Hill from 6 P.M. on July 2 to noon on July 3. Its position earlier in the day on July 2 was one mile to the northeast. The brigade's estimated battle strength was 1104.[1] It was commanded during the battle by Colonel J.M. Williams.

143. STEUART'S BRIGADE
Tablet on granite pedestal.
Located east of East Confederate Avenue, .25 mile north of Spangler Meadow.
Erected 1910-1911, replacing earlier tablet erected 1899.

TEXT

C.S.A. Army of Northern Virginia. Ewell's Corps, Johnson's Division, Steuart's Brigade. 1st Maryland Battalion, 1st and 3rd North Carolina, 10th, 23rd and 37th Virginia Infantry.

July 1. Arrived about nightfall and took position near Hanover Road about a mile east of Rock Creek with left wing at edge of woods.

July 2. Crossing Rock Creek at 6 P.M. the 3rd N.C. and 1st Md. attacked the lesser summit of Culp's Hill. Reinforced later by the other regiments, the Union breastworks, thinly manned at some points, were occupied to the southern base of the main summit but only after a vigorous and desperate conflict.

July 3. The Union troops reinforced the conflict at dawn and it raged fiercely until 11 A.M. when this Brigade and the entire line fell back to the base of the Hill and from thence moved about midnight to Seminary Ridge northwest of the town.

July 4. Occupied Seminary Ridge. About 10 P.M. began the march to Hagerstown.

Present about 1700. Killed 83, wounded 409, missing 190. Total 682.

COMMENTARY

From the evening of July 2 until noon on July 3 Steuart's brigade fought at and near the summit of South Culp's Hill, about ¼ mile to the southeast of this marker. For the position reached by the 1st Maryland Battalion during this fighting, see Nos. 32 and 35. On the morning and afternoon of July 2 the brigade was posted with its division about one mile to the northeast of this marker. The brigade had an estimated battle strength of 2121.[1]

144. WALKER'S BRIGADE

Tablet on granite pedestal.
Located east of East Confederate Avenue, .15 mile north of Spangler Meadow.
Erected 1910-1911, replacing earlier tablet erected 1899.

TEXT

C.S.A. Army of Northern Virginia. Ewell's Corps, Johnson's Division, Walker's Brigade. 2nd, 4th, 5th, 27th, 33rd Virginia Infantry.

July 1. Arrived about nightfall and took position east of Rock Creek near Hanover Road at border of woods on left of Division.

July 2. Guarded Division all day on its flank from Union forces in woods near by, skirmishing with them sharply at times and finally driving them away. After dark crossed Rock Creek and rejoined the Division which had crossed about 6 P.M. and occupied part of the Union breastworks.

July 3. Took part in the unsuccessful struggle lasting from daybreak until near noon and then retired to the foot of the Hill and from thence about midnight moved with the Division and Corps to Seminary Ridge.

July 4. Occupied Seminary Ridge. About 10 P.M. began the march to Hagerstown.

Present about 1450. Killed 35, wounded 208, missing 87. Total 330.

COMMENTARY

This marker is located about ¼ mile southeast of the position held by the brigade during its attack on Culp's Hill on the morning of July 3. This brigade, better known as the "Stonewall Brigade," had an estimated battle strength of 1323.[1]

145. LATIMER'S BATTALION

Tablet on granite pedestal.Located on Benner's Hill, .1 mile south of Hanover Road.
Erected 1910-1911, replacing earlier tablet erected 1905.

TEXT

C.S.A. Army of Northern Virginia. Ewell's Corps, Johnson's Division, Latimer's Battalion. Brown's, Carpenter's, Dement's and Raine's Batteries. Two 20 pounder Parrotts, five 10 pounder Parrotts, three 3 inch rifles and six Napoleons.

July 1. After dark crossed Rock Creek and encamped on this ridge.

July 2. At 4 P.M. the Battalion except the 20 pounder Parrotts took position here and was engaged more than two hours in a heavy cannonade with the Union Artillery on Cemetery Hill, Stevens' Knoll, and Culp's Hill. Ammunition exhausted and losses severe, the guns were withdrawn except four to cover the advance of Johnson's Infantry against Culp's Hill. In the renewed firing Major S.W. Latimer was mortally wounded. In the cannonading the 20 pounder Parrotts in position half a mile north took an active part.

July 3. The 20 pounder Parrotts took part in the great cannonade while the other Batteries were in reserve.
July 4. The Battalion withdrew and began the march to Hagerstown.
Losses. Killed 10, wounded 40. Horses killed 30.

COMMENTARY

This marker shows the position held by the battalion from 4 to 6:30 P.M. on July 2. The battalion then retired to a new position out of enemy range about one mile to the northeast. For the specific positions held by each battery of the battalion, see Nos. 36 (Brown), 37 (Dement) 50 (Carpenter), and 71 (Raine). The battalion had an estimated battle strength of 356.[1]

146. RODES' DIVISION
Tablet on granite marker.
Located north of North Confederate Avenue on Oak Hill, 30 feet southeast of rear of Peace Memorial.
Erected 1909.

TEXT

C.S.A. Army of Northern Virginia. Second Army Corps. Rodes's Division. Maj. Gen. R.E. Rodes. Daniel's Brigade. Brig. Gen. Junius Daniel. Doles's Brigade. Brig. Gen. George Doles. Iverson's Brigade. Brig. Gen. Alfred Iverson. Ramseur's Brigade. Brig. Gen. S.D. Ramseur. O'Neal's Brigade. Col. E.A. O'Neal. Artillery Battalion. Four Batteries. Lieut. Col. Thomas H. Carter.
July 1. Rodes's Division advancing by the Newville Road occupied Oak Ridge about noon. The line formed and advanced in the following order: Doles's Brigade deployed in the Valley north of Town and left of Division and was opposed by troops of the Eleventh Corps; O'Neal's and Iverson's Brigades advanced on Ridge and meeting a portion of First Union Corps were driven back with heavy loss; Daniel's Brigade was ordered to the support of Iverson but became separated by a change of direction. Moved to the Railroad on the right where Heth's Division was engaged. Ramseur held in reserve. After a severe conflict the Union troops retired.
July 2. The Division occupied ground near and west of town and was not engaged.
July 3. The Brigades of Daniel and O'Neal were ordered to report to Gen. E. Johnson on the left early in the morning and joined in the attack on Culp's Hill. The remainder of the Division held the position of day before and at night retired to Seminary Ridge.
July 4. The Division took up the line of march during the night.
Casualties. Killed 421, wounded 1728, missing 704. Total 2853.

COMMENTARY

This marker is located at the position held by the division's right flank from noon to 4 P.M. on July 1. The marker's text neglects to mention that a part of O'Neal's brigade was engaged against the left flank of the Union Eleventh Corps at this time. On July 2 the division was posted 1½ mile south of this marker. For its position on July 4, see No. 147. The division's estimated battle strength was 7873.[1]

147. RODES' BREASTWORKS ON SEMINARY RIDGE
Metal marker.
Located east of Seminary Avenue, 130 feet south of Chambersburg Pike.
Erected ca. 1903.

TEXT

This breastwork was constructed by Rodes' division C.S.A. July 4, 1863.

COMMENTARY

This marker shows the position held by Rodes' division from the evening of July 3 until it left the field on the evening of July 4. For the division's position on July 1, see No. 146. General Rodes speaks in his official battle report of the construction of these breastworks after the division withdrew from its positions at Culp's Hill and along Long Lane: "During the night of the 3d, my division fell back to the ridge which had been wrested from the enemy in the first day's attack, and, being reunited, was posted so that the railroad divided it about equally. Expecting to give battle in this position, it was strengthened early on the morning of the 4th. We were not disturbed, however, in the least during the day."[1]

148. DANIEL'S BRIGADE (JULY 1)
Tablet on granite pedestal.
Located on Oak Hill, 50 feet west of Peace Memorial.
Erected 1910-1911, replacing earlier tablet erected 1905.

TEXT

C.S.A. Army of Northern Virginia. Ewell's Corps, Rodes's Division, Daniel's Brigade. 32nd, 43rd, 45th, 53rd Regiments and 2nd Battalion North Carolina Infantry.

July 1. The Brigade formed the right of Division and its line extended from Forney Field to the railroad near the McPherson Barn. The regiments did not at first move together nor attack the same troops. The 43rd and 53rd Regiments, aided by O'Neal's 3rd Alabama and Iverson's 12th North Carolina attacked the Union line in the Sheads and Forney Woods. The 45th Regiment and 2nd Battalion fought the 2nd Brigade, 3rd Division, First Corps near the railroad cuts, and being joined by the 32nd Regiment and other troops compelled retreat. The Regiments fought under a heavy Artillery fire. The Brigade was reunited and lost heavily in the struggle which dislodged the Union forces from Seminary Ridge.

July 2. On Seminary Ridge all day. After night moved into town.

July 3. Marched before daylight to Culp's Hill to aid Johnson's Division.

July 4. Occupied Seminary Ridge. At night began the march to Hagerstown.

Present 2100. Killed 165. Wounded 636. Missing 116. Total 916.

COMMENTARY

This marker is located in the general area where the brigade fought on the right of Rodes' division from noon to 4 P.M. on July 1. During the heaviest part of the conflict, the right portion of the brigade (35th and 42nd regiments and 2nd Battalion) attacked the Union line one mile southwest of this marker, and the left portion of the brigade (43rd and 53rd regiments) fought ½ mile south of here. On July 2, the brigade was posted on Seminary Ridge between the Cashtown and Fairfield Roads. For its position on July 3, see No. 149. The brigade had an estimated battle strength of 2052.[1]

149. DANIEL'S BRIGADE (JULY 3)

Tablet on granite pedestal.
Located east of East Confederate Avenue, .4 mile north of Spangler Meadow, opposite Culp's Hill.
Erected 1910-1911, replacing earlier tablet erected 1899.

TEXT

C.S.A. Army of Northern Virginia. Ewell's Corps, Rodes' Division, Daniel's Brigade. 32nd, 43rd, 45th, 53rd Regiments and 2nd Battalion North Carolina Infantry.

July 3. After taking part in the battles of the First and Second Days elsewhere on the field, the Brigade marched about 1:30 A.M. from its position in the town to Culp's Hill to reinforce Johnson's Division. Arriving about 4 A.M. it fought at different points wherever ordered through the long and fierce conflict, its main position being in the ravine between the two summits of Culp's Hill. At the close of the struggle near noon it was withdrawn by Gen. Johnson with the rest of the line to the base of the Hill from whence it moved during the night to Seminary Ridge west of the town and there rejoined Rodes's Division.

July 4. Occupied Seminary Ridge. Late at night began the march to Hagerstown.

Present 2100. Killed 165, wounded 635, missing 116. Total 916.

COMMENTARY

This marker is located in the general position from which the brigade attacked the Union positions on Culp's Hill from 4 to 11 A.M. on July

3. For the brigade's strength and movements on July 1 and 2, see No. 148. For the position of the 43rd North Carolina on July 3, see No. 201.

150.   DOLES' BRIGADE

Tablet on granite pedestal.
Located north of West Howard Avenue, 280 feet west of Carlisle Road.
Erected 1910-1911, replacing earlier tablet erected 1905

TEXT

C.S.A. Army of Northern Virginia. Ewell's Corps, Rodes's Division, Doles's Brigade. 4th, 12th, 21st, 44th Georgia Infantry.

July 1. About 1 P.M. the Brigade formed line in the fields east of Oak Hill and skirmished with Union 2nd Brigade 1st Cavalry Division and aided Gordon's Brigade in dislodging the Union forces from Barlow Knoll and their line from thence to the Heidlersburg Road. Then joined Ramseur and others in their attack upon the rear of First Corps which after a long struggle was compelled to retire from Seminary Ridge. The Brigade took many prisoners from the First and Eleventh Corps which it pursued to the southern borders of the town.

July 2. Lay all day in the town on West Middle Street. After dark moved out to aid in a contemplated attack on Cemetery Hill.

July 3. In line with other Brigades in the sunken road southwest of town.

July 4. On Seminary Ridge all day. At night began the march to Hagerstown.

Present 1369. Killed 86, wounded 124, missing 31. Total 241.

COMMENTARY

This marker shows the position at which the brigade attacked von Amsberg's brigade of the Union Eleventh Corps from 3:30 to 4 P.M. on July 1. Its battle strength was about 1323[1]. The army's Medical Director reported its losses to be 179—24 killed, 124 wounded, and 31 captured or missing.[2]

151.   IVERSON'S BRIGADE

Tablet on granite pedestal.
Located on Oak Hill, 180 feet southeast of Peace Memorial.
Erected 1910-1911, replacing earlier tablet erected 1905.

TEXT

C.S.A. Army of Northern Virginia. Ewell's Corps, Rodes's Division, Iverson's Brigade. 5th, 12th, 20th, 23rd North Carolina Infantry.

July 1. The Brigade was one of the first of the Division in the battle. It advanced against the Union line posted behind stone fence east of Forney Field. Its right being assailed by 2nd Brigade First Corps and its left exposed by the repulse of O'Neal, a vigorous assault by Union forces in front and on left flank almost annihilated three regiments. The

12th regiment on the right being sheltered by the knoll suffered slight loss and the remnants of the others joined Ramseur's Brigade and served with it throughout the battle.

July 2. Lay all day in the town. At dusk moved to aid in an attack on Cemetery Hill, but two of Early's Brigades having been repulsed, the Brigade withdrew.

July 3. With other Brigades in the sunken road southwest of the town. At night withdrew to Seminary Ridge.

July 4. Marched at 2 P.M. as wagon train guard on road to Hagerstown. Present 1470. Killed 130, wounded 328, missing 308. Total 820.

COMMENTARY

About 2:30 P.M. on July 1 this brigade advanced over the position indicated by this marker on its way to attack the Union line ½ mile to the south. During this attack the regiments of the brigade were in the following order from east to west: 5-20-23-12. The brigade's right was attacked by the 2nd Brigade, 2nd Division, 1st Corps, whose full title is not given in the marker's text. The brigade had an estimated battle strength of 1384.[1]

152.   O'NEAL'S BRIGADE (JULY 1)

Tablet on granite pedestal.
Located southeast of Peace Memorial, on west side of North Confederate Avenue, .1 mile north of intersection of North Confederate Avenue and Mummasburg Road. Erected 1910-1911, replacing earlier tablet erected 1905.

TEXT

C.S.A. Army of Northern Virginia. Ewell's Corps, Rodes's Division, O'Neal's Brigade. 3rd, 5th, 6th, 12th, 26th Alabama Infantry.

July 1. Soon after arriving at this position three regiments attacked the Union flank, the 5th regiment being ordered to guard the wide interval between the Brigade and Doles's Brigade in the valley on the left, and the 3rd regiment joining Daniel's and afterwards Ramseur's Brigade. The three regiments were repulsed with heavy loss but the entire Brigade took part in the general attack soon made by the Confederates which finally dislodged the Union forces from Seminary Ridge.

July 2. The Brigade in position all day in or near the town but not engaged.

July 3. The 5th regiment lay in the southern borders of the town firing upon the Union Artillery with their long range rifles. The other regiments moved to Culp's Hill to reinforce Johnson's Division.

July 4. Moved to Seminary Ridge. At night began the march to Hagerstown.

Present 1794. Killed 73, Wounded 430, Missing 193. Total 696.

COMMENTARY

This marker is located at the position held by the right of the brigade's line from 1 to 4 P.M. on July 1. On July 2, the brigade was held in reserve along the Chambersburg Pike between Gettysburg and Seminary Ridge. For its position on July 3, see No. 153. The brigade had an estimated battle strength of 1688.[1]

153. O'NEAL'S BRIGADE (JULY 3)

Tablet on granite pedestal. Located east of East Confederate Avenue, .45 mile north of Spangler Meadow, opposite Culp's Hill.
Erected 1910-1911, replacing earlier tablet erected 1899.

TEXT

C.S.A. Army of Northern Virginia. Ewell's Corps, Rodes's Division, O'Neal's Brigade. 3rd, 5th, 6th, 12th, 26th Alabama Infantry.

July 3. After taking part in the battle of the First and Second Days elsewhere on the field, the Brigade leaving the 5th Regiment on guard marched at 2 A.M. from its position in town to Culp's Hill to reinforce Johnson's Division. Arrived at daybreak and was soon under fire but not actively engaged until 8 A.M. when it advanced against the breastworks on the eastern slope of the main summit of the Hill, gaining there a position near the Union works and holding it under a terrific fire for three hours until withdrawn by Gen. Johnson with his entire line to the base of the hill near the Creek. From thence it moved during the night to Seminary Ridge west of the town and rejoined Rodes's Division.

July 4. Occupied Seminary Ridge. Late at night began the march to Hagerstown.

Present 1650. Killed 73, wounded 430, missing 193. Total 696.

COMMENTARY

This marker shows the general position held by the brigade from 4 to 11 A.M. on July 3 when it was attacking the Union lines on Culp's Hill. For the brigade's strength and movements on July 1 and 2, see No. 152.

154. RAMSEUR'S BRIGADE

Tablet on granite pedestal.
Located southwest of Peace Memorial on north side of North Confederate Avenue, .1 mile north of Mummasburg Road.
Erected 1910-1911, replacing earlier tablet erected 1905.

TEXT

C.S.A. Army of Northern Virginia. Ewell's Corps, Rodes's Division, Ramseur's Brigade. 2nd, 4th, 14th, 30th North Carolina Infantry.

July 1. Soon after Iverson's and O'Neal's Brigades had each suffered the repulse of three regiments with heavy losses, Ramseur's Brigade moved from its position here and vigorously assailed the right wing of the Union forces. The 14th and 30th regiments with O'Neal's 3rd Alabama turned the flank of the Union troops while the 2nd and 4th regiments together with Doles's Brigade and part of O'Neal's struck them in the rear. A struggle ensued in which both sides suffered severely and the conflict here only ended with the retreat of the Union Corps from Seminary Ridge. In that retreat the Brigade made active pursuit and captured many prisoners.

July 2. Skirmishing on the southern borders of the town.

July 3. In sunken lane southwest of town.

July 4. In line on Seminary Ridge. At night began the march to Hagerstown.

Present 1909. Killed 23, wounded 129, missing 44.

COMMENTARY

This marker shows the position held by the right flank of the brigade from 2 to 4 P.M. on July 1. The brigade had an estimated battle strength of 1027.[1] Its losses as reported by the army's Medical Director totaled 177—23 killed, 122 wounded, and 32 captured or missing.[2]

155.   T. CARTER'S BATTALION

Tablet on granite pedestal.
Located on Oak Hill, 200 feet southeast of Peace Memorial.
Erected 1910-1911, replacing earlier tablet erected 1906.

TEXT

C.S.A. Army of Northern Virginia. Ewell's Corps, Rodes's Division, Carter's Battalion. Carter's, Fry's, Page's and Reese's Batteries. Four 10 pounder Parrotts, six 3 inch rifles and six Napoleons.

July 1. Arrived on the field soon after noon and rendered very effective service in the day's battle.

July 2. Held in readiness for action but was not engaged.

July 3. The Parrotts and Rifled guns were placed on Seminary Ridge near the railroad cut and took part in the great cannonade preceding Longstreet's assault.

July 4. After nightfall began the march to Hagerstown.

Losses. Killed 6, wounded 35, missing 24. Total 65. Ammunition expended 1898 rounds.

COMMENTARY

This marker shows the position held by the battalion from noon on July 1 until the end of the day. On July 2 the battalion was moved to a reserve position between the Mummasburg and Carlisle Roads 1⅛ mile southeast of this marker. On July 3 the battalion's rifled guns were placed on Seminary Ridge just north of the Chambersburg Pike, about one mile south of this marker. For the specific positions held by the battalion's batteries, see Nos. 16 (Reese), 70 (W. Carter), 75 (Page), and 76 (Fry). The battalion had an estimated battle strength of 385.[1]

156. HILL'S CORPS

Tablet on granite marker.
Located west of West Confederate Avenue, .48 mile north of Virginia Monument (just south of McMillan Woods).
Erected 1907.

TEXT

Army of Northern Virginia. Third Army Corps. Lieutenant General Ambrose P. Hill. Anderson's Division. Major General R.H. Anderson. Heth's Division. Major General Henry Heth, Brigadier General J.J. Pettigrew. Pender's Division. Major General William D. Pender, Brigadier General James H. Lane, Major General I.R. Trimble. Artillery Reserve. Nine Batteries. Colonel R. Lindsay Walker.

July 1. The Corps was near Cashtown. Heth's Division at 5 A.M. moved towards Gettysburg. Two Brigades with Artillery advancing across Willoughby Run were soon engaged. Archer's Brigade was driven across the run. After resting an hour Heth's Division formed in line west of Willoughby Run and advanced with Pender's Division in reserve. 2:30 P.M. the right of Ewell's Corps appeared on the left. Pender's Division was ordered forward. After a severe contest the Union forces were driven back and through the town. The two Divisions bivouacked on the ground gained. Anderson's Division bivouacked two miles in rear.

July 2. Anderson's Division extended to the right along the crest of hills facing Cemetery Ridge, Pender's Division occupying the crest from the Seminary and joining Anderson's Division with Heth's Division in reserve, the Artillery in position on Seminary Ridge. The First Corps ordered to attack the left of Union forces, the Third Corps to co-operate. General Anderson moved forward three Brigades connecting with left of McLaws's Division and drove the Union forces from their position. Anderson's right becoming separated from McLaws's left and no support coming to these Brigades, they returned to their former lines.

July 3. The Corps occupied the same position. Reserve Batteries were placed facing the Union lines. The Confederate line held by Anderson's Division, half of Pender's and half of Heth's, the remainder of Corps ordered to report to General Longstreet as a support in the assault to be made on the Union position on Cemetery Ridge. About 1 P.M. the Artillery along the line opened fire. 3 P.M. the assault was made and failed Anderson's Division was held in reserve. The troops fell back to former positions.

July 4. The Corps took up the line of march during the night.
Casualties. Killed 837, wounded 4407, missing 1491. Total 6735.

COMMENTARY

This marker is located on the left of the line held by the Corps on July 2 and 3. Its text neglects to mention that a large part of Davis' brigade was captured in the opening part of the engagement on July 1. The Corps had an estimated battle strength of 22,026.[1]

157. HILL'S HEADQUARTERS

Cannon barrel in granite base.
Located west of West Confederate Avenue, .32 mile northeast of Virginia Monument.
Erected 1920-1921.

TEXT

C.S.A. Army of Northern Virginia. 3rd Corps Headquarters. Lieut. General Ambrose P. Hill. Divisions. Major Genl. R.H. Anderson. Major Genl. Henry Heth. Major Genl. William D. Pender. July 1, 2, 3, 4, 1863. These headquarters were located at a farmhouse 540 yards westerly.

COMMENTARY

The farmhouse occupied by Hill's headquarters during the battle belonged to E. Pitzer.

158. MCINTOSH'S BATTALION

Tablet on granite pedestal.
Located 100 feet west of West Confederate Avenue, .11 mile south of Fairfield Road.
Erected 1910-1911, replacing earlier tablet erected ca. 1903.

TEXT

C.S.A. Army of Northern Virginia. Hill's Corps, Artillery Reserve, McIntosh's Battalion. Johnson's, Rice's, Hurt's and Wallace's Batteries. Six Napoleons, two Whitworths, eight 3 inch rifles.
July 1-4. The Battalion was actively engaged on each of the three days of the battle and withdrew from the field under orders in the evening of the fourth day.
Losses. 7 men killed, 25 wounded of whom 16 were captured. 38 horses killed or disabled.

COMMENTARY

This marker shows the position held by most of the battalion on July 2, 3 and 4; its two Whitworth rifles were placed on Oak Hill on July 3. On July 1 the battalion fought against the First Union Corps from a position on Herr Ridge, 1½ mile northwest of this marker (see No. A-9). For the positions held by each battery of the battalion, see Nos. 14 and 15 (Hurt), 60 and 61 (Rice), 68 and 69 (M. Johnson), and 87 (Wallace). The battalion had an estimated battle strength of 357.[1]

159. PEGRAM'S BATTALION

Tablet on granite pedestal.

Located east of West Confederate Avenue, .53 mile northeast of Virginia Monument (opposite McMillan Woods).
Erected 1910-1911, replacing earlier tablet erected ca. 1903.

TEXT

C.S.A. Army of Northern Virginia. Hill's Corps, Artillery Reserve, Pegram's Battalion. Marye's, Crenshaw's, Zimmerman's, McGraw's and Brander's Batteries. Ten Napoleons, four 10 pounder Parrotts, four 3 inch rifles, two 12 pounder howitzers.

July 1-3. The Battalion was actively engaged on each of the three days of the battle. The first cannon-shot of the battle was fired by one of the Batteries from a point near the south side of Chambersburg Pike on the ridge west of Herr's Tavern.

July 4. About sunset withdrew and began the march to Hagerstown.

Losses. Killed 10, wounded 37. Total 47. Ammunition expended 3800 rounds. Horses killed or disabled 38.

COMMENTARY

This marker shows the position held by the battalion on July 2, 3 and 4. On July 1 it engaged the First Union Corps from a position on Herr Ridge, two miles northwest of this marker (see No. A-10). For the positions held by the individual batteries of the battalion, see Nos. 48 (Zimmerman), 59 (Crenshaw), 64 (Marye), 72 (Brander) and 80 (McGraw). The battalion had an estimated battle strength of 375.[1] Its losses were reported by the army's Medical Director to total 48—10 killed, 37 wounded, and 1 missing.[2]

160. R.H. ANDERSON'S DIVISION

Tablet on granite marker.
Located west of West Confederate Avenue, .4 mile southwest of Virginia Monument.
Erected 1909.

TEXT

Army of Northern Virginia. Third Army Corps, Anderson's Division. Major Gen. R.H. Anderson. Wilcox's Brigade. Brig. Gen. Cadmus M. Wilcox. Mahone's Brigade. Brig. Gen. William Mahone. Wright's Brigade. Gen. A.R. Wright, Col. William Gibson. Perry's Brigade. Col. David Lang. Posey's Brigade. Brig. Gen. Carnot Posey. Artillery Battalion. Three Batteries. Major John Lane.

July 1. Anderson's Division on the march to Gettysburg was directed about dark to occupy the position vacated by Heth's Division and to send a Brigade and Battery a mile or more to the right.

July 2. In the morning a new line of battle formed extending further to the right. About noon Longstreet's Corps placed on the right nearly at right angles to the line directed to assault the Union left, the Division to advance as the attack progressed to keep in touch with Longstreet's left. The Union troops were forced from the first line and a portion of the ridge beyond; Union re-inforcements pressing on the right flank which had become disconnected from McLaws's left made the position gained untenable. The Brigades withdrew to their position in line.

July 3. The Division remained in position until 3:30 P.M. Orders were given to support Lieut. Gen. Longstreet's attack on the Union centre; Wilcox and Perry moved forward. The assault failed; the order to advance was countermanded.

July 4. The Division after dark took up the line of march.

Casualties. Killed 147, wounded 1128, missing 840. Total 2115.

COMMENTARY

This marker is located at the center of the position held by the division on July 2, 3 and 4. It had a battle strength estimated at 7136.[1]

161. MAHONE'S BRIGADE

Tablet on granite pedestal.
Located west of West Confederate Avenue, .15 mile northeast of Virginia Monument.
Erected 1910-1911, replacing earlier tablet erected 1901-1902.

TEXT

C.S.A. Army of Northern Virginia. Hill's Corps, Anderson's Division, Mahone's Brigade. 6th, 12th, 16th, 41st, 61st Virginia Infantry.

July 2. Arrived and took position here in the forenoon under orders to support the Artillery. A strong skirmish line was sent out which was constantly engaged and did effective service.

July 3. Remained here in support of the Artillery. Took no active part in the battle except by skirmishers.

July 4. In line here all day. At dark began the march to Hagerstown. Present 1500. Killed 8, wounded 55, missing 39. Total 102.

COMMENTARY

This marker shows the position held by the brigade on July 2. On July 3 it was posted on this same ridge ½ mile to the north of this marker. The brigade had an estimated battle strength of 1542.[1]

162. PERRY'S BRIGADE

Tablet on granite pedestal.
Located west of West Confederate Avenue, .2 mile southwest of Virginia Monument.
Erected 1910-1911, replacing earlier tablet erected 1901-1902.

TEXT

C.S.A. Army of Northern Virginia. Hill's' Corps, Anderson's Division, Perry's Brigade. 2nd, 5th, 8th Florida Infantry.

July 2. Formed line in forenoon in the eastern border of these woods. Advanced at 6 P.M. and assisted in forcing the Union line on the Emmitsburg Road and by rapid pursuit compelled the temporary abandonment of several guns. At the foot of the slope met fresh Union forces and the line on its right retiring it also fell back. The Color-bearer of the 8th Florida fell and its flag was lost.

July 3. Ordered to join Wilcox's Brigade on its left and conform to its movements. Supported Artillery until Longstreet's column started and then advanced in aid of his assault. But dense smoke hiding his oblique course, the Brigade moved directly forward. In the gap caused thereby a strong force struck its left flank capturing about half of the 2nd Florida and its colors.

July 4. In line here and at dark began the march to Hagerstown.

Present 700. Killed 33, wounded 217, missing 205. Total 455.

COMMENTARY

This marker shows the position held by the brigade on July 2, 3 and 4. From here it advanced to attack the Union line ⅞ mile to the east on two occasions, the evening of July 2 (see No. 163) and the afternoon of July 3. The brigade had a battle strength of about 742.[1] It was commanded during the battle by Col. David Lang.

163. PERRY'S BRIGADE (ADVANCE POSITION)

Cast iron tablet.
Located west of Emitsburg Road, .2 mile south-southwest of Codori Farm.
Erected 1907-1908.

TEXT

Army of Northern Virginia. Hill's Corps, Anderson's Division. Perry's Brigade. 2nd, 5th, 8th Florida Infantry.

July 2. Formed line in forenoon in the Western border of these woods. Advanced at 6 P.M. and assisted in driving back the Union lines on Emmitsburg Road and by rapid pursuit compelled the temporary abandonment of several guns. At the foot of the slope met Union infantry and the line on the right retiring also fell back. The color bearer of the 8th Florida fell and its flag was lost.

COMMENTARY

This marker shows the position at which the brigade crossed the Emmitsburg Road' at about 7:45 P.M. on July 2 on its way to attack the Union lines on Cemetery Ridge. Within half an hour the brigade streamed back across this position after its attack was repulsed. The brigade's attack on July 3 reached a position ¼ mile to the northwest of this marker before it was repulsed. Both attacks began from the position marked by No. 162.

164. POSEY'S BRIGADE

Tablet on granite pedestal.
Located west of West Confederate Avenue, .03 mile northeast of Virginia Monument.
Erected 1910-1911, replacing earlier tablet erected 1901-1902.

TEXT

C.S.A. Army of Northern Virginia. Hill's Corps, Anderson's Division, Posey's Brigade. 12th, 16th, 19th, 48th Mississippi Infantry.

July 2. Arrived and took position here in the morning. Through some misunderstanding of orders instead of the Brigade advancing in compact ranks in support of the troops on its right in their assault on the Union lines, the regiments were ordered forward at different times. Deployed as skirmishers and fighting in detachments they pushed back the Union outposts and drove some artillerists for awhile from their guns but did not join in the attack upon the Union position on Cemetery Ridge.

July 3. Was held in reserve here supporting Artillery in its front.

July 4. In line here all day. At dark began the march to Hagerstown. Present 1150. Killed 12, wounded 71. Total 83.

COMMENTARY

On July 2, 3 and 4 the brigade was posted ½ mile north of this marker. Through a misunderstanding of orders it advanced only ½ mile to the east during the Confederate attacks on the evening of July 2. The brigade had a battle strength of about 1322.[1]

165. WILCOX'S BRIGADE

Tablet on granite pedestal.
Located west of West Confederate Avenue, .45 mile southwest of Virginia Monument.
Erected 1910-1911, replacing earlier tablet erected 1901-1902.

TEXT

C.S.A. Army of Northern Virginia. Hill's Corps, Anderson's Division, Wilcox's Brigade. 8th, 9th, 10th, 11th, 14th Alabama Infantry.

July 2. Formed line here in forenoon. The 10th and 11th Regiments taking position on the right after a severe skirmish with Union outpost. Advanced at 6 P.M. and broke the Union line on Emmitsburg Road, capturing two guns and pursuing rapidly took many prisoners and six more guns. At Plum Run was met by a heavy fire of Artillery and fresh Infantry and being unsupported, after severe losses fell back without being able to bring off the captured guns.

July 3. Took position west of Emmitsburg Road in support of Artillery. Soon after Longstreet's Column started an order was received to advance and support it, but smoke hiding the oblique course of Pickett's Division, the Brigade moving straightforward found itself engaged in a separate and useless conflict and was promptly withdrawn.

July 4. In line here all day and at dark began the march to Hagerstown. Present 1777. Killed 51, wounded 469, missing 261. Total 781.

COMMENTARY

This marker shows the position held by the brigade on July 2, 3 and 4. From here it advanced to attack the Union line ⅞ mile to the east on two occasions, the evening of July 2 and the afternoon of July 3 (see No. 166). The brigade had an estimated battle strength of 1726.[1] Its casualties were reported by the army's Medical Director to total 777—51 killed, 469 wounded, and 257 captured or missing.[2]

166. WILCOX'S BRIGADE (ADVANCE POSITION)
Cast iron tablet.
Located west of Emmitsburg Road, ⅜ mile north-northeast of Peach Orchard (opposite Klingel house).
Erected 1907-1908.

TEXT

Army of Northern Virginia. Hill's Corps, Anderson's Division, Wilcox's Brigade. 8th, 9th, 10th, 11th, 14th Alabama Infantry.

July 2. Formed line in forenoon, the 10th and 11th Regiments taking position on the right after a severe skirmish with a Union outpost. Advanced at 6 P.M. and broke the Union line on Emmitsburg Road capturing two guns and pursuing rapidly took many prisoners and six more guns. At Plum Run was met by a heavy fire of artillery and Infantry and being unsupported after severe loss fell back without being able to bring off the captured guns.

COMMENTARY

This marker shows the position of the right wing of the brigade's battle line as it advanced about 7:15 P.M. on July 2 to attack the Union lines located ¼ mile to the east; the brigade's line stretched from here north ⅛ mile to the Rogers house. About 3:30 P.M. on July 3 the brigade again crossed the Emmitsburg Road slightly north of this position as it advanced belatedly to the support of Pickett's division. This attack was repulsed about ¼ mile east of this marker. Both attacks began from the position marked by No. 165.

167. WRIGHT'S BRIGADE
Tablet on granite pedestal.
Located west of West Confederate Avenue, opposite Virginia Monument.
Erected 1910-1911, replacing earlier tablet erected 1901-1902.

TEXT

C.S.A. Army of Northern Virginia. Hill's Corps, Anderson's Division, Wright's Brigade. 3rd, 22nd, 48th Regiments and 2nd Battalion Georgia Infantry.

July 2. Formed line here in the forenoon. Advanced at 6 P.M. and dislodged Union troops posted near the Codori House, capturing several guns and many prisoners. Pushing on broke the Union line at

the stone wall south of the Angle and reached the crest of the ridge beyond capturing more guns. The supports on the right being repulsed and those on the left not coming up, with both flanks assailed and converging columns threatening its rear, it withdrew fighting its way out with heavy losses and unable to bring off the captured guns.
July 3. Advanced 600 yards to cover the retreat of Pickett's Division. Afterward was moved to the right to meet a threatened attack.
July 4. In line here all day. At dark began the march to Hagerstown. Present 1450. Killed 146, wounded 394, missing 333. Total 873.

COMMENTARY

This marker shows the position held by the brigade on July 2, 3 and 4. For the course of its attack on Cemetery Ridge on the evening of July 2, see No. 168. On July 3 the brigade advanced late in the afternoon to a position ⅜ mile east of this marker. The brigade's battle strength was about 1413.[1] The army's Medical Director reported a total of 668 casualties for the brigade—40 killed, 295 wounded and 333 captured or missing.[2]

168. WRIGHT'S BRIGADE (ADVANCE POSITION)
Cast iron tablet.
Located west of Emmitsburg Road, .05 mile southwest of Codori farm.
Erected 1907-1908.

TEXT
Army of Northern Virginia. Hill's Corps, Anderson's Division, Wright's Brigade. 3rd, 22nd, 48th Regiments and 2nd Battalion Georgia Infantry. July 2. Formed line in forenoon. Advanced at 6 P.M. and dislodged Union troops posted near the Codori House, Capturing several guns and many prisoners. Pursuing on broke the Union line at the stone wall south of the angle, reached the crest of the ridge beyond, capturing more guns. The supports on the right being repulsed and those on the left not coming up, with both flanks assailed and converging columns threatening its rear, it withdrew fighting its way out with heavy losses and unable to bring off the captured guns.

COMMENTARY
At about 7:15 P.M. on July 2 the brigade crossed the Emmitsburg Road about ⅛ mile northeast of this marker as it advanced from the position marked by No. 167 to attack the Union line on Cemetery Ridge. This attack was replused half an hour later about ¼ mile east of this marker.

169. JOHN LANE'S BATTALION
Tablet on granite pedestal.
Located east of West Confederate Avenue, .4 mile northeast of Virginia Monument, just north of North Carolina Monument.

Erected 1910-1911, replacing earlier tablet erected ca. 1903.

TEXT

C.S.A. Army of Northern Virginia. Hill's Corps, Anderson's Division, Lane's Battalion. Patterson's, Wingfield's and Ross's Batteries. Three Napoleons, two 20 pounder Parrotts, three 10 pounder Parrotts, four 3 inch Navy Parrotts, and five 12 pounder howitzers.

July 2-3. Took part in the battle.

July 4. Remained in position near here and about sunset began the march to Hagerstown.

Losses. Killed 3, wounded 21, missing 6. Total 30.

Ammunition expended 1082 rounds. Horses killed or disabled 36.

COMMENTARY

   This marker shows the position held by half of the guns of the battalion on July 2, and by the whole battalion on July 3 and 4. For the positions occupied by the individual batteries of the battalion, see Nos. 19 (Ross), 20 (Patterson) and 21 (Wingfield). The battalion had a battle strength of about 384.[1]

170.   HETH'S DIVISION
Tablet on granite marker.
Located west of West Confederate Avenue, .39 mile northeast of Virginia Monument.
Erected 1909.

TEXT

C.S.A. Army of Northern Virginia. Third Army Corps, Heth's Division. Major Gen. Henry Heth, Brig. Gen. J.J. Pettigrew. First Brigade. Brig. Gen. J.J. Pettigrew, Col. J.K. Marshall. Second Brigade. Col. J.M. Brockenbrough. Third Brigade. Brig. Gen. James A. Archer, Col. B.D. Fry, Col. S.G. Shepard. Fourth Brigade. Brig. Gen. Joseph R. Davis. Artillery Brigade. Four Batteries. Lieut. Col. John J. Garnett.

July 1. The Division moved at 5 A.M. from Cashtown toward Gettysburg. About 3 miles from town the advance met the Union forces. Archer's and Davis's Brigades moved forward on the right and left of the turnpike; were soon engaged. The Brigades were forced to retire with heavy loss. After resting for an hour the Division was advanced in line of battle to the right of the Pike and met with stubborn resistance. Rodes's Division Second Corps appeared on the left and formed a line at right angles. The Union troops retired to a wooded hill in the rear and finally gave way. The Division bivouacked on the ground won.

July 2. The Division in the morning was relieved by Anderson and held in reserve.

July 3. The Division occupied the position of the day before and was ordered to report to Lieut. Gen. Longstreet to unite in the attack on the

Union centre. The assault was made and failed. The Division returned to its former position.

July 4. At night the Division took up the line of march.

Casualties. Killed 411, wounded 1905, missing 534. Total 2850.

COMMENTARY

This marker shows the division's position on July 3 before it advanced at 3 P.M. to support Pickett's left during Longstreet's Assault. On July 2 the division was held in reserve 1½ mile northwest of this marker. The division had an estimated battle strength of 7458.[1]

171. ARCHER'S BRIGADE (July 1)

Tablet on granite pedestal.
Located southwest of Meredith Avenue, .3 mile west of South Reynolds Avenue.
Erected 1910-1911, replacing earlier tablet erected 1907.

TEXT

C.S.A. Army of Northern Virginia. Hill's Corps, Heth's Division, Archer's Brigade. 5th Battalion and 13th Alabama, 1st, 7th, 14th Tennessee Infantry.

July 1. The Brigade moved from Cashtown early in the morning towards Gettysburg. After a march of six miles came in view of the Union forces. The Brigade was deployed on the west side of Willoughby Run and about 10 A.M. advanced; encountered 1st Brigade 1st Division First Corps beyond the run. The firing continued for a short time when a large force appearing on the right flank and opening a cross fire the position became untenable, the Brigade was forced back across the run but advanced with the Division later in the day. The advance in the morning reached this position.

July 2. Not engaged.

July 3. Formed part of the column of Longstreet's assault.

July 4. The Brigade took up the line of march during the night to Hagerstown.

COMMENTARY

This marker shows the position at which the brigade was repulsed by the Union "Iron Brigade" at about 10:30 A.M. on July 1. The marker neglects to mention that the brigade's commander, General Archer, was captured nearby—the first General from Lee's army to be captured during the war. On the afternoon of July 1 the brigade was posted on the Corps' right flank ¾ mile to the southwest. On July 2 the brigade was held in reserve ⅝ mile west of this marker. For its position on July 3, see No. 172. The brigade had an estimated battle strength of 1197.[1] I Its losses were reported by the army's Medical Director to total 677-16 killed, 144 wounded, and 517 captured or missing.[2]

172. ARCHER'S BRIGADE (JULY 3)

Tablet on granite pedestal.
Located west of West Confederate Avenue, .25 mile northeast of Virginia Monument.
Erected 1910-1911, replacing earlier tablet erected 1901-1902.

TEXT

C.S.A. Army of Northern Virginia. Hill's Corps, Heth's Division, Archer's Brigade. 5th Battalion and 13th Alabama, 1st, 7th, 14th Tennessee Infantry.

July 1. Reached the field in the morning. The Battalion was ordered to watch Cavalry on the right. The four Regiments advancing into Reynolds Woods were met and flanked by the 1st Brigade, 1st Division, First Corps, and fell back across the Run losing 75 prisoners, including Brig.General Archer.

July 2. In the evening marched from the Woods west of Willoughby Run and took position here.

July 3. In Longstreet's assault was the right Brigade of Pettigrew's Division. Advanced to the stone wall at the Angle and some of the men leaped over it. Had 13 color bearers shot, 4 of them at the wall. Lost 4 of the 5 flags and 5 of the 7 field officers, with company officers and men in nearly the same proportion.

July 4. After night withdrew and began the march to Hagerstown.

Present 1048. Killed and wounded 160, missing 517. Total 677.

COMMENTARY

On July 3 the brigade formed .2 mile south of this marker before advancing as part of Longstreet's assault about 3 P.M. For its position on July 1, see No. 171. On July 2 the brigade was held in reserve 1½ mile northwest of this marker. The brigade had an estimated battle strength of 1197, [1] and lost 16 killed, 144 wounded, and 517 missing or captured.[2]

173. BROCKENBROUGH'S BRIGADE

Tablet on granite pedestal.
Located west of West Confederate Avenue, .45 mile northeast of Virginia Monument, .05 mile south of McMillan Woods.
Erected 1910-1911, replacing earlier tablet erected 1901-1902.

TEXT

C.S.A. Army of Northern Virginia. Hill's Corps, Heth's Division, Brockenbrough's Brigade. 40th, 47th, 55th Regiments and 22nd Battalion Virginia Infantry.

July 1. Crossed the Run at 2 P.M. between Chambersburg Pike and Reynolds Woods. Engaged Union forces on McPherson Ridge and with other troops on left drove them back to next ridge capturing two flags and many prisoners with some sharpshooters in the barn. Soon afterwards the Brigade was relieved by Pender's Division.

July 2. Lay in the Woods west of the Run. In the evening took position near here.

July 3. In Longstreet's assault this Brigade was on the left flank of the column and as it approached the Union position was exposed to a severe fire of musketry on the left flank and of Artillery and musketry in front. It pushed on beyond the Emmitsburg Road but was met by a heavy front and flank fire from the Union lines north of the Bryan Barn and compelled to fall back.

July 4. After night withdrew and began the march to Hagerstown. Present about 1100. Killed 25, wounded 123, missing 60. Total 208.

COMMENTARY

This marker shows the position occupied by the brigade on July 3 before it advanced as part of Longstreet's assault about 3 P.M. On July 2, the brigade was held in reserve 1½ mile northwest of this marker. For the brigade's position on July 1, see No. A-11. It had an estimated battle strength of 971.[1]

174. DAVIS' BRIGADE (July 1)

Tablet on granite pedestal.
Located west of North Reynolds Avenue, .15 mile north of Chambersburg Pike.
Erected 1910-1911, replacing earlier tablet erected 1901-1902.

TEXT

C.S.A. Army of Northern Virginia. Hill's Corps, Heth's Division, Davis's Brigade. 2nd, 11th, 42nd Mississippi, 55th North Carolina Infantry.

July 1. Formed west of Herr's Tavern; crossed Willoughby Run about 10 A.M. Advanced in line and soon encountered Artillery supported by 2nd Brigade 1st Division First Corps. The engagement was stubborn. The advance was made to the railroad cut; after a short interval the attack was renewed at the cut and the Brigade was forced back losing many killed and wounded. A large force advancing on the right and rear opening a heavy flank fire, the order was given to retire. About 3 P.M. the Brigade again moved forward with the Division and reached the suburbs of the town. The Brigade in the advance in the morning reached the railroad cut.

July 2. Not engaged.

July 3. Formed part of the column of Longstreet's assault.

July 4. The Brigade took up the line of march during the night to Hagerstown.

COMMENTARY

This marker shows the position at which a large portion of the brigade was captured about 10:30 A.M. on July 1; this fact is not clearly stated by the marker's text. The marker also does not report that the 11th Mississippi was not present on the battlefield on July 1. On July 2 the brigade was held in reserve one mile to the west of this marker. For the brigade's position on July 3, see No. 175. It had a battle strength of about 2305.[1] Its losses are given on No. 175. The brigade's commander, Joseph R. Davis, was a nephew of Confederate President Jefferson Davis.

175. DAVIS' BRIGADE (JULY 3)

Tablet on granite pedestal.
Located west of West Confederate Avenue, .35 mile northeast of Virginia Monument.
Erected 1910-1911, replacing earlier tablet erected 1901-1902.

TEXT

C.S.A. Army of Northern Virginia. Hill's Corps, Heth's Division, Davis's Brigade. 55th North Carolina and 2nd, 11th, 42nd Mississippi Infantry.

July 1. Formed line west of Herr's Tavern and crossing the Run at 10 A.M. dislodged 2nd Maine Battery and the 2nd Brigade, 1st Division, First Corps. Threatened on the right, it wheeled and occupied railroad cut too deep and steep for defense, whereby it lost many prisoners and a stand of colors. Joined later by the 11th regiment previously on duty guarding trains, the Brigade fought until the day's contest ended.

July 2. Lay all day west of the Run. At evening took position near here.

July 3. In Longstreet's assault the Brigade formed the left centre of Pettigrew's Division and advanced to the stone wall south of the Bryan Barn where with regiments shrunken to companies and field officers all disabled further effort was useless.

July 4. After night withdrew and began the march to Hagerstown.

Present on the first day about 2000. Killed 180, wounded 717, missing about 500. Total 1397.

COMMENTARY

This marker shows the position held by the brigade on July 3 before it advanced as part of Longstreet's assault about 3 P.M. For its position on July 1, see No. 174. The marker's text errs by not stating clearly that the 11th Mississippi remained at Cashtown all day on July 1 and so was not engaged in the fighting that day. The brigade had an estimated battle strength or 2305.[1]

176. PETTIGREW'S BRIGADE

Tablet on granite pedestal.
Located west of West Confederate Avenue, .3 mile northeast of Virginia Monument.
Erected 1910-1911, replacing earlier tablet erected 1901-1902.

TEXT
C.S.A. Army of Northern Virginia. Hill's Corps, Heth's Division, Pettigrew's Brigade. 11th, 26th, 47th, 52nd North Carolina Infantry.

July 1. Crossing Willoughby Run at 2 P.M. met the 1st Brigade, 1st Division, First Corps in Reynolds Woods and drove it back after a bloody struggle. Advancing to the summit of the ridge encountered and broke a second Union line and was then relieved by troops of Pender's Division.

July 2. Lay in Woods west of the Run. In evening took position near here.

July 3. In Longstreet's assault the Brigade occupied the right center of the Division and the course of the charge brought it in front of the high stone wall north of the Angle and 80 yards farther east, it advanced very nearly to that wall. A few reached it but were captured. The skeleton regiments retired led by Lieutenants and the Brigade by a Major, the only field officer left.

July 4. After night withdrew and began the march to Hagerstown.

Present on the first day about 2000. Killed 190, wounded 915, missing about 300. Total 1405.

COMMENTARY
This marker shows the position held by the brigade on July 3 before it advanced as part of Longstreet's assault about 3 P.M. For its position on July 1 see No. A-12. On July 2 it was held in reserve about one mile west of this marker. The brigade had a battle strength of about 2581.[1]

177. J. GARNETT'S BATTALION
Tablet on granite pedestal.
Located east of West Confederate Avenue, .4 mile south of Fairfield Road.
Erected 1910-1911, replacing earlier tablet erected ca. 1903.

TEXT
C.S.A. Army of Northern Virginia. Hill's Corps, Heth's Division, Garnett's Battalion. Grandy's, Moore's, Lewis's and Maurin's Batteries. Four Napoleons, two 10 pounder Parrotts, seven 3 inch rifles, two 12 pounder howitzers. July 1, 2, 3, 4. The Parrotts and Rifles took part in the battle in a different position on each of the three days, their most active service being on the second day in this position. The Napoleons and Howitzers were in reserve and not actively engaged at any time. All withdrew from the field on the fourth day but not at the same hour nor by the same route.

Losses. Wounded 5, missing 17. Total 22. Ammunition expended 1000 rounds. Horses killed or disabled 13.

COMMENTARY
This marker shows the position held by the battalion's rifled guns

on July 2, and by the Napoleons and howitzers on July 4. On July 2 the Napoleons and howitzers were held in reserve ¼ mile west of this marker. On July 3 the whole battalion was held in reserve one mile south of this marker. On the afternoon of July 1 six of the battalion's rifled guns were deployed in action on Herr Ridge, 1¾ mile northwest of this marker (see No. A-13). For the specific positions held by each of the battalion's batteries, see Nos. 24 (Maurin), 66 (Moore), 73 (Lewis) and 76 (Grandy). The battalion had an estimated battle strength of 396.[1]

178. PENDER'S DIVISION
Tablet on granite marker.
Located west of West Confederate Avenue, .1 mile northeast of McMillan Woods and .63 mile northeast of Virginia Monument.
Erected 1909.

TEXT
Army of Northern Virginia. Third Army Corps. Pender's Division. Major Gen. William D. Pender, Brig. Gen. James H. Lane, Major Gen. I.R. Trimble. First Brigade. Col. Abner Perrin. Second Brigade. Brig. Gen. James H. Lane. Third Brigade. Brig. Gen. Edward L. Thomas. Fourth Brigade. Brig. Gen. A.M. Scales, Lieut. Col. G. T. Gordon, Col. W. Lee J. Lowrance. Artillery Battalion. Four Batteries. Major William T. Poague.

July 1. The Division moved about 8 A.M. in the direction of Gettysburg following Heth's Division. A line of battle was formed on the right and left of the pike 3 miles from the town. About 3 P.M. a part of Ewell's Corps appeared on the left and the Union forces making a strong demonstration, an advance was ordered. Heth became vigorously engaged. The Division moved to the support, passing through the lines, forced the Union troops to Seminary Ridge. Scales's Brigade moved to the left flanking this position; the Union troops gave way retiring to Cemetery Ridge. The Division reformed on the Ridge, the left resting on Fairfield Road.

July 2. In position on the Ridge; not engaged except heavy skirmishing along the line.

July 3. During the morning two Brigades ordered to report to Lieut. Gen. Longstreet as a support to Gen. Pettigrew and were placed in rear of right of Heth's Division, which formed a portion of the column of assault. The line moved forward one mile in view of the fortified position on Cemetery Ridge, exposed to severe fire. The extreme right reached the works but was compelled to fall back. The Division reformed where it rested before making the attack.

July 4. The Division during the night took up the line of march. Casualties. Killed 262, wounded 1312, missing 116. Total 1690.

COMMENTARY

This marker shows the center of the line occupied by the division on the evening of July 1 and held until the night of July 4. On July 1 the division attacked the Union line on Seminary Ridge ½ mile north of this marker. At 1 P.M. on July 3 Scales' and J.H. Lane's brigades, under the command of Major General Trimble, formed one mile southeast of this marker in the rear of Heth's division. They then formed part of the left wing of Longstreet's 3 P.M. assault against the Union center. The division had an estimated battle strength of 6681.[1]

179. J.H. LANE'S BRIGADE

Tablet on granite pedestal.
Located west of West Confederate Avenue, .56 mile northeast of Virginia Monument
(.05 mile north of McMillan Woods).
Erected 1910-1911, replacing earlier tablet erected 1901-1902.

TEXT

C.S.A. Army of Northern Virginia. Hill's Corps, Pender's Division, Lane's Brigade. 7th, 18th, 28th, 33rd, 37th North Carolina Infantry.

July 1. Crossed Willoughby Run about 3:30 P.M. and advanced on the right of the Division in the final and successful movement against the Union forces on Seminary Ridge; held back Union Cavalry which threatened the flank and had a sharp conflict at the stone wall on Seminary Ridge just south of Fairfield Road.

July 2. Lay with its right in McMillan's Woods with skirmish line advanced.

July 3. In Longstreet's assault the Brigade supported the centre of Pettigrew's Division, advancing in good order under the storm of shot and shell and when near the Union works north of the Angle pushed forward to aid the fragments of the front line in the final struggle and was among the last to retire.

July 4. After night withdrew and began the march to Hagerstown.

Present 1355. Killed 41, wounded 348, missing 271. Total 660.

COMMENTARY

At about 4 P.M. on July 1 the brigade passed by the position shown by this marker as it moved to attack the left end of the Union line on Seminary Ridge. The brigade then formed on the ridge at this position and remained here all of July 2. At 1 P.M. on July 3 it was put under General Trimble's command and formed in rear of Heth's division ¾ mile southeast of this marker. It then formed part of the left wing of Longstreet's 3 P.M. assault on the Union center. The brigade had a battle strength of about 1734.[1]

180. PERRIN'S BRIGADE

Tablet on granite pedestal.

Located west of West Confederate Avenue, .5 mile south of Fairfield Road.
Erected 1910-1911, replacing earlier tablet erected 1901-1902.

TEXT

C.S.A. Army of Northern Virginia. Hill's Corps, Pender's Division, Perrin's Brigade. 1st Rifles, 12th, 13th, 14th Regiments and 1st Provisional South Carolina Infantry.

July 1. Crossed Willoughby Run about 3:30 P.M. with its left in Reynolds Woods and advancing relieved Heth's line. Took a prominent part in the struggle by which the Union forces were dislodged from Seminary Ridge and pursuing them into the town captured many prisoners. The Rifle regiment was on duty as train guard and not in the battle of this day.

July 2. Supported Artillery south of Fairfield Road. At 6 P.M. advanced a Battalion of sharpshooters which skirmished with the Union outposts until dark. At 10 P.M. took, position on Ramseur's right in the Long Lane leading from the town to the Bliss House and Barn.

July 3. In the same position and constantly engaged in skirmishing.

July 4. After night withdrew and began the'march to Hagerstown. Present about 1600. Killed 100. Wounded 477. Total 577.

COMMENTARY

This marker shows the general position held by the brigade while it was supporting the artillery line on July 2. Late in the day the brigade advanced ¼ mile southeast to Long Lane and remained there until the night of July 3. It then returned to the position indicated by this marker. About 5:30 P.M. on July 1 the brigade attacked the Union line at the Lutheran Seminary about ⅝ mile north of this marker (see No. A-14). The brigade had a battle strength of about 1882.[1]

181. SCALES' BRIGADE

Tablet on granite pedestal.
Located west of West Confederate Avenue, .5 mile northeast of Virginia Monument (at McMillan Woods).
Erected 1910-1911, replacing earlier tablet erected 1901-1902.

TEXT

C.S.A. Army of Northern Virginia. Hill's Corps, Pender's Division, Scales's Brigade. 13th, 16th, 22nd, 38th North Carolina Infantry.

July 1. Crossed Willoughby Run about 3:30 P.M. relieving Heth's line and advancing with left flank on Chambersburg Pike; took part in the struggle until it ended. When the Union forces made their final stand on Seminary Ridge the Brigade charged and aided in dislodging them but suffered heavy losses. Gen. A.M. Scales was wounded and all the field officers but one were killed or wounded.

July 2. In position near here with skirmishers out in front and on flank.

July 3. In Longstreet's assault the Brigade supported the right wing of Pettigrew's Division. With few officers to lead them the men advanced in good order through a storm of shot and shell and when the front line neared the Union works they pushed forward to aid it in the final struggle and were among the last to retire.

July 4. After night withdrew and began the march to Hagerstown. Present about 1250. Killed 102, wounded 381, missing 116. Total 599.

COMMENTARY

This marker shows the position occupied by the brigade on the evening of July 1 and held until 1 P.M. on July 3. The brigade was then put under General Trimble's command and formed in rear of Heth's division ¾ mile southwest of this marker. From there it advanced at 3 P.M. as part of the left wing of Longstreet's assault against the Union center. About 3:30 P.M. on July 1 the brigade attacked the Union line on Seminary Ridge one mile north of this marker (see No. A-15). The brigade had an estimated battle strength of 1351.[1] Its casualties as reported by the army's Medical Director were 535—102 killed, 323 wounded and 110 captured or missing.[2]

182. THOMAS' BRIGADE

Tablet on granite pedestal.
Located west of West Confederate Avenue, .6 mile northeast of Virginia Monument (.1 mile north of McMillan Woods).
Erected 1910-1911, replacing earlier tablet erected 1901-1902.

TEXT

C.S.A. Army of Northern Virginia. Hill's Corps, Pender's Division, Thomas's Brigade. 14th, 35th, 45th, 49th Georgia Infantry.

July 1. In reserve north of Chambersburg Pike on left of the Division. At sunset moved to position in McMillan's Woods.

July 2. On duty in support of Artillery. At 10 P.M. advancing took position in Long Lane with the left flank in touch with McGowan's Brigade and the right near the Bliss House and Barn.

July 3. Engaged most of the day in severe skirmishing and exposed to a heavy fire of Artillery. After dark retired to this Ridge.

July 4. At night withdrew and began the march to Hagerstown. Present about 1200. Killed 34, wounded 179, missing 57. Total 270.

COMMENTARY

This marker shows the general position held by the brigade from the evening of July 1 to the night of July 2. At 10 P.M. on July 2 it advanced ¼ mile to the southeast to Long Lane, where it formed the left of the division's line facing Cemetery Hill. It remained there until the night of July 3, when it returned to the position indicated by this marker. For the brigade's position on July 1, see No. A-16. The brigade had an estimated battle strength of 1326.[1] Its casualties were reported by the army's Medical Director to be 152—16 killed and 136 wounded.[2]

183. POAGUE'S BATTALION
Tablet on granite pedestal.
Located east of West Confederate Avenue, .25 mile northeast of Virginia Monument.
Erected 1910-1911, replacing earlier tablet erected ca. 1903.

TEXT
C.S.A. Army of Northern Virginia. Hill's Corps, Pender's Division, Poague's Battalion. Ward's, Brooke's, Wyatt's and Graham's Batteries. Seven Napoleons, six 12 pounder howitzers, one 10 pounder Parrott, two 3 inch rifles.
July 2. Late in the evening ten of the guns were placed in position at different points ready for service next day. The Howitzers were kept in the rear as no place was found from which they could be used with advantage.
July 3. The ten guns were actively engaged.
July 4. In the evening about dusk began the march to Hagerstown.
Killed 2, wounded 24, missing 6. Total 32. Ammunition expended 657 rounds. Horses killed or disabled 17.

COMMENTARY
This marker shows the position held by the battalion's Napoleons and rifled guns from the evening of July 2 to dusk on July 4. Early on July 2 the entire battalion had taken up a reserve position west of Spangler Woods, .3 mile southwest of this marker. In the evening the Napoleons and rifled guns moved to this position, and the howitzers moved to the position marked by No. 184. For the specific positions occupied by the guns of each of the battalion's batteries, see Nos. 38 (Ward), 41 (J. Graham), 49 (Wyatt) and 56 (Brooke). The battalion had an estimated battle strength of 377.[1]

184. POAGUE'S HOWITZERS
Cast iron tablet.
Located west of West Confederate Avenue, .05 mile north of Virginia Monument.
Erected ca 1906.

TEXT
Army of Northern Virginia. Hill's Corps, Pender's Division. Poague's Howitzers.
July 2. The Howitzers in the lunettes nearby belonged to the batteries of Poague's Battalion, one to Ward's, two to Brooke's, one to Wyatt's, one to Graham's. But on this day they were detached and kept under shelter from the fire of the Union Artillery which they could not return by reason of their short range.
July 3. In the morning the lunettes were constructed and the Howitzers

placed in them to meet a possible advance of the Union forces but as this did not occur they took no active part in the battle.

July 4. At dusk they withdrew from the field with their Battalion and began the march to Hagerstown.

COMMENTARY

This marker shows the position occupied by the howitzers of Poague's battalion from the evening of July 2 to the evening of July 4. They moved to this position from a reserve position .2 mile southwest of this marker that had been formed early on July 2 (see No. 183).

185. STUART'S DIVISION

Tablet on granite marker.
Located west of Confederate Cavalry Avenue; .52 mile north of intersection of
Confederate Cavalry Avenue and Gregg Avenue.
Erected 1913.

TEXT

Army of Northern Virginia. Cavalry Division. Stuart's Division. Major General J.E.B. Stuart. Hampton's Brigade. Brig. Gen. Wade Hampton, Col. L.S. Baker. Robertson's Brigade. Brig. Gen. Beverly H. Robertson. Fitz Lee's Brigade. Brig. Gen. Fitzhugh Lee. Jenkins's Brigade. Brig. Gen. A.G. Jenkins, Col. M.J. Ferguson. Jones's Brigade. Brig. Gen. William E. Jones. W.H.F. Lee's Brigade. Col. J.R. Chambliss Jr. Stuart's Horse Artillery. Six Batteries. Major R.F. Beckham. Robertson's and Jones's Brigades with 3 Batteries detached, operating on right flank of the Army.

July 1. The Division on the march from Dover to Carlisle received information that the Confederate Army was concentrating at Gettysburg.

July 2. The advance near Gettysburg late in the afternoon engaged with Custer's Cavalry Brigade at Hunterstown on the left and rear of Early's Division.

July 3. Pursuant to order the Cavalry Division of four Brigades took position on the left in advance of Early on a ridge which controlled the open ground toward Hanover. Gregg's Union Cavalry was massed in full view. The sharpshooters were advanced and soon became engaged. The battle continued until near night, being hotly contested. At night the Division withdrew to the York Road.

July 4. The Division was posted on the flanks and rear of the Army. Casualties. Killed 36, wounded 140, missing 64. Total 240.

COMMENTARY

This marker is located on the field of the great cavalry battle fought on the afternoon of July 3. The units of the division engaged on this field from noon until sunset were Hampton's, F. Lee's, Jenkins' and

Chambliss' brigades, plus three batteries of Beckham's battalion. These units had a combined battle strength of about 6442.[1]

186. CHAMBLISS' BRIGADE

Tablet on granite pedestal.
Located west of Confederate Cavalry Avenue, .24 mile north of Gregg Avenue.
Erected 1910-1911, replacing earlier tablet erected 1906.

TEXT

C.S.A. Army of Northern Virginia. Stuart's Cavalry Division, Chambliss' Brigade. 2nd North Carolina and 9th, 10th, 13th Virginia Cavalry.

July 3. The Brigade reached here about noon and took an active part in the fight until it ended. Some of the men serving as sharpshooters in the vicinity of the Rummel Barn but most of the Command participating in the charges made by the Cavalry during the afternoon. It left the field after nightfall.

Losses. Killed 8, wounded 41, missing 25. Total 74.

COMMENTARY

This marker is located at the general position held by the brigade on the right wing of Stuart's cavalry line from noon to dark on July 3. During the fighting from noon to 3 P.M., some sharpshooters from the brigade were stationed at the Rummel farm, ¼ mile east of this marker. Several mounted charges were made from this position toward the southeast, passing east of the Rummel farm. The brigade had a battle strength of about 1173.[1] Its casualties were reported by the army's Medical Director to be 41—2 killed, 26 wounded and 13 captured or missing.[2]

187. HAMPTON'S BRIGADE

Tablet on granite pedestal.
Located west of Confederate Cavalry Avenue, .55 mile north of Gregg Avenue.
Erected 1910-1911, replacing earlier tablet erected 1906.

TEXT

C.S.A. Army of Northern Virginia. Stuart's Cavalry Division, Hampton's Brigade. 1st North Carolina, 1st and 2nd South Carolina Cavalry, Jeff Davis (Miss.) and Cobb's and Phillips's (Ga.) Legions.

July 2. Engaged in the evening with 3rd Division Cavalry Corps near Hunterstown. Cobb's Legion led the attack and lost a number of officers and men killed and wounded.

July 3. The Brigade arrived here about noon and skirmished with Union sharpshooters. In the afternoon the 1st North Carolina and Jeff Davis Legion advancing in support of Chambliss' Brigade drove back the Union cavalry but met their reserve and were in a critical position when the Brigade went to their support and a hand to hand fight ensued in which Brig. Gen. Wade Hampton was severely wounded. The conflict ended in the failure of the Confederates in their purpose to assail the rear of the Union Army.

Losses. Killed 17, wounded 58, missing 16. Total 91.

COMMENTARY

This marker shows the position held by the brigade at the center of Stuart's cavalry line from noon to dusk on July 3. During the fighting the brigade made several charges from this position to the Union lines located ⅜ mile south of this marker. The brigade had a battle strength of about 1751.[1]

188. JENKINS' BRIGADE

Tablet on granite pedestal.
Located west of Confederate Cavalry Avenue, .14 mile north of intersection of
Confederate Cavalry Avenue and Gregg Avenue. Erected 1910-1911, replacing earlier
tablet erected 1906.

TEXT

C.S.A. Army of Northern Virginia. Stuart's Cavalry Division, Jenkins's Brigade. 14th, 16th, 17th Virginia Cavalry, 34th and 36th Virginia Cavalry Battalions.

July 3. The Brigade had been with Ewell's Corps but rejoined the Cavalry Division here on this day about noon. It was armed with Enfield Rifles but by an oversight brought to this field only about ten rounds of ammunition. While this lasted it was actively engaged mainly on foot as sharpshooters around and in front of the Rummel Barn and out-houses. It was withdrawn from the field at an early hour in the evening.

Losses not reported.

COMMENTARY

This marker is located on the right wing of the line held by the brigade from noon to evening on July 3. From here the brigade's line stretched ¼ mile to the east to the Rummel farm. The 17th Regiment and six companies of the 16th Regiment were detached from the brigade on July 3 and were not present on this part of the battlefield.[1] The brigade's total battle strength was approximately 1179.[2]

189. W.E. JONES' BRIGADE

Tablet on granite pedestal.
Located west of South Reynolds Avenue, 50 feet north of Fairfield Road.
Erected 1910-1911.

TEXT

C.S.A. Army of Northern Virginia. Stuart's Cavalry Division, Jones's

Brigade. 6th, 7th, 11th, 12th Virginia Cavalry Regiments and 35th Virginia Cavalry Battalion.

July 1. The 12th Regiment was detached and remained on the south side of the Potomac River. White's 35th Virginia Battalion was also detached. The remaining regiments crossed the Potomac at Williamsport Md.

July 2. Marched from near Greencastle Pa. to Chambersburg Pa.

July 3. The Brigade marched from Chambersburg Pa. via Cashtown to Fairfield Pa. Met the 6th U.S. Cavalry about two miles from Fairfield. The 7th Virginia charged in the advance and was repulsed. The 6th Virginia in support charged and forced the Union Regiment to retire with heavy loss. The Brigade encamped at Fairfield for the night.

July 4. The Brigade held the Mountain Passes and picketed the left flank of the Army. Casualties. Killed 11, wounded 30, missing 6. Total 47.

COMMENTARY

This marker describes the movements of the brigade, but does not mark its position since the brigade never reached the battlefield proper. See No. 190 for the position it occupied near Orrtanna. The brigade's losses were reported by the army's Medical Director to be 58—12 killed, 40 wounded, and 6 captured or missing.[1]

190.   W.E. JONES' BRIGADE (ORRTANNA)
Cast iron tablet.
Located west of Fairfield–Orrtanna Road, .18 mile south of Marshall and Culberson House, about 2.4 miles north of Pa. Route 116 and 9½ miles west of Gettysburg. Date erected not known (ca. 1906-1910).

TEXT

Army of Northern Virginia. Stuart's Cavalry Division, Jones's Brigade. 6th, 7th, 11th, 12th Cavalry Regiments and 35th Virginia Cavalry Battalion.

July 1. The 12th Regiment was detached and remained on the south side of the Potomac River. White's 35th Virginia Battalion was also detached. The remaining regiments crossed the Potomac at Williamsport, Md.

July 2. Marched from near Greencastle Pa. to Chambersburg Pa.

July 3. The Brigade marched from Chambersburg Pa. via Cashtown to Fairfield Pa. Met the 6th U.S. Cavalry about two miles from Fairfield. The 7th Virginia charged in the advance and was repulsed. The 6th Virginia in support charged and forced the Union Regiment to retire with heavy losses. The Brigade encamped at Fairfield for the night.

July 4. The Brigade held the Mountain Passes and picketed the left flank of the Army.

Casualties. Killed 11, wounded 30, missing 6. Total 47.

COMMENTARY

On the afternoon of July 3 the brigade met and defeated the 6th U.S. Cavalry at the position shown by this marker. This Confederate victory was significant because it kept open Lee's most direct line of retreat from Gettysburg. White's 35th Battalion, with a strength of about 250, was absent, from the brigade on July 3 serving with Ewell's Corps. The rest of the brigade had a battle strength of about 1500.[1] The brigade's casualties were reported by the army's Medical Director to be 58—12 killed, 40 wounded, and 6 captured or missing.[2]

191.   F. LEE'S BRIGADE

Tablet on granite pedestal.
Located east of Confederate Cavalry Avenue, .73 mile north of intersection of
Confederate Cavalry Avenue and Gregg Avenue.
Erected 1910-1911, replacing earlier tablet erected 1906.

TEXT

C.S.A. Army of Northern Virginia. Stuart's Cavalry Division, Fitzhugh Lee's Brigade. 1st Maryland Battalion and 1st, 2nd, 3rd, 4th, 5th Virginia Cavalry.

July 3. The Battalion being on duty with Ewell's Corps, the Brigade brought only five regiments to this field where it arrived soon after midday and took position on the left of Hampton's Brigade on the edge of the neighboring woods. It participated actively in the conflict which ensued.

Losses. Killed 5, wounded 16, missing 29. Total 50.

COMMENTARY

This marker shows the extreme right of the brigade line held from noon to dusk on July 3. The brigade, which held the left flank of the division's line, held a position extending ¼ mile east of this marker and almost at a right angle to Hampton's line on the right. During the fighting from noon to 3 P.M. the brigade charged the Union position ½ mile south of this marker. During this time the 4th Virginia was stationed to guard the division's far left flank and did not participate in the fighting. The 1st Maryland Battalion with a strength of about 310[1] was not present with the brigade on this part of the field on July 3. The estimated battle strength of the brigade (less the 1st Maryland Battalion) was 1603.[2]

192.   B.H. ROBERTSON'S BRIGADE

Tablet on granite pedestal.
Located west of South Reynolds Avenue, 70 feet north of Fairfield Road.
Erected 1910-1911.

TEXT

C.S.A. Army of Northern Virginia. Stuart's Cavalry Division, Robertson's Brigade. 4th and 5th North Carolina Cavalry.

July 1. The Brigade crossed the Potomac at Williamsport Md. and marched to Greencastle Pa.

July 2. Marched from Greencastle Pa. to Chambersburg Pa.

July 3. Marched to Cashtown and in the direction of Fairfield, guarding the flank of the Army.

July 4. Held Jack's Mountain and picketed the left flank of the Army of Northern Virginia.

No report nor details of losses made.

COMMENTARY

This marker describes the movements of the brigade, but does not mark its position since the brigade never reached the battlefield proper. See No. 193 for its strength and the position it held near Orrtanna.

193.   B.H. ROBERTSON'S BRIGADE (ORRTANNA)
Cast iron tablet.
*Located at Orrtanna, 3.8 miles north of Pa. Route 116 on east side of
Fairfield–Orrtanna Road.*
Date erected not known (ca. 1906-1910).

TEXT

Army of Northern Virginia. Stuart's Cavalry Division, Robertson's Brigade. 4th and 5th North Carolina Cavalry.

July 1. The Brigade crossed the Potomac at Williamsport, Md., and marched to Greencastle, Pa.

July 2. Marched from Greencastle, Pa., to Chambersburg, Pa.

July 3. Marched to Cashtown and in the direction of Fairfield guarding the flank of the Army.

July 4. Held Jack's Mountain and picketed the left flank of the Army. No report nor details of losses.

COMMENTARY

This marker shows the general position held by the brigade for most of July 3. It had a battle strength of about 850,[1] but was not engaged with any Union forces.

194.   BECKHAM'S BATTALION
Tablet on granite pedestal.
Located west of Confederate Cavalry Avenue, .54 mile north of Gregg Avenue.
Erected 1910-1911, replacing earlier tablet erected 1906.

TEXT

C.S.A. Army of Northern Virginia. Stuart's Cavalry Division, Horse Artillery. Major R.F. Beckham Commanding. Breathed's Virginia Battery, Chew's Virginia Battery, Griffin's Maryland Battery, Hart's

South Carolina Battery, McGregor's Virginia Battery, Moorman's
Virginia Battery.
July 3. These Batteries were not permanently attached to the Cavalry
Brigades but were sent to them when needed; Breathed's Battery with
Brig. General W.H.F. Lee's Brigade; Chew's Battery with Brig. General
W.E. Jones's Brigade; Griffin's Battery with the Second Army Corps;
Hart's Battery attached to the Washington Artillery with the Army
Trains; McGregor's Battery with Brig. Gen. Wade Hampton's Brigade;
Moorman's Battery, No report.
Casualties not reported.

COMMENTARY

This marker shows the position held by two of the battalion's
batteries from noon to dusk on July 3. McGregor's battery fought at the
position indicated by No. 74, and Breathed's battery at that shown by
No. 55. Jackson's battery (No. 67) and Green's battery (No. 26) did not
belong to the battalion but assisted it on this portion of the battlefield.
At this time four batteries were detached from the battalion. W. Griffin's
battery was posted on Oak Hill (see No. A-l); Hart's battery was serving
with Longstreet's Corps on the army's right wing (see No. A-2); Chew's
battery was serving with W.E. Jones' brigade west of Gettysburg (see
No. A-3); and Moorman's battery was guarding the army's rear (see
No. A-4). The two batteries serving with the battalion on this field had
a combined battle strength of about 212.[1]

195. IMBODEN'S BRIGADE

Tablet on granite pedestal.
Located west of South Reynolds Avenue, 90 feet north of Fairfield Road.
Erected 1910-1911.

TEXT

C.S.A. Army of Northern Virginia. Stuart's Cavalry Division. Imboden's
Brigade. 18th Virginia Cavalry, 62nd Virginia Infantry, Virginia Partisan
Rangers and McClanahan's Virginia Battery.
July 3. Command guarding ammunition and supply trains. Reached
the field at noon and retired with the supply trains at night.
No report nor details of losses made.

COMMENTARY

This marker describes the movements of the brigade, but does not
mark its position since the brigade never reached the battlefield proper.
See No. 196 for the position occupied by the brigade at Cashtown.

196. IMBODEN'S BRIGADE (CASHTOWN)

Cast iron tablet.
*Located at Cashtown, north of Cashtown-Gettysburg Road, just west of Old
Cashtown Inn and about 7 miles west of Gettysburg.*

Date erected not known (ca. 1906-1910).

TEXT

Army of Northern Virginia. Stuart's Cavalry Division, Imboden's Brigade. 18th Virginia Cavalry, 62nd Virginia Infantry, Virginia Partisan Rangers and Virginia Battery.

July 3. Command guarding trains. Reached the field at noon and retired with the trains that night.

No report nor details of losses.

COMMENTARY

This marker shows the position held by the brigade from noon to 5:30 P.M. on July 3. During the retreat to Virginia the brigade served as an escort to a seventeen mile long wagon train of wounded. The brigade had a battle strength of about 2000.[1] The battery attached to the brigade was the Staunton (Va.) Horse Artillery, commanded by McClanahan.

197. HIGH WATER MARK MONUMENT

Large bronze open book on granite base.
Located 60 feet west of Hancock Avenue at the Angle, .1 mile south of Bryan farm.
Designed by John B. Bachelder.
Dedicated June 2, 1892.

TEXT (BOOK)

High Water Mark of the Rebellion. This copse of trees was the landmark towards which Longstreet's assault was directed July 3, 1863.

The assaulting column was composed of Kemper's, Garnett's and Armistead's Brigades of Pickett's Division, Archer's, Davis', Pettigrew's and Brockenbrough's Brigades of Heth's Division, and Scales' and Lane's Brigades of Pender's Division.

Supported on the right by Wilcox's and Perry's Brigades of Anderson's Division; on the left by Thomas' and McGowan's Brigades of Pender's Division; and in rear by Wright's, Posey's and Mahone's Brigades of Anderson's Division, and assisted by the following artillery: Cabell's Battalion, consisting of Manly's, Fraser's, McCarthy's and Carlton's Batteries. Alexander's Battalion, Woolfolk's, Jordan's, Gilbert's, Moody's, Parker's and Taylor's Batteries. Eshleman's Battalion, Squires', Richardson's, Miller's and Norcom's Batteries. Dearing's Battalion, Stribling's, Caskie's, Macon's and Blount's Batteries. Cutts' Battalion, Ross', Patterson's and Wingfield's Batteries. Poague's Battalion, Wyatt's, Graham's, Ward's and Brooke's Batteries. Pegram's Battalion, McGraw's, Zimmerman's, Brander's, Marye's and Crenshaw's Batteries. McIntosh's Battalion, Rice's, Hurt's, Wallace's and Johnson's Batteries. Carters Battalion, Reese's, Carter's, Page's and Fry's Batteries. Brown's Battalion, Watson's, Smith's, Cunningham's and Griffin's Batteries.

Repulse of Longstreet's Assault. Longstreet's Assault was repulsed by Webb's, Hall's and Harrow's Brigades of Gibbon's Division Second Army Corps; Smyth's and Willard's Brigades and portions of Carroll's Brigade of Hays' Division Second Army Corps; and the First Massachusetts Sharpshooters (unattached), portions of Rowley's and Stannard's Brigades of Doubleday's Division First Army Corps; Hazard's Second Corps Artillery Brigade, consisting of Woodruff's, Arnold's, Cushing's, Brown's and Rorty's Batteries. Assisted on the right by Hill's, Edgell's, Eakin's, Bancroft's, Dilger's and Taft's Batteries on Cemetery Hill; and on the left by Cowan's, Fitzhugh's, Parson's, Wheeler's, Thomas', Daniels' and Sterling's Batteries and McGilvery's Artillery Brigade, consisting of Thompson's, Phillips', Hart's, Cooper's, Dow's and Ames' Batteries, and by Hazlett's Battery on Little Round Top. And supported by Doubleday's Division of the First Army Corps, which was in position on the immediate left of the troops assaulted.

The Third Army Corps moved up to within supporting distance on the left, and Robinson's Division of the First Army Corps moved into position to support the right.

TEXT (EAST BASE)
Commands honored. In recognition of the patriotism and gallantry displayed by their respective troops who met or assisted to repulse Longstreet's Assault, the following states have contributed to erect this tablet. Maine, New Hampshire, Vermont, Massachusetts, Rhode Island, Connecticut, New York, New Jersey, Delaware, Pennsylvania, West Virginia, Ohio, Michigan and Minnesota.

TEXT (SOUTH BASE)
Infantry Commands in Longstreet's Charging Column. Pickett's Division. Kemper's Va. Brigade. 1st, 3d, 7th, 11th & 24th Regiments. Garnett's Va. Brigade. 8th, 18th, 19th, 28th & 56th Regiments. Armistead's Va. Brigade. 9th, 14th, 38th, 53d & 57th Regiments.
Heth's Division. Archer's Tenn. Brigade. 13th Ala., 5th Ala. Batt., 1st, 7th & 14th Tenn. Regiments. Davis' Miss. Brigade. 2d, 11th, 42d Miss. & 55th N.C. Regiments. Pettigrew's N.C. Brigade. 11th, 26th, 44th, 47th & 52d Regiments. Brockenbrough's Va. Brigade. 40th, 47th & 55th Reg'ts. & 22d Battalion.
Pender's Division. Lane's North Carolina Brigade. 7th, 18th, 28th, 33d, 37th Regiments. Scales' North Carolina Brigade. 13th, 16th, 22d, 34th & 38th Regiments.

TEXT (NORTH BASE)
Infantry Commands Which Met Longstreet's Assault. Second Corps (Hancock's). Second Division (Gibbon's). The First Brigade, Harrow's, was composed of the 19th Maine, 15th Massachusetts, 1st Minnesota, and 82d New York Regiments. Second Brigade, Webb's, 69th, 71st, 72d,

and 106th Pennsylvania. Third Brigade, Hall's, 19th and 20th Massachusetts, 42d and 59th New York and 7th Michigan. United States Sharpshooters. First Regiment. Companies A, B, D, H, New York, C, I, K, (detached), Mich., E, N.H., F, Vt., G, Wis. Second Regiment. Companies A, Minn., B, Mich., C, Penn., D, Maine, E, H, Vt., F, G, N.H. First Co. Mass. Sharpshooters. Second Co. Minn. Sharpshooters.

Third Division, Hays' First Brigade, Carroll's 8th Ohio. Second Brigade, Smyth's, 14th Connecticut, 1st Delaware, 12th New Jersey, 108th New York and 10th New York Battalion. Third Brigade, Willard's, 39th, 111th, 125th and 126th New York.

First Army Corps, Newton's. Third Division, Doubleday's First Brigade, Rowley's, 80th New York, and the 151st Pennsylvania. Third Brigade, Stannard's, 13th, 14th and 16th Vermont. Assisted by the artillery, the 1st Pennsylvania Cavalry and Co's. D and K 6th New York Cavalry.

TEXT (WEST BASE)

Gettysburg Battlefield Memorial Association. Organized April 30, 1864. Directors 1895. President, Governor Daniel H. Hastings. Vice President, Colonel Charles H. Buehler. Secretary, Calvin Hamilton. Treasurer, J. Lawrence Schick. John B. Bachelder, Colonel George G. Briggs, Brevet Major Gen. Joseph B. Carr, Major Gen. S.W. Crawford, Brigadier Gen. Lucius W. Fairchild, Brevet Major Gen. D. McM. Gregg, Brevet Major Gen. George S. Greene, Lieut. C.E. Goldsborough, Brevet Major Chill. W. Hazzard, Jacob A. Kitzmiller, John C. Linehan, Captain Edward McPherson, Captain H.W. McKnight, Major Gen. Daniel E. Sickles, Major Gen. Henry W. Slocum, Captain Frank D. Sloat, Samuel McC. Swope, Colonel Wheelock G. Veazey, John M. Vanderslice, Brevet Brig. Gen. Louis Wagner, Brevet Major Gen. Alex. S. Webb, Brevet Lieut. Col. Charles L. Young, Brevet Lieut. Col. John P. Nicholson.

COMMENTARY

The High Water Mark monument is the only monument on the battlefield that lists both Union and Confederate combat troops in detail by name. It is dedicated to the Union troops who repulsed Longstreet's assault, and is located at the farthest point reached by Pickett's men at about 3:30 P.M. on July 3. As such it symbolically represents the high point reached by the Confederacy during the war. The monument was designed by John B. Bachelder in 1887 at the request of the Gettysburg Battlefield Memorial Association. Its form and location were approved on May 10, 1891. The monument was erected at a cost of $6500 with funds donated by the fifteen northern states listed on its inscription. Pennsylvania Governor James A. Beaver was the principal speaker at the monument's dedication ceremonies, which were held on June 2,

1892. In his speech he emphasized how the monument was a national memorial since it commemorates both Northern and Southern troops.

The monument is 9 feet tall and consists of an open bronze book resting on a granite plinth and base. It has a subbase of Gettysburg granite, and is surrounded by a cement esplanade that provides a walkway as well as a platform for two field cannons that are placed on the north and south sides of the monument. The entire monumental complex covers an area 18 feet 6 inches by 48 feet 6 inches.

The monument's base is made of Quincy granite from Massachusetts. It is 7 feet 4 inches deep, 9 feet wide, and 1 foot 4 inches high. The plinth, which is made of Fox Island granite from Maine, measures 8 feet 4 inches by 6 feet 3 inches. Attached to each face of the plinth are bronze inscriptional tablets. The central feature of the monument is a large open bronze book that is tilted toward the viewer. The book measures 6 feet 9 inches by 4 feet 6 inches and is supported by a post and two piles of cannonballs. It symbolizes the "record of history" and has listed on its pages the southern troops that formed or supported Longstreet's assault (better known as "Pickett's Charge") and the northern troops that repulsed them. These same troops are listed in more detail on tablets that were attached to the monument's plinth in 1902. Apparently several veterans of Union regiments who fought at the Angle objected that the original monument listed no units below brigade level and so did not name individual regiments. These veterans were anxious for everyone to know that they had helped to repulse "Pickett's Charge." They finally got their way in 1902 when two new tablets were added to the monument's plinth listing the Union and Confederate regiments and batteries that formed the brigades and divisions listed in the original text of the monument.

198. MCPHERSON BARN HOSPITAL
Tablet.
Attached to north side of barn wall, 100 yards south of Chambersburg Pike 200 yards east of Meredith Avenue.
Date erected not known.

TEXT
This barn was used as a Hospital and sheltered the wounded of both the Union and Confederate Armies, July 1, 2, 3, 4, 1863.

COMMENTARY
This barn was the scene of heavy fighting on the afternoon of July 1. It was then used as a hospital as the marker states. The barn, which belonged to the E. McPherson farm, has recently been restored to its war time appearance. The farm's other buildings are not extant.

199. ETERNAL LIGHT PEACE MEMORIAL

Large limestone memorial.
Located on Oak Hill, north of Confederate Avenue and .1 mile north of Mummasburg Road.
Sculpted by Lee Lawrie.
Dedicated July 3, 1938.

TEXT

Peace Eternal in a Nation United. An enduring light to guide us in unity and friendship.

United States Commission. Harry H. Woodring. Hugh L. White. Joseph F. Guffey. Harry L. Haines. Marvin Jones.

Contributing states. Pennsylvania, New York, Wisconsin, Indiana, Tennessee, Virginia, Illinois.

Penn. State Commission. John S. Rice, Chairman. Willis D. Hall, Henry W.A. Hanson, Frederick B. Kerr, Victor C. Mather, William S. McLean Jr., Gerald P. O'Neill, William A. Schadner, Edward C. Shannon, Paul L. Roy, Exec. Secy.

Paul Philippe Cret, Architect.

"With firmness in the right as God gives us to see the right." Lincoln. Eternal Light Peace Memorial dedicated by President Franklin D. Roosevelt during the observance of the 75th Anniversary of the Battle of Gettysburg, July 3, 1938.

COMMENTARY

The Eternal Light Peace Memorial is the only monument on the battlefield dedicated to peace and a reunited country. Its dedication on July 3, 1938, was the highlight of the ceremonies marking the 75th anniversary of the battle. Such a monument had not been conceivable in the decades following the battle because of the sectional tensions during the Reconstruction era. By the time of the battle's 50th anniversary in 1913, these tensions had subsided enough that plans were being made for a Peace Memorial to show the successful reunification of the country. The cornerstone for such a monument was supposed to be laid on July 4, 1913, but the project had to be postponed for several reasons.[1]

Plans for the Peace Memorial lay dormant until they were revived by Pennsylvanian John S. Rice in 1935. Rice, who had been elected to Pennsylvania's State Senate in 1932, was the principal supporter of the movement to celebrate the battle's 75th anniversary in 1938. His proposal to form a 75th Anniversary Commission for the Battle of Gettysburg was approved by Pennsylvania's Governor George H. Earle on April 30, 1935. One month later Rice was appointed Chairman of the Anniversary Commission, with Paul L. Roy as Executive Secretary.

Rice's major goal was the erection of the Eternal Light Peace

Memorial. Twenty-one states were approached for funds, but only seven responded. The first after Pennsylvania was Virginia, which appropriated funds for the monument on March 7, 1936. She was followed by one other Southern state, Tennessee. Four Northern states—New York, Wisconsin, Indiana and Illinois—joined Pennsylvania in helping to build the Memorial. Thus the Peace Memorial is the only monument on the battlefield to be constructed jointly by states that had been foes in the Civil War.

The Memorial was designed by Paul Philippe Cret and was erected in 1938 on ground occupied by part of Rodes' Confederate division prior to its attack on the Union First Corps on the afternoon of July 1. It is made of veined Alabama limestone and consists of a large platform supporting a tall shaft surmounted by an "eternal flame." The platform measures 42 by 85 feet and is 11 feet high. Around it are pavements of Crab Orchard flagstone. The shaft is 40 feet high and is adorned on its south side by an 8 foot high bas relief that was sculpted by Lee Lawrie (1877-1961) for a fee of $60,000. The relief features two figures that stand side by side and hold a wreath while they embrace each other. In front of them stands an eagle. The symbolism of the relief clearly represents the reunification of the nation and the fraternity of the two sections of the country that once made war on each other. Atop the memorial's shaft is an urn for the "eternal flame." The memorial's inscription contains a quotation from Lincoln's Second Inaugural Address.

The Peace Memorial was dedicated at ceremonies held at 6:30 P.M. on Sunday, July 3, 1938. In attendance was a crowd estimated variously from 200,000 to 450,000, a number that included almost 2000 grizzled Civil War veterans. The ceremonies were presided over by John S. Rice, the Chairman of the 75th Anniversary Committee. The guest of honor for the ceremonies was President Franklin D. Roosevelt, who arrived in Gettysburg on a special train at 6 P.M. that evening. The ceremony's first principal speaker was George H. Earle, the Governor of Pennsylvania. Governor Earle then presented the Memorial to President Roosevelt, who in his acceptance speech commemorated the valor of the soldiers of the Blue and the Gray, stating that he was "thankful that they stand together under one flag now."[2] At the close of his speech, the President gave a signal for the monument to be unveiled. At that moment a huge U.S. garrison flag that had been draped over the monument was lowered by two veterans of the Civil War Northerner George N. Lockwood of California and Southerner A.G. Harris of McDonough, Georgia.

When the monument was unveiled, its gas "eternal light" was lighted by a spark ignited by the rays of the sun. It burned at the rate of 300 cubic feet per hour for over 35 years until it was extinguished during an energy crisis in December 1973. The "eternal light" was then dormant for four and one half years until a sodium vapor light was installed on June 20, 1978. This was lighted during a rededication ceremony held on July 1, 1978. The memorial was again rededicated on the 125th anniversary of the battle in July 1988.

200. SPANGLER'S SPRING

Bronze tablets set in stonework of spring covering.
Located in Spangler Meadow, southwest of intersection of Slocum Avenue and Geary Avenue.
Date erected not known.

TEXT

Spangler's Spring. One Country and One Flag. The strife of brothers is past. This spring supplied Union and Confederate soldiers with water during the battle.

COMMENTARY

During the night of July 2/3 soldiers of both armies came to this spring for water. At that time the spring was located between the opposing lines part of Johnson's Confederate division had seized the Union works on the hill to the north, and Union troops of the Twelfth Corps were posted to the west and south.

201. 43RD NORTH CAROLINA INFANTRY

Bronze tablet on granite marker.
Located east of East Confederate Avenue, .3 mile north of Spangler Meadow.
Dedicated October 22, 1988.

TEXT

Forty-Third North Carolina Infantry Regiment. Army of Northern Virginia. Daniel's Brigade, William Gaston Lewis, Lieutenant Colonel; Ewell's Corps, Thomas Stephen Kenan, Colonel; Rodes' Division, Walter Jones Boggan, Major.

As they approached the field of battle on the morning of July 1, the 43rd North Carolina, along with the rest of Daniel's Brigade, heard the distant booming of cannon. Early in the afternooon the regiment moved to the right and onto open ground where they were met with a furious fire. Their steady progress was checked by the deep railroad cut, but subsequent assaults were successful in breaking the Union line. Having suffered heavily, the regiment rested for the night west of town. The next morning the 43d supported a battery just north of the seminary. Shelling from guns on the nearby heights inflicted some losses. Toward evening the regiment took up a position on the southern edge of town. Before daybreak on July 3, the 43d moved to the extreme left of the Confederate line to take part in an assault on Culp's Hill. Passing this point and advancing under heavy fire, they occupied earthworks abandoned by Union troops. Attempting to push beyond the works, the regiment was exposed to a most severe fire of canister, shrapnel, and shell at short range. During the attack Col. Kenan was wounded and taken from the field and command passed to Lt. Col. Lewis. The regiment retired to this point and remained exposed and under fire until ordered to recross Rock Creek in the early evening.

"All that men could do, was done nobly."

Erected by the State of North Carolina, 1988.

COMMENTARY

This monument is the fourth and most recent Confederate regimental marker erected on the battlefield.[1] It is located on the line of the regiment's advance early on the moring of July 3. For the regiment's role in the fighting on July 1, see No. 148. The 43rd was not engaged on July 2, and before dawn on July 3 moved to support Johnson's attack on Culp's Hill, being stationed about ¼ mile north of this marker. After being held in reserve for a short time, the regiment moved to its left and advanced over the position of this marker en route to relieve some of Johnson's troops that had occupied a portion of the Union works on South Culp's Hill, ⅛ mile to the west. In on e attack from that position, Colonel T.S. Kenan of the 43rd was wounded. After being heavily engaged for most of the morning, the regiment was withdrawn with its brigade past the position of this monument. The 43rd entered the battle on July 1 with an estimeate battle strength of 572.[2]

The monument was erected largely through the efforts of descendants of the 43rd's commander, Colonel Thomas S. Kenan, who was wounded less than ¼ mile to the west of the monument. It was sponsored by the North Caroliniana Society in conjunction with the North Carolina Historical Commission and the North Carolina Department of Cultural Resources. Its shape and structure are similar to that of the 26th North Carolina monument erected on McPherson's Ridge in 1985 (No. 39). William C. Friday, President Emeritus of the University of North Carolina presided over the dedication ceremonies held on October 22, 1988. James R. Leutze, President of Hampden-Sydney College, gave the day's principal address, and Frank H. Kenan presented the monument to the Park on behalf of the people of North Carolina.

202. MASONIC MEMORIAL

Two bronze figures on a granite base.
Located in the National Cemetery Annex, 140 yards southeast of the interseciton of Steinwehr Avenue and Taneytown Road (Washington Street).
Sculpted by Ron Tunison.
Dedicated August 21, 1993.

TEXT

Friend to Friend. A Brotherhood Undivided.

Friend to Friend. A Brotherhood Undivided.

Friend to Friend. Union General Winfield Scott Hancock and Confederate General Lewis Addison Armistead were personal friends and members of the Masonic fraternity. Although they had served and fought side by side in the United States Army prior to the Civil War, Armistead refused to raise his sword against his fellow Southerners and joined the Confederate Army in 1861. Both Hancock and Armistead fought heroically in the previous twenty-seven months of the war. They were destined to meet at Gettysburg. During Pickett's Charge, Armistead led his men gallantly, penetrating Hancock's line. Ironically, when Armistead was mortally wounded, Hancock was also wounded. Depicted in this sculpture is Union Captain Henry Bingham, a Mason and staff assistant to General Hancock, himself wounded, rendering aid to the fallen Confederate General. Armistead is shown handing his watch and personal effects to be taken to his friend, General Hancock. Hancock survived the war and died in 1886. Armistead died at Gettysburg July 5, 1863. Captain Bingham attained the rank of General and later served 32 years in the United States House of Representatives. He was known as the "Father of the House." Shown on the wall surrounding this monument are the names of the States whose soldiers fought at the Battle of Gettysburg.

Friend to Friend. Masonic Memorial. This monument is presented by the Right Worshipful Grand Lodge and Accepted Masons of Pennsylvania and dedicated as a memorial to the Freemasons of the Union and the Confederacy. Their unique bonds of friendship enabled them to remain a brotherhood undivided, even as they fought in a divided nation, faithfully supporting the respective governments under which they lived.

Dedicated August 21, 1993 By The Right Worshipful Grand Lodge Of The most Ancient And Honorable Fraternity Of Free and Accepted Masons of Pennsylvania and Masonic Jurisdiction Thereunto Belonging. Edward H. Fowler, Jr., Right Worshipful Grand Master. George H. Hohenshildt, R.W. Deputy Grand Master, Chairman. Edward O. Weisser, R.W. Senior Grand Warden. James L. Ernette, R.W. Junior Grand Warden. Marvin G. Speicher, R.W. Grand Treasurer. Thomas W. Jackson , R.W. Grand Secretary.

COMMENTARY

The Masonic Memorial commemorates the approximately 18,000 Freemasons who fought at the battle in both armies. It was conceived by Sheldon Munn and consists of two larger than life size figures on a granite base. The two figures, which were sculpted by artist Ron Tunison of Cairo, New York, depict Union Captain Henry Bingham (who was an aide to Major General Winfield S. Hancock) giving aid to Confederate Brigadier General Lewis A. Armistead after Armistead was mortally wounded within the Union lines during the height of Pickett's Charge on July 3 at a position about one-quarter mile southwest of this memorial (see no. 124). Armistead, who was a Freemason, requested Bingham, who was a fellow Freemason, to carry a message to Hancock, who was an old friend of Armistead's and also was a Freemason. Armistead even gave some of his personal effects to Bingham for safe keeping, but the General unfortunately died two days later, before Hancock (who had also been wounded on July 3) could see him. The memorial honors the friendship of Armistead and Hancock as well as "the acts of love and compassion that occurred in the battle despite the political and emotional strains brought on by the Civil War."

Captain Bingham is depicted kneeling and in the act of speaking to General Armistead, who is lying on the ground with his upper body slightly raised. The two figures, each about eight feet in height/length, are sculpted in bronze and together weigh about one ton. The statue is unique because it is the first "polychrome" sculpture on the battlefield: the bronze surface of the statues has been chemically treated so that Bingham's uniform appears to have a blue tint and Armistead's has a gray tint.

The sculpture stands on a base that is 6 feet high and 10 feet 8 inches wide and 8 feet 6 inches deep. It is located in the center of a small plaza that has a granite wall encircling it for 270 degrees. The names of each state, North and South, that sent troops to the battle, are inscribed on the wall, which has 29 panels, one for each state. It was not discovered until after the dedication that Kentucky (which sent no troops to the battle) was included while Mississippi (which did send troops) was not. For this reason, the Kentucky panel had to be removed and a Mississipppi panel was created and inserted in its proper alphabetical position.

The entire memorial was erected at a cost of $500,000. An additional $25,000 was endowed for its perpetual care and maintenance. The Freemasons also donated the cost of new landscaping for the National Cemetery Annex, including an entrance plaza with a lighted flagpole, perimeter fencing, and paved walkways.

The memorial was dedicted on August 21, 1993, amidst elaborate ceremonies attended by over 50,000 people. A parade of some 3000 participants, including reenactors, several marching bands, and numerous Shriner and Masonic groups, marched through town to the site of the memorial. The dedictory address was given by Edward H.

Fowler, Jr., Right Worshipful Grand Master of Pennsylvania's Freemasons.

203. MARYLAND MEMORIAL
Two large bronze figures on a granite base.
Located west of the Taneytown Road at the southwest corner of the Cyclorama parking lot.
Sculpted by Lawrence M. Ludtke.
Dedicated November 13, 1994.

TEXT
A Final Tribute.
More than 3,000 Marylanders served on both sides of the conflict at the Battle of Gettysburg. They could be found in all branches of the Army from the rank of Private to Major General and on all parts of the battlefield. Brother against brother would be their legacy, particularly on the slopes of Culp's Hill. This memorial symbolizes the aftermath of that battle and the war. Brothers again. Marylanders all.
The State of Maryland proudly honors its sons who fought at Gettysburg in defense of the causes they held so dear.
Participating Maryland Commands: Union—1st Eastern Shore Infantry, 1st Potomac Home Brigade Infantry, 3rd Infantry, 1st Cavalry, Co. A Purnell Legion Cavalry, Battery A, 1st Artillery; Confederate—2nd Infantry, 1st Cavalry, 1st Artillery, 2nd Artillery (Baltimore Light), 4th Artillery (Chesapeake).

COMMENTARY
The Maryland Memorial and the High Water Mark Monument (No. 197) are the only two monuments on the battlefield to honor specific units from both the North and the South. As a border state, Maryland sent six Union commands (about 2000 men) and five Confederate units (about 1000 men) to fight in the battle, as noted in the memorial's inscription. Each of the Northern units listed has its own monument on the battlefield, but the only Confederate Maryland unit so commemorated is the 1st Maryland (CSA) Infantry (Nos. 32-35). Maryland was the last of the Southern states that sent troops to Gettysburg, to erect a memorial to honor them. The movement to erect this memorial was begun by James Holechek of Baltimore in 1989. In 1990 he organized a twenty member committee, Citizens for a Maryland Monument at Gettysburg, whose honorary chairman was the state's Governor, William D. Schaefer. The committee raised over $200,000 to cover the cost of the memorial and its landscaping; this amount included a $75,000 grant from the Maryland state legislature. The final cost of the project included a $10,000 endowment required by the National Park Service to cover perpetual care of the memorial.[1]
Reuben Kramer, a Baltimore sculptor, chaired a judging committee

that solicited designs for th memorial in 1990. All together there was a total of 83 entrants, from whom three semi-finalists were selected. Each submitted an 18 inch clay model. The winning design was submitted by Lawrence M. Ludtke of Houston, who was awarded a $75,000 contract. The two runners-up were each given $1500 for their effort.

Ludkte's final design features two larger than life size soldiers, one Union and one Confederate, who are both wounded. They are shown supporting each other after the battle, just as the survivors of the battle were reunited after the war in Maryland and in the country at large. The full size clay model for the figures was completed on July 1, 1994. The final sculpture was cast at the Shidoni Foundry in Tesuque, New Mexico.

The two bronze figures, which are nine feet tall and weigh 2000 pounds together, stand on a granite pedestal four feet six inches high. The word "Maryland" is carved in 10 inch high letters on the front of the base, which also features a bronze state seal copied from the medallion on the monument to Rigby's (Union) Maryland battery, locted on Powers Hill. The north side of the base is adorned by the distinctive badge of Lord Calvert, while the south side has a "Maryland Cross." The memorial's bronze narrative tablet is on the rear (west) side of the base. The pedestal was designed by Roger Lee Katzenbach, and the narrative panel was compiled by J.T Holechek and Daniel Toomey. The memorial is situated in a 24 foot square plaza that features an inlaid "Maryland Cross" design. A time capsule lies under the plaza, and is to be opened in November 2094.

The memorial was dedicated in ceremonies held on Sunday, November 13, 1994. The crowd attending numbered more than 5000, including some 800 reenactors. Featured speakers included Robert P. Casey, the Governor of Pennsylvania; James A. Holechek, chairman of the monument committee; Major General James F. Fretterd, Adjutant General of Maryland; and Maryland Governor William D. Schaefer, who unveiled the memorial. The ceremonies closed, appropriately, with a playing of the song "Maryland, My Maryland."

No Maryland units of either army actually fought on or near the position occupied by the memorial. Most fought on Culp's Hill (5/8 mile to the east) or the East Cavalry Field (3½ miles to the east).

"X" Series Tablets

These ten iron tablets were erected in 1903 west of West Confederate Avenue just south of the intersection of West Confederate Avenue and Fairfield Road. They were taken down in 1974 and are presently in storage.

X-1 CONFEDERATE ITINERARY TABLET, JUNE 26, 1863

Army of Northern Virginia, June 26, 1863. Headquarters Army of Northern Virginia with Hood's Division Longstreet's Corps crossed the Potomac at Williamsport, Md. and marched to Greencastle, Pa. McLaws's Division crossed the river and encamped near Williamsport. Pickett's Division with the Reserve Artillery marched through Hagerstown to Greencastle. Rodes's and Johnson's Divisions Ewell's Corps with Jenkins's Cavalry Brigade were on the road from Chambersburg to Carlisle, Pa. Early's Division with French's Cavalry regiment marched from Greenwood via Cashtown to Mummasburg and his Cavalry advanced and had a skirmish with the 26th Penna. Infantry. Gordon's Brigade passed through Gettysburg halting a short time in the town. Anderson's Division Hill's Corps marched from Hagerstown and encamped two miles north of Greencastle. Hampton's, Chambliss's and Fitz Lee's Brigades of Stuart's Cavalry marched from Buckland via Brentsville to near Wolf Run Shoals on the Occoquan River, Va.

X-2 CONFEDERATE ITINERARY TABLET, JUNE 27, 1863

Army of Northern Virginia, June 27, 1863. Headquarters of the Army moved from Greencastle to Chambersburg, Pa. Rodes's and Johnson's Divisions Ewell's Corps arrived at Carlisle. Early's Division moved from Mummasburg via Hunterstown, New Chester and Hampton to Berlin. Gordon's Brigade reached York. McLaws's Division Longstreet's Corps marched from Williamsport via Hagerstown, Middleburg and Greencastle to camp five miles south of Chambersburg. Hood's Division reached that town and Pickett's Division moved on three miles further north. Anderson's Division Hill's Corps marched via Chambersburg to Fayetteville, Pa. Heth's and Pender's Divisions to the same place by other routes. Hampton's, Chambliss's and Fitz Lee's Brigades of Stuart's Cavalry marched from Wolf Run Shoals on Occoquan River via Fairfax Station, Annandale and Dranesville, Va. and crossed the Potomac into Maryland below Seneca Creek. Robertson's and Jones's Brigades were left in Virginia to guard the passes of the Blue Ridge.

X-3 CONFEDERATE ITINERARY TABLET, JUNE 28, 1863

Army of Northern Virginia, June 28, 1863. Rodes's and Johnson's Divisions Ewell's Corps were at Carlisle. Jenkins's Cavalry Brigade was sent to reconnoitre the defenses of Harrisburg. Early's Division marched from Berlin by way of Weiglestown to York. Gordon's Brigade moving on through York to Wrightsville on the Susquehanna River. Heth's, Pender's and Anderson's Divisions Hill's Corps were in camp at Fayetteville. Hood's, McLaws's and Pickett's Divisions Longstreet's Corps at or near Chambersburg. Hampton's, Chambliss's and Fitz Lee's Brigades of Stuart's Cavalry moved via Darnestown and Rockville, Md.

X-4 CONFEDERATE ITINERARY TABLET, JUNE 29, 1863

Army of Northern Virginia, June 29, 1863. Heth's Division Hill's Corps moved from Fayetteville to Cashtown, Pender's and Anderson's Divisions remaining at Fayetteville. Johnson's Division Ewell's Corps countermarched from Carlisle to Greenville, Pa. Rodes's Division remained at Carlisle and Early's Division at York and Wrightsville. Hood's, McLaws's and Pickett's Divisions Longstreet's Corps remained in position near Chambersburg. Stuart's three Brigades of Cavalry marched through Cooksville, Sykesville and Westminster, Md. to Union Mills, Pa.

X-5 CONFEDERATE ITINERARY TABLET, JUNE 30, 1863

Army of Northern Virginia, June 30, 1863. Heth's Division Hill's Corps at Cashtown. Pettigrew's Brigade marched nearly to Gettysburg but was recalled. Pender's Division moved from Fayetteville to Cashtown. Anderson's Division remained at Fayetteville. Rodes's Division Ewell's Corps moved from Carlisle via Petersburg to Heidlersburg. Johnson's Division marched from Greenville to Scotland, Pa. Early's Division returned from York via Weiglestown and East Berlin and encamped three miles from Heidlersburg. Pickett's Division Longstreet's Corps remained at Chambersburg. McLaws's and Hood's Division moved from there to Fayetteville except Law's Brigade which was sent to New Guilford. Stuart's Brigades of Cavalry moved from Union Mills, Pa. via Hanover to Jefferson and had a sharp fight at Hanover, Pa. with Union Cavalry.

X-6 CONFEDERATE ITINERARY TABLET, JULY 1, 1863

Army of Northern Virginia, July 1, 1863. Heth's and Pender's Divisions Hill's Corps marched from Cashtown to Gettysburg. Anderson's Division marched from Fayetteville via Cashtown to Gettysburg. Rodes's Division Ewell's Corps marched from Heidlersburg via Middletown to Gettysburg. Early's Division to Heidlersburg and thence by the direct road to Gettysburg. Johnson's Division from Scotland via Cashtown to Gettysburg. Pickett's Division Longstreet's Corps remained with the wagon trains at Chambersburg. McLaws's and Hood's Divisions except Law's Brigade on outpost duty at New Guilford marched from Fayetteville to Marsh Creek within four miles of Gettysburg. Stuart's Brigades of Cavalry marched from Jefferson via Dover and Dillsburg to

Carlisle. Robertson's and Jones's Brigades of Cavalry crossed the Potomac at Williamsport and moved to Greencastle, Pa.

X-7 CONFEDERATE ITINERARY TABLET, JULY 2, 1863

Army of Northern Virginia, July 2, 1863. McLaws's and Hood's Divisions Longstreet's Corps moved from Marsh Creek to the field at Gettysburg. Law's Brigade Hood's Division marched from New Guilford to Gettysburg arriving about noon. Pickett's Division marched from Chambersburg and arrived in the vicinity of Gettysburg soon after sunset. Stuart's Brigades of Cavalry marched from Carlisle via Hunterstown to Gettysburg. Hampton's Cavalry Brigade being in front had an engagement with Union Cavalry in the evening at Hunterstown, Pa. Robertson's and Jones's Brigades of Cavalry marched from Greencastle to Chambersburg.

X-8 CONFEDERATE ITINERARY TABLET, JULY 3, 1863

Army of Northern Virginia, July 3, 1863. Pickett's Division Longstreet's Corps arrived on the field early in the morning. Robertson's and Jones's Brigades of Cavalry marched from Chambersburg via Cashtown and Fairfield to a position on the right flank of the Confederate Army. Jones's Brigade had a severe fight with the Sixth United States Cavalry near Fairfield, Pa. Imboden's Brigade of mounted Infantry reached the field at noon.

X-9 CONFEDERATE ITINERARY TABLET, JULY 4, 1863

Army of Northern Virginia, July 4, 1863. Ewell's Corps moved before dawn from the base of Culp's Hill and the streets of Gettysburg to Seminary Ridge and the Army remained in position on that Ridge throughout the day. Soon after dark Hill's Corps withdrew and began the march via Fairfield and Waynesborough on the Hagerstown Road. Pickett's and McLaws's Divisions Longstreet's Corps followed during the night.

X-10 CONFEDERATE ITINERARY TABLET, JULY 5, 1863

Army of Northern Virginia, July 5, 1863. The entire Army on the march to the Potomac. Hill's Corps had the advance, Longstreet's the center, Ewell's the rear. Hood's Division Longstreet's Corps started after sunrise. Early's Division Ewell's Corps started near noon and formed the rear guard. Fitz Lee's and Hampton's Brigades of Cavalry, the latter under Col. Baker, moved via Cashtown and Greenwood en route to Williamsport. Chambliss's and Jenkins's Brigades of Cavalry under General Stuart moved via Emmitsburg. Robertson's and Jones's Brigades of Cavalry held the Jack Mountain Passes. Imboden's Brigade of mounted Infantry in charge of the wagon trains reached Greencastle in the morning and Williamsport in the afternoon.

"A" Series Tablets

These tablets do not stand on the battlefield, but are suggested for erection to give a more complete story of the battle.

A-1 SECOND BALTIMORE (MD.) BATTERY (W. GRIFFIN'S BATTERY)

Cast iron tablet.
To be located on Oak Hill southeast of the Peace Memorial, west of North Confederate Avenue 330 yards north of Mummasburg Road.

SUGGESTED TEXT

Army of Northern Virginia. Stuart's Horse Artillery. Beckham's Battalion. Griffin's Battery. Four 10 pounder Parrotts.
July 2. Arrived on the field and took position here.
July 3. Held this position until about 4 P.M. when was ordered to withdraw to the rear.
July 4. Rejoined Jenkins' Brigade and moved to the southwest towards Hagerstown.
Losses not reported.

COMMENTARY

This marker would be located at the position held by the battery from the evening of July 2 until 4 P.M. on July 3, when it withdrew from the battlefield proper. During the early part of the campaign, the battery served with Jenkins' cavalry brigade. Shortly before the battle it was assigned to Rodes' command. It rejoined Jenkins' brigade on July 4. The battery had a battle strength of about 106.[1]

Several sources place this battery with Jenkins' brigade on the East Cavalry Battlefield during the fighting there on July 3.[2] However, several eye witness accounts place the battery on Oak Hill on July 2 and 3.[3] Perhaps the battery thought to be Griffin's on the East Cavalry Battlefield was actually Jackson's newly organized Virginia Battery.[4] The battery had a battle strength of about 106.[5]

A-2 WASHINGTON (S.C.) ARTILLERY (HART'S BATTERY)

Cast iron tablet.
To be located west of Emmitsburg Road, one half mile south of intersection of Emmitsburg Road and West Confederate Avenue.

SUGGESTED TEXT

Army of Northern Virginia. Stuart's Horse Artillery, Beckham's Battalion. Hart's Battery. Three Blakely rifles.

July 3. The Battery, being detached from its Battalion, reported to Longstreet's Corps and was posted here to support the extreme right flank of the army. In the late afternoon it aided in the repulse of the Union Cavalry attack made against this position.

July 4. Withdrew and reported to General Hampton's Brigade at Cashtown to help guard wagon trains on the retreat to Winchester. Losses not reported.

COMMENTARY

This marker would show the position held by the battery on July 3. The battery served actively during the early stages of the campaign, losing one of its guns at Middleburg on June 21.[1] It was usually attached to Hampton's cavalry brigade, but on July 3 was detached to serve with Longstreet's Corps. It rejoined Hampton's brigade at Cashtown on July 4. Its battle strength on July 3 was about 79.[2]

A-3 ASHBY (VA.) HORSE ARTILLERY (CHEW'S BATTERY)

Cast iron tablet.
To be located west of South Reynolds Avenue, 110 feet north of Fairfield Road.

SUGGESTED TEXT

Army of Northern Virginia. Stuart's Horse Artillery, Beckham's Battalion. Chew's Battery. Number and type of guns not known.

July 3. The Battery, which was serving with Jones's Cavalry Brigade, took part in the engagement at Fairfield in the afternoon.

COMMENTARY

This marker does not show the position of the battery, which did not reach the battlefield proper. It served actively with Jones' brigade throughout the campaign. During the engagement at Fairfield the battery's position was opposite the Marshall house, on the east side of the Fairfield–Orrtanna Road about 2.6 miles north of Pa. Route 116. On July 3 the battery had a battle strength of about 93.[1]

A-4 LYNCHBURG (VA.) HORSE ARTILLERY (MOORMAN'S BATTERY)

Cast iron tablet.
To be located west of South Reynolds Avenue, 130 feet north of Fairfield Road.

SUGGESTED TEXT

Army of Northern Virginia. Stuart's Horse Artillery, Beckham's Battalion. Moorman's Battery. Number and type of guns not known.

July 4. After helping to guard the army's rear during the campaign, the Battery was posted between Fairfield and Emmitsburg:

COMMENTARY

This marker does not show the position of the battery, which did not reach the battlefield proper. During the entire campaign it helped guard the flanks and rear of the army. It had a battle strength on July 4 of about 106.[1]

A-5 LONGSTREET MONUMENT

Bronze equestrian statue.
To be located in Pitzer Woods, 1/8 mile west of West Confederate Avenue.

SUGGESTED TEXT

Lieutenant Gen. James Longstreet. 1821-1904. Commander of the First Corps, Army of Northern Virginia.

COMMENTARY

A movement to erect a monument to Lee's "Old War Horse" began in the 1930s, supported largely by Longstreet's family and their friends. A site was determined and ground was broken west of South Confederate Avenue and the Emmitsburg Road, but the project was later abandoned.[1] The movement to erect a monument to General Longstreet was revived in the early 1990s by the North Carolina Division of the Sons of Confederate Veterans. Sculptor Gary Casteel of Maurertown, Virginia, has been selected to design the monument, and he is planning a life size equestrian statue mounted on a granite base at ground level. A site for the monument has been selected in Pitzer Woods, to the left of the line held by McLaws' division before Longstreet's attack on the afternoon of July 2. It is estimated that the project will cost $250,000, including a payment to the Park for perpetual care of the monument. Donations may be sent to The General Longstreeet Memorial Fund, c/o The North Carolina Division, Sons of Confederate Veterans, PO Box 1896, Raleigh, NC 27602.

A-6 ALEXANDER'S ARTILLERY LINE (JULY 3)

Cast iron tablet.
To be located 200 yards west of Emmitsburg Road, 3/8 mile north of Peach Orchard.

SUGGESTED TEXT

Army of Northern Virginia. Longstreet's Corps, Alexander's Artillery Line.
July 3. Early in the morning 75 guns of Alexander's, Cabell's, Dearing's, Eshleman's and Henry's Battalions were formed on this ridge under the supervision of Col. E.P. Alexander of Longstreet's Reserve Artillery. The guns participated from 1 to 3 P.M. in the great cannonade that preceded Longstreet's assault, the opening shots of which were fired by two guns of Miller's Battery from a position near here.

COMMENTARY

This spot marks the approximate center of Longstreet's artillery line formed by Col. E.P. Alexander on the morning of July 3. This line was about 1300 yards long, running north from the Peach Orchard along this ridge. It consisted of 75 guns from Alexander's, Cabell's, Dearing's, Eshleman's and Henry's battalions. These guns all participated in the great cannonade from 1 to 3 P.M. that preceded Longstreet's assault. Two guns of Miller's battery fired the opening shots for this bombardment shortly after 1 P.M. At 3 P.M. some of the batteries in this line retired for lack of ammunition, while others (such as Miller's) advanced to support the infantry attack.

A-7 HAYS' BRIGADE (JULY 1)

Tablet on granite pedestal.
To be located east of Harrisburg Road north of the junction of Harrisburg Road and Lincoln Avenue.

SUGGESTED TEXT

C.S.A. Army of Northern Virginia. Ewell's Corps, Early's Division, Hays' Brigade. 5th, 6th, 7th, 8th, 9th Louisiana Infantry.

July 1. Arrived about 1 P.M. and formed astride the Harrisburg Road. Advanced with Hoke's Brigade at 3 P.M. to support Gordon's Brigade on the right. Engaged Coster's Brigade of the Union Eleventh Corps near here and captured two guns. Pursued retreating Union troops into the town, capturing many. Late in the evening halted on East High Street.

July 2. Moved forward early into the low ground southeast of town and skirmished all day. At 8 P.M. with Hoke's Brigade charged East Cemetery Hill but was repulsed.

July 3. Occupied a position on High St. in the town.

July 4. At 2 A.M. moved to Seminary Ridge. After midnight began the march to Hagerstown.

Present about 1295. Killed 36, wounded 201, missing 76. Total 313.

COMMENTARY

This marker would show the position from which the brigade attacked Coster's brigade of the Eleventh Corps at about 3:45 P.M. on July 1. At 3 P.M. the brigade advanced from a position astride the Harrisburg Road one mile northeast of here, with the purpose of supporting Gordon's attack on Barlow Knoll. It met Union reserves 1/8 mile south of this point and formed a battle line stretching from the county Almshouse on the right to Stevens Run on the left. The brigade then broke the Union line and captured two guns of Heckman's Battery K 1st Ohio Artillery.[1] During the ensuing Union retreat the brigade captured a number of prisoners greater than its own strength. That night the brigade formed in the town 3/4 mile south of this marker. For the brigade's movements on July 2, 3 and 4, see No. 136.

A-8 HOKE'S BRIGADE (July 1)

Tablet on granite pedestal.

To be located north of Hanover Road, 1000 feet west of bridge over Rock Creek.

SUGGESTED TEXT

C.S.A. Army of Northern Virginia. Ewell's Corps, Early's Division, Hoke's Brigade. 6th, 21st, 57th North Carolina Infantry.

July 1. Arrived between noon and 1 P.M. and formed between the Harrisburg and Hunterstown Roads on the left of the Division. Advanced with Hays' Brigade at 3 P.M. to support Gordon's Brigade on the right. Engaged the Union line near here and outflanked it by advancing along the railroad cut. Helped capture a large number of prisoners. Late in the day formed southeast of town.

July 2. Skirmished all day. At 8 P.M. with Hays' Brigade charged East Cemetery Hill but was repulsed. Its commander Col. Isaac E. Avery was mortally wounded leading the charge.

July 3. Ordered to railroad cut in rear and later to High Street in town.

July 4. At 2 A.M. moved to Seminary Ridge. After midnight began the march to Hagerstown.

Present about 1244. Killed 35, wounded 216, missing 94. Total 345.

COMMENTARY

This marker would be located about ¼ mile south of the position from which the brigade attacked Coster's brigade of the Eleventh Corps at about 3:45 P.M. on July 1. At 3 P.M. the brigade advanced on the left of the division line from a position between the Harrisburg and Hunterstown Roads 1¼ mile northeast of here. After crossing Rock Creek under heavy artillery fire it met Union reserves posted ¼ mile west of here. The brigade formed with its left on the railroad and its right on Stevens Run. It then advanced along the railroad cut and outflanked the Union line. That night the brigade formed southeast of town about ½ mile southwest of here. For the brigade's movements on July 2, 3 and 4, see No. 137.

A-9 MCINTOSH'S BATTALION (July 1)

Tablet on granite pedestal.
To be located south of Chambersburg Pike near Herr Tavern.

SUGGESTED TEXT

C.S.A. Army of Northern Virginia. Hill's Corps, Artillery Reserve, McIntosh's Battalion. Johnson's, Rice's, Hurt's and Wallace's Batteries. Six Napoleons, two Whitworths, eight 3 inch rifles.

July 1. Late in the morning Rice's and Wallace's Batteries and the Whitworth rifles were placed on this ridge near here. Later Johnson's Battery and Hurt's two 3 inch rifles were posted on the Corps' right near the Fairfield Road. Engaged the Union guns one mile to the east until their lines began to collapse. Two batteries accompanied Pender's Division as it advanced towards the town.

July 2-4. The Battalion was actively engaged from a position on Seminary Ridge south of Fairfield Road.

Losses. 7 men killed, 25 wounded of whom 16 were captured. 38 horses killed or disabled.

COMMENTARY

This marker would show the position held by most of the battalion from 11 A.M. to dusk on July 1. During this time Johnson's battery and Hurt's two 3 inch rifles were posted one mile directly to the south of here. From July 2-4 most of the battalion was posted 1½ mile to the southeast (see No. 158).

A-10 PEGRAM'S BATTALION (JULY 1)

Tablet on granite pedestal.
To be located north of Chambersburg Pike opposite Herr Tavern.

SUGGESTED TEXT

C.S.A. Army of Northern Virginia. Hill's Corps, Artillery Reserve, Pegram's Battalion. Marye's, Crenshaw's, Zimmerman's, McGraw's and Brander's Batteries. Ten Napoleons, four 10 pounder Parrotts, four 3 inch rifles, two 12 pounder howitzers.

July 1. About 10 A.M. the opening artillery shots of the battle were fired by Marye's battery from a position on the Pike about one mile to the west of here. The battalion then formed at this position and was actively engaged. One of Zimmerman's rifled guns was disabled, and Johnson's howitzers were not engaged. Later Brander's Battery was detached ½ mile to the northeast. Camped nearby.

July 2-3. Engaged with the Union forces from a position on Seminary Ridge near McMillan Woods.

July 4. About sunset withdrew and began the march to Hagerstown.

Losses. Killed 10, wounded 37. Total 47. Ammunition expended 3800 rounds. Horses killed or disabled 38.

COMMENTARY

This marker would show the position held by most of the battalion from 10:30 A.M. on July 1 to early morning on July 2. At about 10 A.M. on July 1 the rifled guns of Marye's battery fired the first Confederate artillery shots of the battle from a position along the Pike about a mile west of here. The battalion's position here extended from this marker north to the woods at the edge of Willoughby Run. For the battery's position on July 2-4, see No. 159.

A-11 BROCKENBROUGH'S BRIGADE (JULY 1)

Tablet on granite pedestal.
To be located west of Meredith Avenue, ⅛ mile south of Chambersburg Pike.

SUGGESTED TEXT

C.S.A. Army of Northern Virginia. Hill's Corps, Heth's Division,

Brockenbrough's Brigade. 40th, 47th, 55th Regiments and 22nd Battalion Virginia Infantry.

July 1. Crossed Willoughby Run at 2 P.M. between Chambersburg Pike and Reynolds Woods. Engaged Union forces at this position and with other troops on left drove them back to next ridge capturing two flags and many prisoners with some sharpshooters in the barn. Soon afterwards the Brigade was relieved by Pender's Division.

July 2. Lay in the Woods west of the Run. In the evening took position on Seminary Ridge south of McMillan Woods.

July 3. In Longstreet's Assault the Brigade was on the left flank of the attacking column. It was repulsed near the Emmitsburg Road by heavy fire from the front and flank.

July 4. After night withdrew and began the march to Hagerstown.

Present about 971. Killed 25, wounded 123, missing 60. Total 208.

COMMENTARY

This marker would show the position at which the brigade attacked the center of the Union First Corps from 2 to 3 P.M. on July 1. The brigade was present on the field during the morning's engagement but was held in reserve behind Herr Ridge about ¾ mile to the northwest. On July 2 the brigade was held in reserve ¾ mile west of here. For its movements on July 3 and 4, see No. 173.

A-12 PETTIGREW'S BRIGADE (JULY 1)

Tablet on granite pedestal.
To be located west of South Reynolds Avenue, ⅜ mile south of Chambersburg Pike.

SUGGESTED TEXT

C.S.A. Army of Northern Virginia. Hill's Corps, Heth's Division, Pettigrew's Brigade. 11th, 26th, 47th, 52nd North Carolina Infantry.

July 1. Crossing Willoughby Run at 2 P.M. met the 1st Brigade, 1st Division, First Corps in Reynolds Woods near here and drove it back after a bloody struggle. Advancing to the summit of the ridge encountered and broke a second Union line and was then relieved by troops of Pender's Division.

July 2. Lay in Woods west of the Run. In evening took position on central Seminary Ridge.

July 3. In Longstreet's Assault the Brigade occupied the right center of the Division. The few who reached the line north of the Angle were forced to surrender.

July 4. After night withdrew and began the march to Hagerstown.

Strength about 2584. Killed 190, wounded 915, missing about 300. Total 1405.

COMMENTARY

This marker would show the position at which the brigade attacked

Meredith's and Biddle's brigades from 2 to 3 P.M. on July 1. When Biddle's brigade was forced back from its open position south of this marker, the "Iron Brigade" was finally outflanked and forced from its stronghold in McPherson's Woods. During this combat the 26th North Carolina Regiment lost most of the 588 casualties it suffered during the battle—the highest number of battle losses for any Confederate regiment in any battle.[1] The position at which the 26th North Carolina made its last attack against the "Iron Brigade" in McPherson's Woods is marked by No. 39. The brigade then assaulted the second Union line east of this ridge, but was relieved by Pender's division shortly before 4 P.M. The brigade was present on the field during the morning's engagement but was held in reserve behind Herr Ridge 1½ mile to the northwest. On July 2 the brigade was held in reserve ¾ mile west of here. For its movements on July 3 and 4, see No. 176.

A-13 GARNETT'S BATTALION (July 1)
Tablet on granite pedestal.
To be located south of Chambersburg Pike at Herr Tavern.

SUGGESTED TEXT
C.S.A. Army of Northern Virginia. Hill's Corps, Heth's Division, Garnett's Battalion. Grandy's, Moore's, Lewis' and Maurin's Batteries. Four Napoleons, two 10 pounder Parrotts, seven 3 inch rifles, two 12 pound howitzers.

July 1. The Battalion was at Cashtown when the battle commenced and did not reach the battlefield until early in the afternoon. About 2 P.M. Captain Maurin was sent with six rifled guns to relieve one of Pegram's Batteries near this point, where they were engaged for about an hour until the Union lines began to retire.

July 2, 3, 4. The Battalion was posted at the center of the army's line on Seminary Ridge. The Parrotts and rifles were engaged at different positions. The Napoleons and howitzers were in reserve and not actively engaged at any time. All withdrew from the field on the fourth day but not at the same hour nor by the same route.

Losses. Wounded 5, missing 17. Total 22. Ammunition expended 1000 rounds. Horses killed or disabled 13.

COMMENTARY
This marker would show the position held by 6 rifled guns of the battalion from about 2 to 3 P.M. on July 1. The rest of the battalion was held in reserve north of the Chambersburg Pike about ½ mile west of this marker. For the positions held by the guns of the battalion on July 2, 3 and 4, see No. 177 and the markers of the individual batteries—Nos. 24 (Maurin), 66 (Moore), 73 (Lewis), and 76 (Grandy).

A-14 PERRIN'S BRIGADE (JULY 1)

Tablet on granite pedestal.
To be located west of Seminary Avenue, ⅛ mile north of Fairfield Road.

SUGGESTED TEXT

C.S.A. Army of Northern Virginia. Hill's Corps, Pender's Division, Perrin's Brigade. 1st Rifles, 12th, 13th, 14th Regiments and 1st Provisional South Carolina Infantry.

July 1. Crossed Willoughby Run about 3:30 P.M. with its left in Reynolds Woods and advanced relieving Pettigrew's Brigade. Took a prominent part in the struggle here by which the Union forces were dislodged from Seminary Ridge and pursuing them into the town captured many prisoners. The Rifle regiment was on duty as train guard and not in the battle of this day.

July 2. Supported Artillery south of Fairfield Road. At 6 P.M. advanced a Battalion of sharpshooters which skirmished with the Union outposts until dark. At 10 P.M. took position on Ramseur's right in the Long Lane leading from the town to the Bliss House and Barn.

July 3. In the same position and constantly engaged in skirmishing.

July 4. After night withdrew and began the march to Hagerstown.
Present about 1882. Killed 100, wounded 477. Total 577.

COMMENTARY

This marker would show the position at which the brigade attacked the line held by Biddle's brigade of the Union First Corps at about 4 P.M. on July 1. During the final 200 yards of its charge on this position the brigade did not stop to return the terrific fire that it was receiving.[1] Since Scales' brigade was stalled on the left and Lane's brigade did not advance promptly on the right, this brigade carried the brunt of the division's final charge. When the Union line was broken, the 1st (P.A.) and 14th Regiments led the pursuit into town until they were exhausted and recalled. On the morning of July 2 the brigade was posted in support of the artillery formed on this ridge one half mile to the south. For its movements later in the battle, see No. 180.

A-15 SCALES' BRIGADE (July 1)

Tablet on granite pedestal.
To be located west of Seminary Avenue, ⅛ mile south of Chambersburg Pike.

SUGGESTED TEXT

C.S.A. Army of Northern Virginia. Hill's Corps, Pender's Division, Scales' Brigade. 13th, 16th, 22nd, 34th, 38th North Carolina Infantry.

July 1. Crossed Willoughby Run about 3:30 P.M. relieving Heth's Division and advanced with left flank on Chambersburg Pike; took part in the struggle until it ended. When the Union forces made their final stand here on Seminary Ridge the Brigade charged and aided in

dislodging them but suffered heavy losses. Gen. A.M. Scales was wounded and all the field officers but one were killed or wounded.
July 2. In position on Seminary Ridge with skirmishers out and in flank.
July 3. Supported the right wing of Pettigrew's Division during Longstreet's Assault. Was among the last to retire following the assault.
July 4. After night withdrew and began the march to Hagerstown.
Present about 1405. Killed 102, wounded 323, missing 110. Total 535.

COMMENTARY

This marker would be located 500 yards east of the position at which the brigade attacked Stone's and Meredith's brigades of the Union First Corps at 4 P.M. on July 1. The brigade's line extended from the railroad cut on the left to the Seminary on the right, with its regiments in the following order from north to south—38-13-34-22-16. During this attack the brigade lost heavily in officers and men, including General Scales, who was wounded by a shell 200 or 300 yards west of this marker. At the close of the day's fighting the brigade remained in this area. Late at night it was shifted ¾ mile south along the ridge. For its position on July 2, 3 and 4, see No. 181.

A-16 THOMAS' BRIGADE (July 1)

Tablet on granite pedestal.
To be located north of Chambersburg Pike opposite Herr Tavern.

SUGGESTED TEXT

C.S.A. Army of Northern Virginia. Hill's Corps, Pender's Division, Thomas's Brigade. 14th, 35th, 45th, 49th Georgia Infantry.
July 1. The Brigade formed supporting Pegram's Battalion at this position but was held in reserve and was not engaged. At sunset moved to McMillan's Woods on Seminary Ridge.
July 2. On duty in support of Artillery. At 10 P.M. advancing took position in Long Lane with the left flank in touch with McGowan's Brigade and the right near the Bliss House and Barn.
July 3. Engaged most of the day in severe skirmishing and exposed to a heavy fire of artillery. After dark retired to this Ridge.
July 4. At night withdrew and began the march to Hagerstown.
Present about 1326. Killed 16, wounded 136. Total 152.

COMMENTARY

This marker would show the position held by the brigade during the afternoon of July 1. Its line extended north from here along the ridge to Willoughby Run. For the brigade's position on July 2-4, see No. 182.

A-17 LONG LANE

Cast iron tablet.
To be located south of Long Lane, ⅜ mile east of Emmitsburg Road.

SUGGESTED TEXT

C.S.A. Army of Northern Virginia. Ewell's Corps, Rodes's Division and Hill's Corps, Pender's Division.

July 2. At dusk Thomas' and Perrin's Brigades of Pender's Division and Ramseur's, Iverson's and Dole's Brigades of Rodes's Division occupied a sunken farm lane that extended northwest from here to the town. Rodes's brigades moved forward to attack Cemetery Hill at 9 P.M. but the attack was canceled.

July 3. This line was held all day under heavy fire of Union skirmishers and artillery on Cemetery Hill. Units withdrew in evening to Seminary Ridge.

COMMENTARY

At the time of the battle Long Lane (100 yards west) extended from near this point northwesterly to the town. Portions of this farm road were sunken and furnished a natural defensive position. At dusk on July 2 this line was occupied by Thomas' and Perrin's brigades of Pender's division and Ramseur's, Iverson's and Doles' brigades of Rodes' division. Rodes' brigades moved forward to assault Cemetery Hill at 9 P.M. but the attack was canceled. These units remained in this position on July 3 under heavy fire of Union skirmishers and artillery from Cemetery Hill. They withdrew at evening to Seminary Ridge.

A-18 BLISS HOUSE AND BARN

Cast iron marker.
To be located south of Long Lane, ⅜ mile east of Emmitsburg Road.

SUGGESTED TEXT

In the field to the south was located the Bliss House and its Stone Barn. These served as a base for Confederate sharpshooters on July 2 and 3 until they were captured and burned by Union troops late on the morning of the 3rd.

COMMENTARY

One quarter mile south of here was located the Bliss farm house with its stone barn. The barn was used as a fortress by Confederate sharpshooters on July 2 and 3. Skirmishing was especially sharp in this sector on the morning of July 3. At 7:30 A.M. five companies of the 12th New Jersey briefly captured the barn. Later in the morning the barn and house were captured and burned by four companies of the 14th Connecticut. Late in the afternoon the position was again attacked by the 1st Delaware.

A-19 ROSE FARM

Cast iron tablet.
To be located south of Wheatfield Road, ⅛ mile east of Emmitsburg Road.

SUGGESTED TEXT

To the south lies the Rose Farm, over which Kershaw's Brigade and other Confederate troops advanced to battle late on the afternoon of July 2. Its buildings were then used as a Hospital.

COMMENTARY

One quarter mile to the south of this marker is the Rose farm, past which Kershaw's brigade advanced under heavy fire about 5:45 P.M. on July 2. Its buildings were then used as a Confederate hospital. The Rose farm house has been restored, but the shell-marked walls of the barn were knocked down in 1984-1985.

Appendices

APPENDIX I:
Monuments by Date

Dedication dates are given where known. Otherwise erection dates are used.

November 19, 1886
1st Maryland Infantry (No. 32)
1st Maryland Infantry, Left Flank (No. 33)
1st Maryland Infantry, Right Flank (No. 34)
1st Maryland Infantry (Advance Position) (No. 35)
Early 1888
Armistead Marker (No. 124)
June 2, 1892
High Water Mark Monument (No. 197)
1898-1899
Taylor's (Va.) Battery (No. 91)
Ashland (Va.) Artillery (Woolfolk's Battery) (No. 52)
Parker's (Va.) Battery (No. 78)
Bedford (Va.) Artillery (Jordan's Battery) (No. 53)
Battery "A" First North Carolina Artillery (Manly's Battery) (No. 42)
Pulaski (Ga.) Artillery (Fraser's Battery) (No. 18)
First Richmond (Va.) Howitzers (McCarthy's Battery) (No. 82)
Troup (Ga.) Artillery (First Section) (Carlton's Battery) (No. 22)
Troup (Ga.) Artillery (Second Section) (Carlton's Battery) (No. 23)
German (S.C.) Artillery (Bachman's Battery) (No. 46)
Palmetto (S.C.) Light Artillery (Garden's Battery) (No. 47)
Branch (N.C.) Artillery (Latham's Battery) (No. 40)
Rowan (N.C.) Artillery (Reilly's Battery) (No. 43)
Rowan (N.C.) Artillery (Section) (Reilly's Battery) (No. 44)
M. Johnson's (Va.) Battery (West Position) (No. 68)
M. Johnson's (Va.) Battery (East Position) (No. 69)
Danville (Va.) Artillery (West Position) (Rice's Battery) (No. 60)
Danville (Va.) Artillery (East Position) (Rice's Battery) (No. 61)
Hardaway (Ala.) Artillery (Hurt's Battery) (No. 14)
Second Rockbridge (Va.) Artillery (Wallace's Battery) (No. 87)
Powhaten (Va.) Artillery (Cunningham's Battery) (No. 79)
Second Richmond (Va.) Howitzers (West Position) (Watson's Battery) (No. 83)
Second Richmond (Va.) Howitzers (East Position) (Watson's Battery) (No. 84)

Third Richmond (Va.) Howitzers (Smith's Battery) (No. 85)
1899 (Replaced 1910-1911)
Semmes' Brigade (No. 117)
Kershaw's Brigade (No. 114)
G.T. Anderson's Brigade (No. 100)
J.B. Robertson's Brigade (No. 106)
Benning's Brigade (No. 102)
Law's Brigade (No. 104)
Hays' Brigade (No. 136)
Gordon's Brigade (July 2 and 3) (No. 135)
Hoke's Brigade (No. 137)
J. Jones' Brigade (No. 141)
Nicholls' Brigade (No. 142)
O'Neal's Brigade (July 3) (No. 153)
Daniel's Brigade (July 3) (No. 149)
Steuart's Brigade (No. 143)
Walker's Brigade (No. 144)
Smith's Brigade (No. 138)
November 1, 1900
Right of the Army of Northern Virginia (No. 93)
1901-1902 (Replaced 1910-1911)
Barksdale's Brigade (No. 112)
Wofford's Brigade (No. 119)
Kemper's Brigade (No. 126)
R.B. Garnett's Brigade (No. 125)
Armistead's Brigade (No. 123)
Wilcox's Brigade (No. 165)
Perry's Brigade (No. 162)
Wright's Brigade (No. 167)
Posey's Brigade (No. 164)
Mahone's Brigade (No. 161)
Archer's Brigade (July 3) (No. 172)
Pettigrew's Brigade (No. 176)
Davis' Brigade (No. 175)
Brockenbrough's Brigade (No. 173)
Scales' Brigade (No. 181)
J.H. Lane's Brigade (No. 179)
Perrin's Brigade (No. 180)
Thomas' Brigade (No. 182)
1901-1902
Madison (La.) Light Artillery (Moody's Battery) (No. 27)
Brooks (S.C.) Artillery (Rhett's Battery) (No. 45)
3rd Company Washington (La.) Artillery (Miller's Battery) (No. 30)
1st Company Washington (La.) Artillery (Squires' Battery) (No. 28)
2nd Company Washington (La.) Artillery (Richardson's Battery) (No. 29)
4th Company Washington (La.) Artillery (Norcom's Battery) (No. 31)
Fauquier (Va.) Artillery (Stribling's Battery) (No. 62)

Hampden (Va.) Artillery (Caskie's Battery) (No. 65)
Richmond (Va.) Fayette Artillery (Macon's Battery) (No. 81)
Blount's (Va.) Battery (No. 54)
Madison (Miss.) Light Artillery (Ward's Battery) (No. 38)
Brooke's (Va.) Battery (No. 56)
Albemarle (Va.) Artillery (Wyatt's Battery) (No. 49)
Charlotte (N.C.) Artillery (J. Graham's Battery) (No. 41)
Company "B" Sumter (Ga.) Artillery (Patterson's Battery) (No. 20)
Company "C" Sumter (Ga.) Artillery (Wingfield's Battery) (No. 21)
Company "A" Sumter (Ga.) Artillery (Ross' Battery) (No. 19)
Fredericksburg (Va.) Artillery (Marye's Battery) (No. 64)
Crenshaw's (Va.) Battery (No. 59)
Pee Dee (S.C.) Artillery (Zimmerman's Battery) (No. 48)
Purcell (Va.) Artillery (McGraw's Battery) (No. 80)
Letcher (Va.) Artillery (Brander's Battery) (No. 69)
Norfolk (Va.) Light Artillery Blues (Grandy's Battery) (No. 76)
Huger (Va.) Artillery (Moore's Battery) (No. 66)
Lewis' (Va.) Battery (No. 73)
Donaldsonville (La.) Artillery (Maurin's Battery) (No. 24)
Salem (Va.) Artillery (July 3) (C. Griffin's Battery) (No. 89)

Ca. 1903 (Replaced 1910-1911)
Dance's Battalion (No. 131)
Nelson's Battalion (No. 132)
McIntosh's Battalion (No. 158)
J. Garnett's Battalion (No. 177)
Pegram's Battalion (No. 159)
John Lane's Battalion (No. 169)
Poague's Battalion (No. 183)
Dearing's Battalion (No. 127)
Alexander's Battalion (No. 97)
Eshleman's Battalion (No. 98)
Cabell's Battalion (No. 121)
Henry's Battalion (No. 109)

Ca. 1903
McLaws' and Pickett's Divisions (No. 111)
Ewell's Corps (July 4) (No. 129)
Rodes' Breastworks on Seminary Ridge (No. 147)

1903 (Taken down in 1974)
Confederate Itinerary Tablet, June 26, 1863 (No. X-1)
Confederate Itinerary Tablet, June 27, 1863 (No. X-2)
Confederate Itinerary Tablet, June 28, 1863 (No. X-3)
Confederate Itinerary Tablet, June 29, 1863 (No. X-4)
Confederate Itinerary Tablet, June 30, 1863 (No. X-5)
Confederate Itinerary Tablet, July 1, 1863 (No. X-6)
Confederate Itinerary Tablet, July 2, 1863 (No. X-7)
Confederate Itinerary Tablet, July 3, 1863 (No. X-8)
Confederate Itinerary Tablet, July 4, 1863 (No. X-9)

Confederate Itinerary Tablet, July 5, 1863 (No. X-10)

March 4, 1904

4th Alabama Infantry (No. 13)

1905 (Replaced 1910-1911)

Ramseur's Brigade (No. 154)

Daniel's Brigade (July 1) (No. 148)

Iverson's Brigade (No. 151)

O'Neal's Brigade (July 1) (No. 152)

Doles' Brigade (No. 150)

Latimer's Battalion (No. 145)

1905

Chesapeake (Md.) Artillery (Brown's Battery) (No. 36)

Alleghany (Va.) Artillery (Carpenter's Battery) (No. 50)

First Maryland Battery (Dement's Battery) (No. 37)

Lee (Va.) Artillery (Raine's Battery) (No. 71)

Fluvanna (Va.) Artillery (Massie's Battery) (No. 63)

Amherst (Va.) Artillery (Kirkpatrick's Battery) (No. 51)

Milledge's (Ga.) Battery (No. 17)

First Rockbridge (Va.) Artillery (A. Graham's Battery) (No. 86)

1906 (Replaced 1910-1911)

F. Lee's Brigade (No. 191)

Hampton's Brigade (No. 187)

Chambliss' Brigade (No. 186)

Jenkins' Brigade (No. 188)

Beckham's Battalion (No. 194)

T. Carter's Battalion (No. 155)

1906

Louisiana Guard Artillery (July 3) (Green's Battery) (No. 26)

1st Stuart (Va.) Horse Artillery (Breathed's Battery) (No. 55)

2nd Stuart (Va.) Horse Artillery (McGregor's Battery) (No. 74)

Jackson's (Va.) Battery (No. 67)

Orange (Va.) Artillery (Fry's Battery) (No. 77)

King William (Va.) Artillery (W. Carter's Battery) (No. 70)

Morris (Va.) Artillery (Page's Battery) (No. 75)

Jeff Davis (Ala.) Artillery (Reese's Battery) (No. 16)

Ca. 1906

Hardaway (Ala.) Artillery (Whitworth Section) (Hurt's Battery) (No. 15)

Salem (Va.) Artillery (July 2) (C. Griffin's Battery) (No. 88)

Poague's Howitzers (No. 184)

Gordon's Brigade (July 1) (No. 134)

1906-1907 (Replaced 1910-1911)

Archer's Brigade (July 1) (No. 171)

1907 (Replaced 1910-1911)

Davis' Brigade (July 1) (No. 174)

H. Jones' Battalion (No. 139)

1907

Charlottesville (Va.) Artillery (Carrington's Battery) (No. 57)

Courtney (Va.) Artillery (Tanner's Battery) (No. 58)
Louisiana Guard Artillery (July 3) (Green's Battery) (No. 26)
Staunton (Va.) Artillery (Garber's Battery) (No. 90)
Longstreet's Corps (No. 95)
Ewell's Corps (No. 128)
Hill's Corps (No. 156)
McLaws' Division (No. 110)

1907-1908

G.T. Anderson's Brigade (Advance Position) (No. 101)
Barksdale's Brigade (Advance Position) (No. 113)
Benning's Brigade (Advance Position) (No. 103)
Kershaw's Brigade (Advance Position) (No. 115)
J.B. Robertson's Brigade (Advance Position) (No. 107)
Semmes' Brigade (Advance Position) (No. 118)
Perry's Brigade (Advance Position) (No. 163)
Wilcox's Brigade (Advance Position) (No. 166)
Wright's Brigade (Advance Position) (No. 168)
Law's Brigade (Advance Position) (No. 105)
Wofford's Brigade (Advance Position) (No. 120)

Summer 1908

Army of Northern Virginia (No. 92)

1909

R.H. Anderson's Division (No. 160)
Early's Division (No. 133)
Heth's Division (No. 170)
Hood's Division (No. 99)
Johnson's Division (No. 140)
Pender's Division (No. 178)
Pickett's Division (No. 122)
Rodes' Division (No. 146)

1910-1911

Imboden's Brigade (No. 195)
B.H. Robertson's Brigade (No. 192)
W.E. Jones' Brigade (No. 189)

September 27, 1913

Hood's Texas Brigade Monument (No. 108)

1913

Stuart's Division (No. 185)

June 8, 1917

Virginia Monument (No. 11)

1920-1921

Lee's Headquarters (No. 94)
Longstreet's Headquarters (No. 96)
Ewell's Headquarters (No. 130)
Hill's Headquarters (No. 156)

July 3, 1929

North Carolina Monument (No. 7)

November 12, 1933
Alabama Monument (No. 1)
July 3, 1938
Eternal Light Peace Memorial (No. 199)
September 21, 1961
Georgia Monument (No. 4)
July 2, 1963
South Carolina Monument (No. 8)
July 3, 1963
Florida Memorial (No. 3)
September 1964
Texas Monument (No. 10)
August 25, 1965
Memorial to the Soldiers and Sailors of the Confederacy (No.12)
June 18, 1966
Arkansas Memorial (No. 2)
November 21, 1970
Kershaw's Brigade Marker (No. 116)
June 11, 1971
Louisiana Memorial (No. 5)
October 19, 1973
Mississippi Monument (No. 6)
July 3, 1982
Tennessee Monument (No. 9)
October 5, 1985
26th North Carolina Infantry (No. 39)
October 22, 1988
43rd North Crolina Infantry (No. 201)
August 21, 1993
Masonic Memorial (No. 202)
November 13, 1994
Maryland Memorial (No. 203)
Unknown Date (ca. 1906-1910)
Imboden's Brigade (Cashtown) (No. 196)
B.H. Robertson's Brigade (Orrtanna) (No. 193)
W.E. Jones' Brigade (Orrtanna) (No. 190)
Unknown Date
McPherson Barn Hospital (No. 198)
Spangler's Spring (No. 200)

APPENDIX II:
Designers and Sculptors of the Monuments

Bachelder, John B. Designer of High Water Mark Monument (No. 197).

Borglum, Gutzon. Sculptor of North Carolina Monument (No. 7).

Cret, Paul Phillipe. Architect of Eternal Peace Light Memorial (No. 199).

Dacy, William Henry. Architect of Virginia Monument (No. 11).

DeLue, Donald. Sculptor of Louisiana Memorial (No. 5), Mississippi Monument (No. 6), and Memorial to the Soldiers and Sailors of the Confederacy (No. 12).

Hill, J.B. Designer of Florida Memorial (No. 3) and South Carolina Monument (No. 8).

Lawrie, Lee. Sculptor of Eternal Light Peace Memorial (No. 199).

Ludtke, Lawrence M. Sculptor of Maryland Memorial (No. 203).

Sellers, Harry. Designer of Georgia Monument (No. 4).

Sievers, F. William. Sculptor of Virginia Monument (No. 11).

Tunison, Ron. Sculptor of the Masonic Memorial (No. 202).

Urner, Joseph W. Sculptor of Alabama Monument (No. 1).

APPENDIX III:
Number of Monuments by State

No. of
Monts. State (Monument Numbers)

61   **VIRGINIA** (Nos. 11, 49, 50, 51, 52, 53, 54, 55, 56, 57, 58, 59, 60, 61, 62, 63, 64, 65, 66, 67, 68, 69, 70, 71, 72, 73, 74, 75, 76, 77, 78, 79, 80, 81, 82, 83, 84, 85, 86, 87, 88, 89, 90, 91, 123, 124, 125, 126, 138, 141, 143, 144, 161, 173, 186, 188, 189, 190, 191, 195, 196; also A-3, A-4, A-11)

23   **GEORGIA** (Nos. 4, 17, 18, 19, 20, 21, 22, 23, 100, 101, 102, 103, 117, 118, 119, 120, 134, 135, 150, 167, 168, 182, 187; also A-16)

23   **NORTH CAROLINA** (Nos. 7, 39, 40, 41, 42, 43, 44, 137, 143, 148, 149, 151, 154, 174, 175, 176, 179, 181, 186, 187, 192, 193, 201; also A-8, A-12, A-15)

13   **ALABAMA** (Nos. 1, 13, 14, 15, 16, 104, 105, 152, 153, 165, 166, 171, 172)

11   **LOUISIANA** (Nos. 5, 24, 25, 26, 27, 28, 29, 30, 31, 136, 142; also A-7)

10   **SOUTH CAROLINA** (Nos. 8, 45, 46, 47, 48, 114, 115, 116, 180, 187; also A-2, A-14)

9   **MARYLAND** (Nos. 32, 33, 34, 35, 36, 37, 143, 191, 203; also A-1, A-20)

8   **MISSISSIPPI** (Nos. 6, 38, 112, 113, 164, 174, 175, 187)

4   **ARKANSAS** (Nos. 2, 106, 107, 108)

4   **TEXAS** (Nos. 10, 106, 107, 108)

3   **FLORIDA** (Nos. 3, 162, 163)

3   **TENNESSEE** (Nos. 10, 106, 107, 108)

APPENDIX IV:
Organization of The Army of Northern Virginia at Gettysburg

ARMY OF NORTHERN VIRGINIA (Nos. 92, 93, 94)—Gen. Robert E. Lee
FIRST ARMY CORPS (Nos. 95, 96)—Lieut. Gen. James Longstreet
RESERVE ARTILLERY—Col. J.B. Walton
Alexander's Battalion (No. 97)—Col. E.P. Alexander
  Madison (La.) Light Artillery (Moody's Battery) (No. 27)
  Brooks (S.C.) Light Artillery (Rhett's Battery) (No. 45)
  Ashland (Va.) Artillery (Woolfolk's Battery) (No. 52)
  Bedford (Va.) Artillery (Jordan's Battery) (No. 53)
  Parker's (Va.) Battery (No. 78)
  Taylor's (Va.) Battery (No. 91)
Eshleman's Battalion (Washington La. Artillery) (No. 98)—Maj. B.F. Eshleman
  1st Company (Squires' Battery) (No. 28)
  2nd Company (Richardson's Battery) (No. 29)
  3rd Company (Miller's Battery) (No. 30)
  4th Company (Norcom's Battery) (No. 31)
HOOD'S DIVISION (No. 99)—Maj. Gen. John B. Hood (w)
G.T. Anderson's Brigade (Nos. 100, 101)—Brig. Gen. George T. Anderson (w)
  7 Ga.
  8 Ga.
  9 Ga.
  11 Ga.
  59 Ga.
Benning's Brigade (Nos. 102, 103)—Brig. Gen. Henry L. Benning
  2 Ga.
  15 Ga.
  17 Ga.
  20 Ga.
Law's Brigade (Nos. 104, 105)—Brig. Gen. E.M. Law
  4 Ala.(No. 13)
  15 Ala.
  44 Ala.
  47 Ala.
  48 Ala.
J.B. Robertson's Brigade (Nos. 106, 107, 108)—Brig. Gen. Jerome B. Robertson (w)
  3 Ark.
  1 Tex.
  4 Tex.
  5 Tex.
Henry's Battalion (No. 109)—Maj. M.W. Henry
  Branch (N.C.) Artillery (Latham's Battery) (No. 40)

German (S.C.) Artillery (Bachman's Battery) (No. 46)
Palmetto (S.C.) Light Artillery (Garden's Battery) (No. 47)
Rowan (N.C.) Artillery (Reilly's Battery) (Nos. 43, 44)
MCLAWS' DIVISION (Nos. 110, 111)—Maj. Gen. Lafayette McLaws
Barksdale's Brigade (Nos. 112, 113)—Brig. Gen. William Barksdale (mw)
  13 Miss.
  17 Miss.
  18 Miss.
  21 Miss.
Kershaw's Brigade (Nos. 114, 115, 116)—Brig. Gen. Joseph B. Kershaw
  2 S.C.
  3 S.C.
  7 S.C.
  8 S.C.
  15 S.C.
  3 S.C. Batn.
Semmes' Brigade (Nos. 117, 118)—Brig. Gen. Paul J. Semmes (mw)
  10 Ga.
  50 Ga.
  51 Ga.
  53 Ga.
Wofford's Brigade (Nos. 119, 120)—Brig. Gen. William T. Wofford
  16 Ga.
  18 Ga.
  24 Ga.
  Cobb's (Ga.) Legion
  Phillips' (Ga.) Legion
Cabell's Battalion (No. 121)—Col. Henry C. Cabell
  Battery "A" First North Carolina Artillery (Manly's Battery) (No. 42)
  Pulaski (Ga.) Artillery (Fraser's Battery) (No. 18)
  First Richmond (Va.) Howitzers (McCarthy's Battery) (No. 82)
  Troup (Ga.) Artillery (Carlton's Battery) (Nos. 22, 23)
PICKETT'S DIVISION (Nos. 111, 122)—Maj. Gen. George E. Pickett
Armistead's Brigade (Nos. 123, 124, 202)—Brig. Gen. Lewis A. Armistead (k)
  9 Va.
  14 Va.
  38 Va.
  53 Va.
  57 Va.
R.B. Garnett's Brigade (No. 125)—Brig. Gen. Richard B. Garnett (k)
  8 Va.
  18 Va.
  19 Va.
  28 Va.
  56 Va.
Kemper's Brigade (No. 126)—Brig. Gen. James L. Kemper (w and c)
  1 Va.

3 Va.
7 Va.
11 Va.
24 Va.
Dearing's Battalion (No. 127)—Maj. James Dearing
 Fauquier (Va.) Artillery (Stribling's Battery) (No. 62)
 Hampden (Va.) Artillery (Caskie's Battery) (No. 65)
 Richmond (Va.) Fayette Artillery (Macon's Battery) (No. 81)
 Blount's (Va.) Battery (No. 54)
SECOND ARMY CORPS (Nos. 128, 129, 130)—Lieut. Gen. Richard S. Ewell
RESERVE ARTILLERY—Col. J. Thompson Brown
Dance's (Brown's) Battalion (No. 131)—Capt. Willis J. Dance
 Second Richmond (Va.) Howitzers (Watson's Battery) (Nos. 83, 84)
 Third Richmond (Va.) Howitzers (Smith's Battery) (No. 85)
 Powhaten (Va.) Artillery (Cunningham's Battery) (No. 79)
 First Rockbridge (Va.) Artillery (A. Graham's Battery) (No. 86)
 Salem (Va.) Artillery (C. Griffin's Battery) (Nos. 88, 89)
Nelson's Battalion (No. 132)—Lieut. Col. William Nelson
 Amherst (Va.) Artillery (Kirkpatrick's Battery) (No. 51)
 Fluvanna (Va.) Artillery (Massie's Battery) (No. 63)
 Milledge's (Ga.) Battery (No. 17)
EARLY'S DIVISION (No. 133)—Maj. Gen. Jubal A. Early
Gordon's Brigade (Nos. 134, 135)—Brig. Gen. John B. Gordon
 13 Ga.
 26 Ga.
 31 Ga.
 38 Ga.
 60 Ga.
 61 Ga.
Hays' Brigade (Nos. 136, A-7)—Brig. Gen. Harry T. Hays
 5 La.
 6 La.
 7 La.
 8 La.
 9 La.
Hoke's (Avery's) Brigade (Nos. 137, A-8)—Col. Isaac E. Avery (mw)
 6 N.C.
 21 N.C.
 57 N.C.
Smith's Brigade (No. 138)—Brig. Gen. William Smith
 31 Va.
 49 Va.
 52 Va.
H. Jones' Battalion (No. 139)—Lieut. Col. H.P. Jones
 Charlottesville (Va.) Artillery (Carrington's Battery) (No. 57)
 Courtney (Va.) Artillery (Tanner's Battery) (No. 58)
 Louisiana Guard Artillery (Green's Battery) (Nos. 25, 26)

Staunton (Va.) Artillery (Garber's Battery) (No. 90)
JOHNSON'S DIVISION (No. 140)—Maj. Gen. Edward Johnson
J. Jones' Brigade (No. 141)—Brig. Gen. John M. Jones (w)
  21 Va.
  25 Va.
  42 Va.
  44 Va.
  48 Va.
  50 Va.
Nicholls' (Williams') Brigade (No. 142)—Col. J.M. Williams
  1 La.
  2 La.
  10 La.
  14 La.
  15 La.
Steuart's Brigade (No. 143)—Brig. Gen. George H. Steuart
  1 Md. Batn. (Nos. 32, 33, 34, 35, 203)
  1 N.C.
  3 N.C.
  10 Va.
  23 Va.
  37 Va.
Walker's ("Stonewall") Brigade (No. 144)—Brig. Gen. James A. Walker
  2 Va.
  4 Va.
  5 Va.
  27 Va.
  33 Va.
Latimer's Battalion (No. 145)—Maj. J.W. Latimer (mw)
  First Maryland Battery (Dement's) (No. 37)
  Allegheny (Va.) Artillery (Carpenter's Battery) (No. 50)
  Chesapeake (Md.) Artillery (Brown's Battery) (No. 36)
  Lee (Va.) Artillery (Raine's Battery) (No. 71)
RODES' DIVISION (Nos. 146, 147)—Maj. Gen. Robert E. Rodes
Daniel's Brigade (No. 148, 149, 201)—Brig. Gen. Junius Daniel
  32 N.C.
  43 N.C.
  45 N.C.
  53 N.C.
  2 N.C. Batn.
Doles' Brigade (No. 150)—Brig. Gen. George Doles
  4 Ga.
  12 Ga.
  21 Ga.
  44 Ga.
Iverson's Brigade (No. 151)—Brig. Gen. Alfred Iverson
  5 N.C.

12 N.C.
20 N.C.
23 N.C.
O'Neal's Brigade (Nos. 152, 153)—Col. Edward A. O'Neal
3 Ala.
5 Ala.
6 Ala.
12 Ala.
26 Ala.
Ramseur's Brigade (No. 154)—Brig. Gen. Stephen D. Ramseur
2 N.C.
4 N.C.
14 N.C.
30 N.C.
T. Carter's Battalion (No. 155)—Lieut. Col. Thomas H. Carter
Jeff Davis (Ala.) Artillery (Reese's Battery) No. 16
King William (Va.) Artillery (W. Carter's Battery) (No. 70)
Morris (Va.) Artillery (Page's Battery) (No. 75)
Orange (Va.) Artillery (Fry's Battery) (No. 77)
THIRD ARMY CORPS (Nos. 156, 157)—Lieut. Gen. A.P. Hill
RESERVE ARTILLERY- Col. R. Lindsay Walker
McIntosh's Battalion (Nos. 158, A-9)—Maj. D.G. McIntosh
Hardaway (Ala.) Artillery (Hurt's Battery) (Nos. 14, 15)
Danville (Va.) Artillery (Rice's Battery) (Nos. 60, 61)
Second Rockbridge (Va.) Artillery (Wallace's Battery) (No. 87)
M. Johnson's (Va.) Battery (Nos. 68, 69)
Pegram's Battalion (Nos. 159, A-10)—Maj. W.J. Pegram
Pee Dee (S.C.) Artillery (Zimmerman's Battery) (No. 48)
Crenshaw's (Va.) Battery (No. 59)
Fredericksburg (Va.) Artillery (Marye's Battery) (No. 64)
Letcher (Va.) Artillery (Brander's Battery) (No. 72)
Purcell (Va.) Artillery (McGraw's Battery) (No. 80)
R.H. ANDERSON'S DIVISION (No. 160)—Maj. Gen. Richard H. Anderson
Mahone's Brigade (No. 161)- Brig. Gen. William Mahone
6 Va.
12 Va.
16 Va.
41 Va.
61 Va.
Perry's (Lang's) Brigade (Nos. 162, 163)—Col. David Lang
2 Fla.
5 Fla.
8 Fla.
Posey's Brigade (No. 164)—Brig. Gen. Carnot Posey
12 Miss.
16 Miss.
19 Miss.

48 Miss.

Wilcox's Brigade (Nos. 165, 166)—Brig. Gen. Cadmus M. Wilcox
  8 Ala.
  9 Ala.
  10 Ala.
  11 Ala.
  14 Ala.
Wright's Brigade (Nos. 167, 168)—Brig. Gen. Ambrose R. Wright
  3 Ga.
  22 Ga.
  48 Ga.
  2 Ga. Batn.
John Lane's Battalion (Sumter Ga. Artillery) (No. 169)—Maj. John Lane
  Company "A" (Ross' Battery) (No. 19)
  Company "B" (Patterson's Battery) (No. 20)
  Company "C" (Springfield Battery) (No. 21)
HETH'S DIVISION (No. 170)—Maj. Gen. Henry Heth (w) Archer's Brigade
  (Nos. 171, 172)—Brig. Gen. James J. Archer
  13 Ala.
  5 Ala. Batn.
  1 Tenn. (P.A.)
  7 Tenn.
  14 Tenn.
Brockenbrough's Brigade (Nos. 173, A-11)—Col. J.M. Brockenbrough
  40 Va.
  47 Va.
  55 Va.
  22 Va. Batn.
Davis' Brigade (Nos. 174, 175)—Brig. Gen. Joseph R. Davis
  2 Miss.
  11 Miss.
  42 Miss.
  55 N.C.
Pettigrew's Brigade (Nos. 176, A-12)—Brig. Gen. J. Johnston Pettigrew
  11 N.C.
  26 N.C. (No. 39)
  47 N.C.
  52 N.C.
J. Garnett's Battalion (Nos. 177, A-13)—Lieut. Col. John J. Garnett
  Donaldsonville (La.) Artillery (Maurin's Battery) (No. 24)
  Huger (Va.) Artillery (Moore's Battery) (No. 66)
  Lewis (Va.) Artillery (Lewis' Battery) (No. 73)
  Norfolk (Va.) Light Artillery Blues (Grandy's Battery) (No. 76)
PENDER'S Division (No. 178)—Maj. Gen. William D. Pender (mw)
J.H. Lane's Brigade (No. 179)—Brig. Gen. James H. Lane
  7 N.C.
  18 N.C.

28 N.C.
33 N.C.
37 N.C.
Perrin's (McGowan's) Brigade (Nos. 180, A-14)—Col. Abner Perrin
1 S.C. (P.A.)
1 S.C. Rifles
12 S.C.
13 S.C.
14 S.C.
Scales' Brigade (Nos. 181, A-15)—Brig. Gen. Alfred M. Scales (w)
13 N.C.
16 N.C.
22 N.C.
34 N.C.
38 N.C.
Thomas' Brigade (Nos. 182, A-16)—Brig. Gen. Edward L. Thomas
14 Ga.
35 Ga.
45 Ga.
49 Ga.
Poague's Battalion (Nos. 183, 184)—Maj. William T. Poague
Albemarle (Va.) Artillery (Wyatt's Battery) (No. 49)
Charlotte (N.C.) Artillery (J. Graham's Battery) (No. 41)
Madison (Miss.) Light Artillery (Ward's Battery) (No. 38)
Brooke's (Va.) Battery (No. 56)
STUART'S DIVISION (No. 185)—Maj. Gen. James E.B. Stuart
Chambliss' (W. Lee's) Brigade (No. 186)—Col. John R. Chambliss
2 N.C. Cav.
9 Va. Cav.
10 Va. Cav.
13 Va. Cav.
Hampton's Brigade (No. 187)—Brig. Gen. Wade Hampton (w)
1 N.C. Cav.
1 S.C. Cav.
2 S.C. Cav.
Cobb's (Ga.) Legion Cav.
Phillips' (Ga.) Legion (Cav.)
Jenkins' Brigade (No. 188)—Brig. Gen. Albert G. Jenkins (w)
14 Va. Cav.
16 Va. Cav.
17 Va. Cav.
34 Va. Cav. Batn.
36 Va. Cav. Batn.
Jackson's (Va.) Battery (No. 67)
W.E. Jones' Brigade (Nos. 189, 190)—Brig. Gen. William E. Jones
6 Va. Cav.
7 Va. Cav.

11 Va. Cav.

35 Va. Cav. Batn.

F. Lee's Brigade (No. 191)—Brig. Gen. Fitzhugh Lee

1 Md. Cav. Batn.

1 Va. Cav.

2 Va. Cav.

3 Va. Cav.

4 Va. Cav.

5 Va. Cav.

B.H. Robertson's Brigade (Nos. 192, 193)—Brig. Gen. Beverly H. Robertson

4 N.C. Cav.

5 N.C. Cav.

Beckham's Battalion (No. 194)—Maj. R.F. Beckham

1st Stuart (Va.) Horse Artillery (Breathed's Battery) (No. 55)

Ashby (Va.) Horse Artillery (Chew's Battery) (No. A-3)

Second Baltimore (Md.) Battery (W. Griffin's) (No. A-1)

Washington (S.C.) Artillery (Hart's Battery) (No. A-2)

2nd Stuart (Va.) Horse Artillery (McGregor's Battery) (No. 74)

Lynchburg (Va.) Horse Artillery (Moorman's Battery) (No. A-4)

Imboden's Brigade (Nos. 195, 196)—Brig. Gen. John D. Imboden

18 Va. Cav.

62 Va.

Va. Partisan Rangers

McClanahan's (Va.) Battery

Notes

Confederate Monuments at Gettysburg

1. Jack McLaughlin, *Gettysburg: The Long Encampment* (New York: Bonanza, 1963), pp. 205-206.
2. W.W. Goldsborough, *The Maryland Line in the Confederate Army* (1900; reprint Gaithersburg, Md.: Butternut Press, 1983), p. 89 note.
3. Notebooks titled "Position of Troops," Gettysburg National Military Park Library.
4. John Vanderslice, *Gettysburg Then and Now* (1899; reprint Dayton, Ohio: Morningside Press, 1983), p. 491.
5. *Annual Reports of the Gettysburg National Military Park Commission to the Secretary of War, 1893-1904* (Washington: GPO, 1905), p. 23.
6. The cast iron narrative tablets stand 4 feet 4 inches high and measure 3 feet 8 1/2 inches by 3 feet. Their inscriptions were written by Park Commissioners William Robbins and C.A. Richardson with the approval of John P. Nicholson. They were cast by Calvin Gilbert of Gettysburg from iron obtained by melting down surplus cannons owned by the GBMA.
7. *Annual Reports of the Gettysburg National Military Park Commission to the Secretary of War, 1893-1904* (Washington: GPO, 1905), p.30.
8. *Ibid.*
9. Date and issue of article uncertain. Copy cited was found in a scrapbook in the Gettysburg National Military Park Library.
10. W.M. Robbins quoting C.A. Richardson in Sept. 27, 1902 letter to J.P. Nicholson, Gettysburg National Military Park Library.
11. Oates to W.M. Robbins in Oct. 2, 1902 letter, Gettysburg National Military Park Library.
12. W.M. Robbins to Oates in Dec. 16, 1902 letter, Gettysburg National Military Park Library.
13. Vanderslice, p. 383.
14. Oates to J.P. Nicholson in letter of March 1, 1905, Gettysburg National Military Park Library.
15. Letter in Gettysburg National Military Park Library. Hought neglects to mention the 1st (2nd) Maryland Infantry marker (No. 32).
16. The brigade tablets cost $115 each. The bronze tablets measure 3 feet 8 inches by 3 feet 4 inches and were cast by Albert Russell Sons and Company. The pedestals, which were made by the Van Amringe Granite Company, are 5 feet 4 inches high with a base circumference of 6 feet 4 inches. They rest on concrete and rubble foundations set by Charles Kappes of Gettysburg in 1910-1911.
17. The original iron tablet for Law's brigade contained the following sentence at the end of its July 3rd entry; it was dropped from the bronze

replacement tablet, probably because it was inaccurate: "At 11 P.M. the brigade took position near here." See photo 30 of the 1899 *Annual Report of the Gettysburg National Military Park Commission to the Secretary of War.* The only evidence of the texts of the replaced iron brigade tablets are the few photos of them in the annual Park Commission reports.

18. The three corps and ten division tablets each consist of a bronze tablet attached to a granite monolith. They were set up by the Van Amringe Granite Company, and are 7 feet high, 50 inches wide, and 2 feet thick. The bronze for the tablets was obtained by melting down surplus cannons. They were designed by E.N. Cope and were cast by Bureau Brothers; their texts were written by L.L. Lomax and John P. Nicholson. The only difference between the corps and division tablets is that the division tablets have a bronze oval "C.S.A." plate on them; six of these plates have been stolen or lost since the markers were set up.

19. The markers each consist of a 12 pounder bronze cannon cemented into a granite die with the muzzle up. A bronze "C.S.A," plate is attached to the trunions. Two bronze tablets give the officer's name and command, and the exact location of the headquarters. The markers stand 10 feet 6 inches high and their bases measure 3 feet 2 inches by 2 feet 7 inches. Their concrete foundations, which are 4 feet deep, were laid in the fall of 1920.

20. *OR* 27.2.361.

21. *OR* 27.2.448.

22. See tablets for Latham's battery (No. 40), Reilly's battery (No. 43), and Garden's battery (No. 47).

23 Edwin B. Coddington, *The Gettysburg Campaign* (1968; reprint Dayton, Ohio: Morningside Press, 1979), p. 676 n. 24.

24. Hightstown, NJ: Longstreet House, 1995. Confederate strengths are given on pages 118-201.

25. *RSLG*, p. 133

26. *RSLG*, p. 159

27. *OR* 27.2.338-346.

28. See Robert K. Krick's *The Gettysburg Death Roster* (Dayton, Ohio: Morningside Bookshop, 1993), pp. 6-17.

29. See Nos. A-7 to A-16 for suggested markers on the first day's battlefield.

30. On hearing of the possibility of a Virginia monument being erected on the battlefield, the GAR chapter in Harrisburg, Pa., objected because of their strong belief that the South had been wrong to fight the war *(Harrisburg Independent,* Jan. 15, 1903).

31. The Secretary of War's precise words were that, "No monument, Federal or Confederate, had been permitted by the Commission since the organization of that body, to be erected at that place, and that none would be permitted in the future;" *Report of the* (Virginia) *Gettysburg Monument Commission,* n.p., n.d.

32. "Preliminary Report on Non-Ferrous Metals in Gettysburg National Military Park," Gettysburg National Military Park Library.

33. These are Rice's battery (Nos. 60 and 61), M. Johnson's battery (Nos. 68 and 69), and Watson's battery (Nos. 83 and 84).

Texts and Descriptions of Monuments (Notes are arranged by monument number.)

1.
1. Act No. 461, S. 519 of 1927.

2.
1. Act No. 275, Acts of Arkansas, 1965.

3.
1. Laws of Florida, Chapter 63-226, Senate Bill No. 806.
2. Figure is killed and wounded only (*OR* 27.2.333)
3. *RSLG* p. 188.

4.
1. SR No. 27, Act No. 58.
2. Information on the dedication ceremony is drawn from "Dedications of Monuments to Georgia Confederate Dead on National Battlefield Sites," n.p.: no publisher, 1961.

5.
1. Letteer, "Report of the Louisiana Gettysburg Memorial Monument Commission" (n.p., n.d.), pp. 9-10.

6.
1. *The Sculptures at Gettysburg* (n.p.: Eastern Acorn Press, 1982), p. 92.
2. Chapter 516, Laws of Mississippi, House Bill No. 394.
3. Chapter 144, Laws of Mississippi, House Bill No. 926.

7.
1. For example, Wayne Craven in *The Sculptures at Gettysburg* (n.p.: Eastern Acorn Press, 1982), p. 86.
2. George R. Stewart, *Pickett's Charge* (Boston: Houghton-Mifflin Company, 1959), p. 232.
3. "North Carolina at Gettysburg," *Confederate Veteran* XXXVII (1929), p. 287.

9.
1. See *RSLG*, p. 177, 219, 220.

10.
1. For details on the monument's background, see Harold B. Simpson's *Red Granite for Gray Heroes, The Monuments to Hood's Texas Brigade on Eastern Battlefields* (n.p., ca. 1963).

11.
1. "Dedication of the Virginia Memorial at Gettysburg, Friday, June 8, 1917," *Southern Historical Society Papers* XLII (1917), p. 112.
2. Quoted in N.A. Meligakes, *Gettysburg The National Shrine* (Gettysburg: The Bookmart, 1975), p. 24.
3. For the monument's background and dedication ceremonies, see "Dedication of the Virginia Memorial at Gettysburg, Friday, June 8, 1917," *Southern Historical Society Papers* XLII (1917), pp. 83-135.

12.
1. Wayne Craven in *The Sculptures at Gettysburg* (Eastern Acorn Press, 1982), pp. 90-91.

13.
1. *RSLG* p. 132.
2. *OR* 27.2.339.

15.
1. *RSLG* p. 192.
2. *RSLG* p. 192.

16.
1. *RSLG* p. 169.

17.
1. *RSLG* p. 171.

18.
1. *RSLG* p. 142.
2. *OR* 27.2.338.

19.
1. *RSLG* p. 191.

20.
1. *RSLG* p. 191.

21.
1. *RSLG* p. 191.

22.
1. *RSLG* p. 142.

23.
1. *RSLG* p. 142.

24.
1. *RSLG* p. 178.

25.
1. *RSLG* p. 162.

27.
1. *RSLG* p. 149.

28.
1. *RSLG* p. 148.

29.
1. *OR* 27.1.243, 890.
2. *OR* 27.2.434.
3. *RSLG* p. 148.

30.
1. *RSLG* p. 148

31.
1. *RSLG* p. 148.

34.

1. For details on the monument's dedication ceremonies, see "The Maryland Confederate Monument at Gettysburg," *Southern Historical Society Papers* 14 (1886), pp. 429-446.
2. *RSLG* p. 152
3. *OR* 27.2.341.

36.

1. *RSLG* p. 156

37.

1. *RSLG* p. 156.

38.

1. *RSLG* p. 184.

39.

1. The first two were the 1st Maryland Infantry Battalion (No. 32), the 4th Alabama Infantry (No. 13).
2. *OR* 27.2.344.
3. William F. Fox, *Regimental Losses in the American Civil War, 1861-1865* (1898; reprint Dayton, Ohio: Morningside Press, 1974), pp. 556-558.
4. *RSLG* p. 174.

40.

1. *RSLG* p. 136.
2. *OR* 27.1.243, 589.

41.

1. *RSLG* p. 184.

42.

1. *RSLG* p. 142.
2. OR 27.2.338.

43.

1. E.P. Alexander, *Military Memoirs of a Confederate* (Bloomington, Ind.: Indiana U.P., 1962J, p. 424.
2. *RSLG* p. 136.
3. *OR* 27.1.243, 589.

45.

1. *RSLG* p. 149.

46.

1. RSLG p. 136.

47.

1. E.P. Alexander, *Military Memoirs of a Confederate* (Bloomington, Ind.: Indiana U.P., 1962j, p. 424.
2. *RSLG* p. 136.

48.

1. *RSLG* p. 193.

49.

1. *RSLG* p. 184.

50.
1. *RSLG* p. 156.

51.
1. *RSLG* p. 171.

52.
1. *RSLG* p. 149.

53.
1. *RSLG* p. 149.

54.
1. *RSLG* p. 147.

55.
1. *RSLG* p. 201.

56.
1. *RSLG* p. 184.

57.
1. *RSLG* p. 162.

58.
1. *RSLG* p. 162.

59.
1. *RSLG* p. 193.

60.
1. *RSLG* p. 192.

62.
1. *RSLG* p. 147.

63.
1. *RSLG* p. 171.

64.
1. *RSLG* p. 193.

65.
1. *RSLG* p. 147.

66.
1. *RSLG* p. 178.

67.
1. *RSLG* p. 199

68.
1. *RSLG* p. 192.

70.
1. *RSLG* p. 169.

71.
1. *RSLG* p. 156.

72.
1. *RSLG* p. 193.

73.
1. *RSLG* p. 178.

74.
1. *RSLG* p. 201.

75.
1. *RSLG* p. 169.

76.
1. *RSLG* p. 178.

77.
1. *RSLG* p. 169.

78.
1. *RSLG* p. 149.

79.
1. *RSLG* p. 170.

80.
1. *RSLG* p. 193.

81.
1. *RSLG* p. 147.

82.
1. *RSLG* p. 142.
2 *OR* 27.2.338.

83.
1. *RSLG* p. 170.

85.
1. *RSLG* p. 170

86.
1. *RSLG* p. 170.

87.
1. *RSLG* p. 192.

88.
1. *RSLG* p. 170.

89.
1. *RSLG* p. 170.

90.
1. *RSLG* p. 162.

91.
1. *OR* 27.2.432.
2. *RSLG* p. 149.

92.
1. *RSLG* p. 129.
2. *OR* 28.2.346.

95.
1. *RSLG* p. 130.
2. *OR* 27.2.338-340.

97.
1. *RSLG* p. 149.

98.
1. *OR* 27.1.243, 890.
2. *OR* 27.2.434.
3. *RSLG* p. 148.

99.
1. *RSLG* p. 131.

100.
1. *RSLG* p. 135.
2. *OR* 27.2.339.

102.
1. *RSLG* p. 134.
2. *OR* 27.2.340.

104.
1. *RSLG* p. 132.
2. *OR* 27.2.339.

106.
1. *RSLG* p. 133.
2. *OR* 27.2.331.

109.
1. *OR* 27.2.428.
2. *OR* 27.1.243, 589.
3. *RSLG* p. 136.

110.
1. *RSLG* p. 137.

112.
1. *RSLG* p. 139.

114.
1. *RSLG* p. 138.
2. *OR* 27.2.338.

117.
1. *RSLG* p. 140.
2. *OR* 27.2.338.

119.
1. *RSLG* p. 141.
2. *OR* 27.2.338.

120.
1. *RSLG* p. 141.

121.
1. *RSLG* p. 142.
2. OR 27.2.338.

122.
1. *RSLG* p. 143.

123.
1. *RSLG* p. 145

125.
1. *RSLG* p. 146.

126.
1. *RSLG* p. 144.

127.
1. *RSLG* p. 147.

128.
1. *RSLG* p. 150.

131.
1. *RSLG* p. 170.

132.
1. *RSLG* p. 171.

133.
1. *RSLG* p. 157.

134.
1. *RSLG* p. 158.

135.
1. *RSLG* p. 158.

136.
1. *RSLG* p. 160.
2. *OR* 27.2.340.

137.
1. *RSLG* p. 159.

138.
1. *RSLG* p. 161.

139.
1. *RSLG* p. 162.
2. *OR* 27.2.341.

140.
1. *RSLG* p. 151.

141.
1. *RSLG* p. 155.

142.
1. *RSLG* p. 153.

143.
1. *RSLG* p. 152.

144.
1. *RSLG* p. 154.

145.
1. *RSLG* p. 156.

146.
1. *RSLG* p. 163.

147.
1. *OR* 27.2.557.

148.
1. *RSLG* p. 164.

150.
1. *RSLG* p. 167.
2. *OR* 27.2.342.

151.
1. *RSLG* p. 165.

152.
1. *RSLG* p. 166.

154.
1. *RSLG* p. 168.
2. *OR* 27.2.342.

155.
1. *RSLG* p. 169.

156.
1. *RSLG* p. 172.

158.
1. *RSLG* p. 192.

159.
1. *RSLG* p. 193.
2. *OR* 27.2.345.

160.
1. *RSLG* p. 185.

161.
1. *RSLG* p. 187.

162.
1. *RSLG* p. 188.

164.
1. *RSLG* p. 189.

165.
1. *RSLG* p. 186.
2. *OR* 27.2.343.

167.
1. *RSLG* p. 190.
2. OR 27.2.343.
169.
1. *RSLG* p. 191.
170.
1. *RSLG* p. 173.
171.
1. *RSLG* p. 177.
2. *OR* 27.2.344.
172.
1. *RSLG* p. 177.
2. OR 27.2.344.
173.
1. *RSLG* p. 176.
174.
1. *RSLG* p. 175.
175.
1. *RSLG* p. 175.
176.
1. *RSLG* p. 174.
177.
1. *RSLG* p. 178.
178.
1. *RSLG* p. 179.
179.
1. *RSLG* p. 181.
180.
1. *RSLG* p. 180.
181.
1. *RSLG* p. 182.
2. *OR* 27.2.345.
182.
1. *RSLG* p. 183.
2. *OR* 27.2.344.
183.
1. *RSLG* p. 184.
185.
1. *RSLG* p. 194.
186.
1. *RSLG* p. 197.
2. *OR* 27.2.345.

187.
1. *RSLG* p. 195.

188.
1. Letter of Col. V.A. Witcher to John Bachelder dated March 19, 1886, Bachelder Papers, New Hampshire Historical Society.
2. *RSLG* p. 199.

189.
1. *OR* 27.2.346.

190.
1. See *RSLG* p. 198.
2. *OR* 27.2.346.

191.
1. *RSLG* p. 196.
2. *RSLG* p. 196.

193.
1. See *RSLG* p. 197.

194.
1. *RSLG* p. 201.

195.
1. *RSLG* p. 200.

199.
1. N.A. Meligakes, *The Spirit of Gettysburg* (Gettysburg, Pa., The Bookmart, 1950), pp. 211, 215.
2. Meligakes, *The Spirit of Gettysburg*, p. 238.

201
1. The other three are the 1st Maryland Infantry (No. 32), the 4th Alabama Infantry (No. 13), and the 26th North Carolina Infantry (No. 39).

203
1. Toomey, *Marylanders at Gettysburg*, (Toomey Press: Baltimore, 1994, pp. 79-80.

"A" SERIES TABLETS

A-1
1. *RSLG* p. 201.
2. For example, David F. Riggs in *East of Gettysburg* (Ft. Collins, Co.: Old Army Press, 1985), pp. 45, 81.
3. Letters written by H.B. McClellan to John B. Bachelder dated June 15, 1884 and May 17, 1886, Bachelder Papers, New Hampshire Historical Society.
4. This interpretation suggested by James M. Clouse.
5. *RSLG* p. 201.

A-2
1. *OR* 27.2.190.
2. *RSLG* p. 201.

A-3

1. *RSLG* p. 201.

A-4

1. *RSLG* p. 201.

A-5

1. Mementos of this ceremony are exhibited in the Gettysburg National Military Park Museum.

A-7

1. *OR* 27.1.755.

A-12

1. William F. Fox, *Regimental Losses in the American Civil War, 1861-1865* (1898; reprint Dayton, Ohio: Morningside Press, 1974), pp. 556-558.

A-14

1. *OR* 27.2.661.

Bibliography

Acts of the State of Alabama, 1927.

Acts of the State of Arkansas, 1965.

Alexander, E.P. *Military Memoirs of a Confederate*. Bloomington, Indiana; Indiana University Press, 1962.

Annual Reports of the Gettysburg National Military Park Commission to the Secretary of War, 1893-1904. Washington, D.C.; Government Printing Office, 1905.

Bachelder, John B. *Map of the Battlefield of Gettysburg, July 1st, 2nd, 3rd, 1863*. Boston: John B. Bachelder, 1876.

John B. Bachelder Papers, New Hampshire Historical Society.

Busey, John W. and David G. Martin. *Regimental Strengths at Gettysburg*. Third Edition. Hightstown, NJ: Longstreet House, 1994.

Coddington, Edwin B. *The Gettysburg Campaign: A Study in Command*. Dayton, Ohio: Morningside Press, 1979 (reprint of 1968 edition).

Craven, Wayne. *The Sculptures at Gettysburg*. N.P.: Eastern Acorn Press, 1982.

"Dedication of the Virginia Memorial at Gettysburg, Friday, June 8, 1917."*Southern Historical Society Papers* XLII (1917), 83-135.

Dedications of Monuments to Georgia Confederate Dead on National Battlefield Sites. N.P.: 1961.

Downey, Fairfax. *The Guns at Gettysburg*. New York: David MacKay Company, 1958.

Fox, William F. *Regimental Losses in the American Civil War, 1861-1865*. Dayton, Ohio: Morningside Press, 1974 (reprint of 1898 edition).

Georg, Kathleen R. *The Location of the Monuments, Markers, and Tablets on Gettysburg Battlefield*. N.P.: Gettysburg National Military Park, 1984.

Gettysburg Battlefield. Markers, memorials and monuments erected since 1863.

Gettysburg National Military Park. Notebooks, scrapbooks, and letters.

Gettysburg Star & Sentinel.

Goldsborough, W.W. *The Maryland Line in the Confederate States Army*. Gaithersburg, Maryland: Butternut Press, 1983 (reprint of 1869 edition).

Harrisburg Independent.

Hought, H.R. Letter to Daniel E. Sickles dated October 17, 1904. Gettysburg National Military Park Library.

Krick, Robert K. *The Gettysburg Death Roster, The Confederate Dead at Gettysburg*. Third Edition. Dayton, Ohio: Morningside Press, 1993.

Laws of the State of Florida, 1965.

Laws of the State of Georgia, 1961.

Laws of the State of Mississippi, 1968.

Letteer, Mrs. Clarence R. *Report of the Louisiana Gettysburg Memorial Monument Commission.* N.P.: n.d.

"The Maryland Confederate Monument at Gettysburg." *Southern Historical Society Papers* XIV (1886), 429-446.

"Maryland State Memorial at Gettysburg." Dedication ceremony booklet, November 13, 1994.

McLaughlin, Jack. *Gettysburg: The Long Encampment.* New York: Bonanza, 1963.

Meligakes, N.A. *Gettysburg The National Shrine.* Gettysburg: The Bookmart, 1975.

_____*The Spirit of Gettysburg.* Gettysburg: The Bookmart, 1950.

"North Carolina at Gettysburg." *Confederate Veteran* XXXVII (1929), 286-288.

William C. Oates Correspondence. Gettysburg National Military Park Library.

Position of Troops. Notebooks in Gettysburg National Military Park Library.

"Preliminary Report on Non-Ferrous Metals in Gettysburg National Military Park." Gettysburg: 1943.

Report of the (Virginia) *Gettysburg Monument Commission.* N.P.: n.d.

Riggs, David F. *East of Gettysburg.* Ft. Collins, Co.: Old Army Press, 1985.

W.M. Robbins Correspondence. Gettysburg National Military Park Library.

Roy, Paul R. *The Last Reunion of the Blue and Gray.* Gettysburg: The Bookmart, 1950.

Simpson, Harold B. *Red Granite for Gray Heroes, The Monuments to Hood's Texas Brigade on Eastern Battlefields.* N.P.: ca. 1963.

Stewart, George R. *Pickett's Charge, A Microhistory of the Final Attack at Gettysburg, July 3, 1863.* Boston: Houghton Mifflin Co., 1959.

Toomey, Daniel C. *Marylanders at Gettysburg.* Toomey Press: Baltimore, 1994.

United States War Department. *The War of the Rebellion: A Compilation of the Official Records of the Union and Confederate Armies.* 128 Volumes. Washington: Government Printing Office, 1880-1901.

Vanderslice, John. *Gettysburg Then and Now.* Dayton, Ohio: Morningside Press, 1983 (reprint of 1899 edition).